ESSAYS ON THE FOUNDATIONS OF ETHICS

Essays on the Foundations of Ethics

CLARENCE IRVING LEWIS

EDITED BY
JOHN LANGE

Cover image of C. I. Lewis / courtesy of Andrew Lewis

Published by State University of New York Press, Albany

For information, contact State University of New York Press, Albany, NY
www.sunypress.edu

Production, Diane Ganeles
Marketing, Fran Keneston

Library of Congress Cataloging-in-Publication Data

Names: Lewis, Clarence Irving, 1883-1964, author. | Lange, John, 1931- editor.
Title: Essays on the foundations of ethics / by C. I. Lewis ; edited by John Lange.
Description: Albany, NY : State University of New York, 2017. | Includes bibliographical references.
Identifiers: LCCN 2016031426 (print) | LCCN 2016039645 (ebook) | ISBN 9781438464930 (hardcover : alk. paper) | ISBN 9781438464947 (e-book)
Subjects: LCSH: Ethics.
Classification: LCC B945.L451 L36 2017 (print) | LCC B945.L451 (ebook) | DDC 170—dc23
LC record available at https://lccn.loc.gov/2016031426

10 9 8 7 6 5 4 3 2 1

Contents

Acknowledgments

It takes a great many people, working together cooperatively, to bring a book to fruition. Most of these are unknown to a book's author or editor. So I accord a cordial thanks, broadcast forth warmly, if not specifically, to all those involved in this project. You know who you are, even if I do not. Thank you.

More specifically, I would like to thank, first, Andrew Kenyon, Acquisitions Editor at SUNY Press, who supervised a long and arduous journey, patiently, courteously, and expertly; he did not always have an easy time of it; second, Fran Keneston, the Director of Marketing and Publicity for SUNY Press; third, Diane Ganeles, Senior Production Editor at the press; and, fourth, a reader whose anonymity will be respected, a reader not only deeply familiar with the work of C. I. Lewis, but one fully sensitive to, and fully aware of, his importance, philosophically, humanly, and culturally. Would that Lewis could lead us back to large issues, those of major human concern. Philosophy can delight in trivia, and that can be innocent and fun, but there are also more important things for her to do, the sorts of thing with which C. I. Lewis was concerned.

I would also like, in particular, to thank Rob Tempio, of Princeton University Press, who kindly brought the availability of the book to the attention of Andrew Kenyon. That is much appreciated.

Stanford University is the repository of the original Lewis papers, to which it invariably, generously, and helpfully provides access. My principal contact in this regard is Mattie Taormina, Head of Public Service and Processing Manuscripts Librarian, Department of Special Collections, the Green Library, Stanford. I herewith include the official credit line for Stanford's permission to publish, supplied by Ms. Taormina. "Courtesy of Department of Special Collections and University Archives, Stanford University Libraries." Thanks to her and the University. Stanford University, however, while housing the physical papers involved, does not own the copyright to the materials, which is owned by the C. I. Lewis Estate. In this regard, I wish to thank Andrew K. Lewis, the Executor of the C. I. Lewis Estate, for permission to publish. Professor Lewis was very fortunate to possess so loving and devoted a son, who took so many pains in so many ways, over so many years, to protect, preserve, and perpetuate the legacy not only of one of the richest, deepest, and greatest of American philosophers, but that of a beloved father. I account myself very fortunate to have studied with Professor Lewis and to have met and known Andrew K. Lewis, not only as an associate in this project, but a friend. I am deeply grieved that Professor Lewis did not live long enough to finish his final book. How marvelous that would have been. It is my hope, however, that our current project, a version of that book, gives us a sense, a good sense, of what might have been.

Editor's Preface

It became evident in the fifties and early sixties of the Twentieth Century that the projected culmination of Professor Lewis' philosophical work, intended to be his crowning achievement, that major gift which he longed to give us, the long-awaited book on ethics, that to be written for all, not merely colleagues, that book which he hoped might make a difference not just to philosophy, but even to civilization, might not be completed.

In his lifetime he published two representative, shorter studies, almost as though taking out insurance against the loss of the race, that desperate labor hurrying against the descent of night: *The Ground and Nature of the Right*, substantially the Woodridge Lectures, given at Columbia in 1954 and published by the Columbia University Press in 1955, and *Our Social Inheritance*, based on a set of lectures given at Indiana University in 1956, under the auspices of the Mahlon Powell Foundation and published by the Indiana University Press in 1957.

And he continued to work to the end, with his customary, dogged exactitude, ignoring, and ultimately defying, declining health and increasing age.

I was a former student of Professor Lewis, meeting him late in his career, when I was a student at the University of Southern California, and had the happy, if challenging, job of assisting him one semester in his legendary Kant course, an in-depth study of the first Critique. I need say no more to those hundreds of students, mostly at Harvard, who know that course. There is a bond there. Some years later, in 1963, when I was a young teacher in the northeast, I came west with my wife and son, on a small grant, to spend a summer at the University of California at Berkeley. Since Professor Lewis lived in Menlo Park, which was nearby, I called up to see if he would mind my dropping by, to say "Hello." It was during this brief visit that I first, personally, became aware of the major project he was trying to finish.

How little did I then understand how much of my own life would be involved in this matter.

He had already accumulated a vast amount of material, literally several feet of draft material, housed in an extensive series of notebooks, here and there about the office, on shelves, by the desk, on the desk, and so on. A Xeroxed copy of this material, for example, without the notebook covers, requires several cartons for its storage.

It was clear even then, in the summer of 1963, that Professor Lewis faced a number of very serious problems, problems serious enough in themselves, but surely exacerbated by age and health. These problems were not only philosophical, those of trying to get things really right, that job in such a field being harrowingly subtle and complex, but, too, easier to understand, many simple logistic problems, those of coordinating, reviewing, managing, and sifting through this enormous amount of material, to extract from it that which might be refined for publication.

It seemed clear that even if Professor Lewis did not need help, and he never had before, he certainly, now, at the least, might be able to use a little.

And there I was, saying "Hello."

One of the things he proposed, to my dismay, was the offer of a collaboration. Naturally I was unwilling to have my name linked with his in such a manner, as though I might be in his league, which I was not, and am not, but, too, more importantly, it was his book, his thinking, his labor of love, not mine. At best I would have been no more than a helper, hopefully a valuable one, but surely not a coequal, worthy of a shared authorship. That offer, it seemed to me, reflected not so much the expectation of any substantive contribution I might make to the project, as Professor Lewis' concern, or fear, that the book might otherwise be lost. Happily, without, as I recall, my saying anything one way or the other, he shortly thereafter rethought this matter and explained to me that he could not actually do a collaboration. He had to have things his way in what he did. That was typical Lewis, one of the things one loved him for. He informed me, to my interest, that even in his famous collaboration with Cooper Harold Langford, *Symbolic Logic*, they had written separate chapters. Thus it was not really a collaboration, so much as a book the separate parts of which were written by separate authors. In any event, we arranged that I would visit him in the summer of 1964, and that we would work on the book together. My job, as I saw it, was not to write the book, or parts of it, but to help Professor Lewis organize and assemble it. Once again I would be an assistant, though now of a rather different sort. My functions would presumably be both seriously editorial and humbly clerical, perhaps locating, reviewing, and editing drafts, offering suggestions, supplying criticisms, and acting as a sounding board for his thinking, and, it may well have been, typing up at least a rough draft that would have served for Professor Lewis' revisions. It is one of the great regrets of my life that this was not to be. Professor Lewis died that winter.

The Lewis Papers, as they came to be called, were donated to Stanford University, where Professor Lewis had taught after his retirement from Harvard. A chair in commemoration of Professor Lewis was also established at that university.

Naturally concern arose pertaining to the unpublished papers.

At this juncture, to my mind, the most important person in this whole business appears, Mr. Andrew K. Lewis, one of Professor Lewis' sons, and the executor of his estate. Mr. Lewis' concern with the papers, and with his father's interests, his father's memory and literary heritage, has made possible a variety of projects. His coordination and support, his attention and interest, his unfailing sensitivity, encouragement, and good will, have again and again proven indispensable and invaluable.

As things began to fall out, Mr. Lewis supplied me with microfilm reels and a Xeroxed copy of the late papers. The book was to be edited by two fine philosophers, both friends of Professor Lewis, William K. Frankena, of the University of Michigan, and Charles A. Baylis, of Duke University. My job here was to index the papers, find the book, select drafts, and reproduce them in a readable form. Professors Frankena and Baylis would then work with these materials. I suspect that none of us, at that time, realized the problems that would be posed by the papers, and the considerable investment of time and effort that would be required just to determine if a publishable manuscript was there, let alone to prepare it, that based on deciphering hundreds of pages of worrisome handscript, for an eventual publication. Professors Frankena and Baylis were both senior philosophers, if not of Professor Lewis' generation, then of one not distantly related to it. Both, I think, were reluctant, and understandably so, as things eventually became clear, to undertake so time-consuming and daunting a task, and possibly so fruitless a task, at that time in their career. And that is how the project came to me. Needless to say, both Professors Frankena and Baylis, the memory of whose friendship I treasure, remained available for consultation, and were invariably supportive.

I, too, feared that no book might materialize or that, if one did, it would come to fruition only in a distant future. Indeed, that was some fifty years ago. Accordingly, it was agreed that I would begin with a small book, drawn on ready, or almost ready, materials, things that Professor Lewis had, at least substantially, himself readied for publication, among them the Wesleyan Lectures, entitled *Foundations of Ethics*, delivered at Wesleyan in 1959. This book was entitled *Values and Imperatives: Studies in Ethics by C. I. Lewis*, and was published by the Stanford University Press in 1969. A bird in the hand, one supposed, was better than encountering the possibility of an empty bush at a later date. Shortly thereafter, in 1970, Professors John D. Goheen and John L. Mothershead, Jr., both of Stanford University, and the latter the first occupant of the newly established C. I. Lewis Chair at Stanford, published their anthology, *Collected Papers of Clarence Irving Lewis*, a major contribution to Lewis Studies. That volume was also published by the Stanford University Press.

Time passed.

It remained my conviction that Professor Lewis' final dream, that project to which he devoted the last years of his life, should one day be realized.

But there was no way that dream could be either soon or easily realized. The papers, as a whole, clearly, were not ready for publication. They were sometimes jumbled and chaotic, and almost invariably rough, and saturated with asides and marginal notes in tiny script, and such, often enough literally difficult to read, even with a strong glass. Sometimes they seemed not merely fragments of a structure never built, but a shambles from which it seemed unlikely anything might arise, let alone touch the sky, and soar. They were a record, substantially, in effect, of a great mind doing philosophy by and for itself, and not yet ready to do it for others. The judgment that they were unpublishable as they stood was not only a judgment one could understand, but it was one which, obviously, and unfortunately, was lamentably correct. Still, where Lewis mined, there was gold. And, all in all, the papers were not so badly off as a relatively cursory study of some weeks might have suggested. Lewis, on closer inspection, was never that badly off. There were themes and shapes there, intellectual geodesics, frequently encountered, precious philosophic minerals. I became gradually more and more certain that the book, or something much like it, was really there, that Lewis had come much closer to it than we had realized.

And so I began again, literally beginning again, working with the handscript, sentence by sentence, and eventually produced a manuscript. This book is not, of course, exactly the book that Lewis himself would have brought to light. We will never have that book. But it is his book, and only his book.

The text, as would be supposed, given its unfinished nature, required considerable, and, alas, heavy editing. I have done this boldly, as there was no real alternative. I have done this editing with a certain amount of trepidation because it remains my impression that good old Professor Lewis could blow a fuse over a misplaced comma. On the whole, of course, as suggested, there was no other choice in the matter. The book simply needed serious editing. I do think the inimitable flavor of Lewis' very personal diction is largely retained. On the other hand, smoothness and readability have been paramount considerations. Philosophically, my editing, for better or for worse, has been determinedly conservative, sometimes preferring to leave ambiguities or dubieties in the text rather than resolve them in such a way as to impose a particular interpretation on the material. I view with equanimity the exposure of the reader to the perils of dialogic interaction with a great mind. It is not my job to save him this exhilarating grief. That sort of thing is part of philosophy.

Lastly, I have chosen to have a continuous manuscript, rather than put together a longer, *variorum* edition consisting of diverse drafts. I do not think that that would be in the best interests of the book. I have also tried to use Professor Lewis' last drafts for the book, rather than select amongst competing drafts, choosing one I might like best. Lewis' last drafts are my first pick in such matters. I would rather rely on his judgment than mine in such matters.

Editor's Introduction

The career of C. I. Lewis was rich, lengthy, remarkable, and profound. He is, in my view, given his solidity, acuity, detail, scope, and depth, the greatest of the American pragmatists. Yet I am personally reluctant to accept this classification, that of pragmatist, uncritically. It is too quick, too facile, too convenient, too limited, perhaps too dismissive, particularly given the intellectual aberrations which are sometimes associated with pragmatism, aberrations of wishful thinking, of murky thinking, of irresponsible thinking, of relativity, of expedience, of subjectivity, and so on. In his thought the strict currents of a rigorous scientific empiricism and an uncompromising logistic rationalism were not only evident, but paramount. There is no Lewis without them. A friend once dismissed C.I. Lewis as a "half-way pragmatist." "He did not go the whole way, he did not go to the end of the line." I responded that C. I. Lewis had gotten off the train when it came to his stop. There are virtues and values in all the great philosophical traditions. If there were not, these traditions could not have arisen and endured. Little survives whose coinage is not legal tender in the house of time. Lewis, as I see it, is not an eclectic philosopher. His work is not a collage. He is himself, and of one piece. He did not patch together a philosophical garment from incompatible fabrics. Rather he saw, or tried to see, the forces and shapes which had originally called these honored, historical, multi-plex fabrics into being, those things which accounted for their perennial fascination, and power, that at which they hinted, in their diverse ways, those things we might call truths, or reali-ties. Accordingly, in Lewis we will find strains of empiricism, rationalism, and pragmatism, though he is not, *simpliciter*, an empiricist, nor a rationalist, nor a pragmatist. He is all of these in his way, and, yet, being himself, can be no single one of them, ever. These elements in Lewis are not assembled, but grown together, afresh, as one living structure, as though from seeds, developed in the light of a fine, decent, sharp mind, one which retained the rare philosophical virtue of knowing the world and philosophy, and yet managing to see them anew. Lewis exceeds categories. In any event, when the train of pragmatism reaches "the end of its line," which is scarcely a virtue, *per se*, and inevitably finds itself awash in the swamps of one silliness or another, having at last fulfilled its destiny of expedient lunacy, political and otherwise, it will find that Lewis got off the train, long ago.

Without delineating bibliography, Lewis' first major works were in the field of mathematical logic. Indeed, in passing, it might be noted that, according to the monumental history of logic, *The Development of Logic*, written by William and Martha Kneale, modern interest in modal logic begins with his work. He then moved, via books and articles, to questions of meaning, knowledge, and valuation, with the ultimate objective of coming to grips with the fundamental problems of the good and the right, of exploring and mapping the country of rational self-governance, the field of ethics. There is a natural progres-sion in this philosophical biography. Surely one must concern oneself with the forms of valid thought, the structure of valid-ity independent of specific content. Such studies constitute the abstract presuppositions of sagacity. They investigate the per-vasive, underlying, invisible values which determine the most basic conditions of rational discourse. And from thence one may proceed, in the logical order of things, to a more familiar world, a visible world, that of embodied forms, if you will, or of contents which may constitute forms fulfilled, the subtleties of semantics, the analysis of meaning. In the logical order of things, one has then prepared oneself for the epistemological quest, the search for knowledge and the conditions of its justifiable acceptance. How must thought work, if it is to serve its tortuously evolved possibility, ultimately that of making possible a well-lived life, a *human* life, a possibility which we may accept or deny, embrace or subvert? And what do we *mean*, and how shall we understand ourselves and others? Meaning is the lens wherewith we attempt to bring the world into focus. It, if only in a prelinguistic form, embodying recollection and anticipation, is a precondition of knowledge, however primitive, however inchoate. Without meaning there is no truth, and without truth no knowledge. And what is the selected-for purpose or utility of knowledge? Like the wings of the bird, and the claws of the lion, what is it good for? Life does not do itself. Death can manage by itself, but life cannot. The human being is a creature of volitional self-consciousness. Its burden or blessing, its fate or opportunity, is self-governance. It must decide; it must act. To claim that there is no better or worse in acting, that nothing matters, is, if not lunacy, an idiocy incapable of being consistently realized in practice. Even the most resolute metaphysical determinist, putting his philosophical money on the arrangement and momenta of gas molecules in the primeval nebula, these dictating the least nuance of the position he has been fated to hold, finds himself, perhaps to his embarrassment, condemned to decide, obligated to act as though free, to inevitably betray in practice what he maintains in theory. The determinist may be right of course, despite the primary data of consciousness and the seeming significance of what he and others are up to. Counter-evidence to his theory may be illusory. That is surely possible. And it is surely possible that the suffering, and the agony, of human beings, their hopes, fears, convictions, arguments, strivings, reasonings, and such may all be an empty charade, rather like a cruel joke of nature, everything being, all the misery and desperation, and such, "in the can," prerecorded, in effect, though we, implicated characters in this self-conscious, authorless film playing to an empty house, are doomed to think it matters, and greatly. That would just be our part. But, as a matter of brute fact, life cannot float; it either sinks or swims; one decides, one acts, or one disintegrates and dies. The universe can doubtless bear with equanimity the extinction of our species, as it has had a great deal of practice in this sort of thing. We may not matter to it, but we matter to us. As a species then, finding ourselves granted, by whatever cause, benevolent or malevolent, benign or satirical, intentional or accidental, the privilege of decision, and the opportunity to act, and the nonrepudiable obligation to do so or die, we must address ourselves to the exigent problems of decision and action, to the problems of self-governance. How shall a human being best act? How shall a human being best be? These are, in effect, the questions to which ethics addresses itself. To claim that there are no better or worse answers to such questions, or no true or false answers to such questions, whatever they may be, self-regarding or other-regarding, is not only to belittle and betray the species, but to espouse hypocrisy. We cannot truly believe that answer, despite whatever ease or license we might seek to draw from it. The problem is not whether there are, or whether we must suppose there to be, better or worse, or true or false, answers to such questions, but what the answers are, or what we must, in consistent rationality, suppose them to be. In our lives we must assume them, because, if we do not, we cannot live. To this troubling, fertile, urgent, necessary field of investigation C. I. Lewis devoted the last years of his life.

Let us now conclude these introductory remarks, utilizing a metaphor, that of oceans, which seems appropriate for philosophy. Here one might distinguish between currents and tides, and ripples, bubbles, and splashes. To understand the philosophical oceans, in all their breadths, depths, and awesomeness, one discovers and charts her mighty features, and seeks to catalog her constants, the regularities of centuries. This is the job of the oceanographers of the spirit. Without diminishing in any respect our admiration for the heroes of the afternoon, who always seem large to us, in their turn, because they are so close to us, until they are inevitably replaced by the heroes of the next afternoon, and without failing to acknowledge the sparkle and fascination of ripples, bubbles, and splashes, which are, after all, real ripples, real bubbles, and real splashes, one sometimes stands on the shore, in one place or another, lonely on the sand, and wonders about continents and horizons. It is at such times that one remembers, with gratitude, and occasionally nostalgia, the special philosophers who taught us a dozen ways to relate to the ultimate mystery, encouraging us to trespass in forbidden meadows, setting us intriguing, inspiring, fearful examples of the exploratory power of the human mind. Humanity, lifting its head above the beer and barley of a quotidian existence, is the richer, and the more exalted, for their work, and their lives. We are grateful to them for their indications and discoveries, even when we are most reluctant to accept them, and for their leadership and guidance, even when we refuse to follow. Without them we could have no proper understanding of the gardens of perhaps, the terrain of possibility.

I remember one young philosopher, a fellow graduate student at the time, who was exasperated with C. I. Lewis, because "like Aristotle, he made too much sense." To be sure, we all have our faults. But I think his criticism was basically motivated not so much by an objection to intelligibility in philosophy, which would seem to be a peculiar property to which to object, as by the fact that the more one read Lewis, the sounder he proved to be, and this meant there was, if one took the trouble to understand him, less and less to object to. There are philosophers, of course, who "live to refute," who would rather have a reputation for the fastest counter-example in the west, or east, than stumble on a truth. In my view, these people are valuable for their homicidal zealotry. They make a valuable contribution to philosophy. If the two symbols of philosophy are the ax and the plowshare, they are the berserkers of the field. Many philosophers, particularly younger ones, who have to establish a reputation for dangerousness before they will be taken seriously, are well advised to adopt this kill-kill-kill, take-no-prisoners approach to the field. On the other hand, when the butchery is done, the blood lust eventually satisfied, and the smoke of battle finally cleared, one wonders if that is all there is. And one hopes there is more. It is then that one thinks about the plowshare, the planting, and the intriguing possibilities of a harvest. C. I. Lewis, when he chose, could be a mean man with an ax, but his ultimate objective was not to cut down more and more trees, but to clear the land for planting. His harvests are among the most important, and most nourishing, in the history of philosophy. He is one of those philosophers whose philosophical contemporaries are not the heroes of this afternoon, but others, the Platos and Aristotles, the Humes and Kants, philosophers who also dealt with deep and important things, brothers in the timeless colloquium of greatness.

This book constitutes an attempt, after a generation of concern, to bring to light a version, however inadequate, of the last great effort to which he applied his considerable talents, a project to which his life's work was intended to be a prolegomena, a treatise on consistency, rationality, and humanity, his final thoughts on ethics.

It is one of the tragedies of not only philosophy, but of the reflective, rational life in general, that he did not live to finish this work.

What we have here is a gesture, a fragment, of what might have been.

On the other hand, this is not a time for lamentation, and regrets.

If we have a fragment here, rough-hewn and incomplete, it is a glorious, stimulatory fragment, a road and horizon, a signpost and a pointing. Once again it is morning, springtime in philosophy.

Lewis, like philosophy, is alive and well.

So we herewith offer this book to the philosophical community, to the intellectual community at large, and to Professor Lewis' family and friends, and his former colleagues and students, and to all who will cherish it, in all humility, and with respect and affection.

Preface—and Confession

In the preface to any piece of writing such as this book attempts to be, it is inexcusable to be autobiographic—even if it is ever excusable to indulge in autobiography, a matter concerning which, for myself at least, I have some doubts. But I find I cannot send this book to print without some manner of such *apologium*.

In 1932, when *Symbolic Logic,* written in collaboration with Cooper Harold Langford, had been sent to print, I decided that any further work in that subject was not my affair. The rapidly mounting volume of new studies in that field would preclude my further command of it unless I should make that my major business. And neither my command of mathematics nor my interest would be compatible with that as a major preoccupation. Indeed, I should not have attempted anything in that field except for the concurrence of two considerations. First, having been introduced to this subject by Josiah Royce, I had been intrigued to follow it through my observance of the insights which could so be afforded and sharpened in the field of epistemology. Something of that, for example, along with other strains of thought, particularly such as derived from a perusal of Charles S. Peirce's as-yet-unpublished literary remains, had already appeared in *Mind and the World-Order,* in 1929. And, the second coincident consideration, I had, in 1911, on first

1

reading Volume I of Alfred North Whitehead's and Bertrand Russell's *Principia Mathematica,* acquired the conviction that the foundations of that work were subtly awry and failed to accord with the basic character of valid inference. Peirce, whose contributions to the development of exact logic were extensive, had himself, briefly but unmistakably, remarked the limitation of material "implication," and I had been surprised that he nowhere in his work had made the correction needed to amend the matter, and delineated, in precise fashion, that relation '*P* implies *Q*' whose properties exactly coincided with those of '*Q* is validly deducible from *P*'. It was very simple: one needed only to reinterpret the Boolean Algebra, in the final form of it due to Ernst Schröder and still current, in order to have a sufficient basis for this emendation. The coincidence of these two considerations, along with a desire for a usable text for my own classes in the subject, was responsible for my first book, *Survey of Symbolic Logic,* published in 1918, and, in 1932, when that work had been out of print for several years, for the volume in cooperation with Langford, in which my own contribution, "strict implication," was a little better and more accurately developed.

But all that was now done, so far as I was concerned.

In the next ten years, such time for writing as I could find was absorbed in studies the final form of which was published in 1946, in *An Analysis of Knowledge and Valuation.*

As is recorded in the preface of *An Analysis of Knowledge and Valuation,* the dominating initial intent had been to say something about ethics. But I had found it impossible to proceed to that goal without a recurrence to topics of epistemology. In particular, there was something altogether omitted in *Mind and the World-Order* which was essential, namely, the thesis that just evaluations are one form of empirical knowledge. Also there was something basic to be carried forward from the logical studies. Consistency is a basic matter, fundamentally the same in logic, in our cognizing, and in the values which we set on things, and in the purpose of action which purpose we take to be justified to pursue. Consistency is a key concept of the normative at large. If that thought had not been explicitly emphasized in *Mind and the World-Order* or even in *An Analysis of Knowledge and Valuation,* it will be in this book. Consistency is of the essence of all rational self-criticism and self-direction. And consistency is definable in the same terms as implication. *P* is consistent with *Q* if and only if it false that the contradictory of *Q* is deducible from *P,* and hence also false that the contradictory of *P* is deducible from *Q.*

Observing this interconnection between the rightness of decisions at large with the logical relations of deducibility and of consistency, and observing that any determination of what is good is something requiring to be empirically determined, and a mode of knowing comparable at bottom with the perception of other characters experimentally to be determined and assessed, gives us the key to the normative in general. But neither of these basic considerations had been developed in anything so far published. The project of developing them became the project of *An Analysis of Knowledge and Valuation,* and its three "books," devoted respectively to the relevant logical considerations, to the basis of empirical knowledge at large, and to the assessments of value, three books which perhaps might better have been, with alterations, published under separate covers.

The projected book in ethics should have promptly followed.

This present volume is hardly what I intended. That it is not is the excuse for these prefatory remarks. The accumulated materials were drawn upon for two less comprehensive efforts, the Woodbridge Lectures, given at Columbia University in 1954, published as *The Ground and Nature of the Right,* and three lectures given under the auspices of the Mahlon Powell Foundation at the University of Indiana in 1956, published as *Our Social Inheritance.* This present book attempts to draw the whole matter together. What in it is retrospective of already presented parts has been better done in *An Analysis of Knowledge and Valuation, The Ground and Nature of the Right,* and *Our Social Inheritance,* and I endeavor only to recapitulate main points already presented, supplying here the connective tissue relating them together, and indicating the connections with ethics, which represents the collation of them, in a resultant theory of the moral. The title of this book, *Essays on the Foundations of Ethics,* rather than *Foundations of Ethics,* is meant to suggest the merely outline character of those portions already dealt with, and the fuller treatment of portions not already covered.

Being beset by "total recall" and having, in any event, a tendency to overwrite, I have found this project, drawing these many things together, developing new material, avoiding undue overlap and such, immensely difficult. If the reader finds this result an unsatisfactory manner of presenting the whole matter in hand, so do I. Hence this untoward kind of preface. At least I have avoided saying all the parts of my little story twice over, and I hope that my impression that, for better or for worse, it all goes together, is not illusory.

ESSAY 1

Introduction

About Philosophy in General and Ethics in Particular

1. Ethics: Its Immediacy and Importance

In that body of studies which presently continue to be grouped under the head of philosophy, it is ethics which has the widest and readiest appeal, and in which one who would attempt any special investigation can be surest that he makes contact with interests which are common and public. Ethics might also claim to be the oldest study. Too, it could hardly fail to be the case that something which is moral in significance is recognizable within, if indeed it is distinguishable from, what comes earliest in, and is even identifiable as, tradition. What is moral in significance represents that community of attitude and of conviction by which a human group is able to remain together and cooperate in action.

Ethics occupies this position of paramountcy as a branch of learning because it addresses itself to the most general and most exigent of all problems, the problem, namely, of what one should choose to do. That question is universal to men and to all occasions on which it is necessary to decide and what is decided upon will make a real difference. The only other kind of

problem which is thus all-pervasive of our living is the question
of what one should think, the question of fact or justified belief,
and that manner of question becomes peremptory to determine
only when and if it becomes necessary to do something affecting it or in the light of it. It is the choosing to do which is the
crux of what has to be decided. Whatever one may think, it
will harm no one, nor, indeed, do anybody any good, so long as
nothing is done about it. By the same token, if we think awry,
we may have a chance to think again. But once action is initiated, the matter is out of our hands; our commitment is made
and the consequences of it are already on their way to happening. Thinking is, mainly at least, for the sake of guidance of our
doing. Except for satisfying our curiosity, thinking has no point
unless it bears upon our doing: one might as well wait and see
what comes about. When we feel ourselves unable to do anything to alter what may happen, we often take this waiting attitude and adjourn any problem of what to expect as one which
does not have to be settled. But problems of doing can have
their peculiar exigency, often absent in the case of determinations of belief, because the question what to do may have to be
settled now; otherwise the opportunity to do anything about
them may pass. Doing has a time limit, and the decision to do
nothing now can be as decisive of consequences as any wrong
decision we could make. But apart from such exigency of what
to do, the question of what to think can always be put over
to another day. As problems of merely believing, they have no
built-in time limit. And later we may have more light on them.

In consequence, if logic, understood broadly as principles
directive of our thinking and concluding, also represents a type
of problem which is universal and unavoidable, it nevertheless takes second place rather than first. And this second question, that of commitments of belief, is likewise universal and
unavoidable because some question of fact to be acknowledged
or found out must be involved in deciding what to do. There
can be no occasion on which what one should choose to do
is independent of the circumstances of the case and of what,
under these circumstances, the act considered will bring about.
Indeed, to act in the human sense of considered and intended
doing is impossible without reference to what lies within our

cognizance, to what we take to be the present fact and what we can expect to happen as a result of what we do. Whatever is done in the sense of choosing to do is something determined in the light of what we think and believe, something done deliberately. And without that ground of it in what we already know, whatever we might be said to do would lack the significance of an act: it will be attributable to us only in that same sense in which we also say that flowers bloom and the wind blows and a compass points to the north. Without the significance of our thought behind it, it may be our behavior but we shall not acknowledge it as anything for which we take responsibility. To be sure, we can say this same thing the other way around: whatever we may believe to be the case, if our so thinking should exercise no influence on any decision, physically, to bring about, then that thinking will be inconsequential—literally. Doing without thinking is blind; but thinking without doing is idle. Thinking is mainly for the sake of doing; it is the doing which is final in significance. What a man responsibly brings about is all he counts for: it represents his total impact on the world he lives in; except for his encumbering the earth, it is all the difference *he* will ever *make*.

Let us now remark a consideration which is further indicative of a perennial and necessary interest in the ethical.

Though it is his doing only which the individual can himself directly govern, and take the responsibility for, still it is not with the consequences of that only, or even preeminently, that he finds it necessary to be concerned. Each of us must be equally and pervasively concerned with what others do, do with results which are of concern to us. Man is a social animal, and whether he survive or perish, prosper or be condemned to misery, depends as much upon what his fellows do to him as upon what he can achieve by his own agency and assure by his own directed doing.

2. Ethics: Its Legitimacy and Autonomy

What we have so far said, tending to found ethics in the business of self-government as a whole, suggests a significance of 'ethics' which is broader than what the term most frequently connotes, namely, that it is to be confined to principles of what we justifiably do to others, though we will now put that in the reverse form—what others—any other—will be justified in doing to us. And it now becomes implicit that in speaking of "principles," it is the intention to refer to such directives or rules only as we assume to be of universal force, imperative for everybody, ourselves included, to find. (That the reader will have taken for granted without mention of it.) But perhaps our inverted way of thus taking it for granted may be expressive of a general fact: we take "rules" to be *binding* on us, obligatory for us, only if and when we have recognized that universal character by way of observing that *we* always desire that others conform to them, and so we should adhere to them ourselves, a conviction which, in any particular instance, may go against the grain, since it is not a psychological verity that we *wish*, automatically, to do what we wish all others would do when their doing has an effect on us. It is one great merit of that simple formulation which expresses the oldest of acknowledged moral insights—the Golden Rule—that it directly commands just that: Whatsoever you would that men should do unto you, do ye even so unto them. Without that adjuration, we should be left free to follow a frequent inclination: though I wish other people would always do thus and so when their doing affects me, there is something about me which is different, and no valid reason for my doing thus and so just on that account when it is *my* doing which is in question. In other words, the Golden Rule announces just what moral skeptics repudiate, namely, that there *are* principles both universal and universally binding, and moral precepts are exactly such: whoever denies that there are universally valid imperatives of doing, and alleges that whatever is, here and there in the world, taken to be such has always some merely provincial and parochial explanation—denies the first and essential premise of ethics. He denies what is precisely the first required presumption for there being any such thing as ethics at all. It is exactly that issue answer to which any supposed foundation of ethics must elicit, even if it may be the last question to be answered, clearly and fully, and decisively, in any such investigation.

Consonantly, it must be a first step, in such an investigation, to ask, "What are the premises which the *skeptic* presumes, and which he takes for granted, as generally admitted facts, which are the support for his adverse conclusion?" Unfortunately for us, there *are* such generally admitted facts, as of now, which he can take as the premises of his argument, and one of these is to be found in a common usage of the word 'ethics', a usage which is at least as well justified as any other, and which is indicative of important facts about ethics, taken in any sense, but nevertheless can operate to confuse the question of ethics in that sense in which ethics calls for some validation of its contentual moral principles.

Any "principles" which are to be adjudged normative demand some ground of their validity, and of their character as imperative.

But first, let us observe some impressive facts—facts which are independent of any usage of the word 'ethics'—facts which are definitely pertinent to, but can confuse, the question: Do moral principles actually have any validity as normative and imperative to heed?

Man is a social animal, and social in a special sense peculiarly relevant to ascribing to him any sensibility to the morally imperative. Many other species are social, have the gregarious bent and habit, and exhibit the phenomenon of group cooperation. But we ascribe moral sensibility to men only. Presumably all gregarious species are subject to some instinctive urge which moves them to associate in groups, whose members behave "imperatively" on occasion, in response to behavior on the part, initially, of a member or members of their group and observable to others. Frighten one crow, and the whole flock flies away. Let one sheep jump the fence, and they all do. Let one cow smell salt, and they are all fighting for a chance at it. Let one member of an audience be startled and the whole audience may panic. Monkey see, monkey do, and all men are part monkey. But they are only part monkey, and that is not what we have in mind by human cooperation, incident to the human social habit. There are peculiarities in the human kind of "social behavior": it is discriminative in its response to group-incited stimulation, and the more intelligent, the more so. This animal social phenomenon could not explain why men have morals and monkeys do not. We must attempt to elicit what is peculiar to the human sociality, and may here be in point.

Human sociality is distinctive in several ways, perhaps each of them a matter of degree, when compared with that of a different form of life, but adding up to a difference of kind. Let us first try to elicit the differential resultants which are pertinent, and then add any explanatory afterthoughts which seem relevant.

It is characteristic of any human social order that it has traditions; it has a group memory, as distinct from the merely personal recollections of its various members in any generation. Members of each generation come by what is thus traditional by being told by members of the preceding generation. And they pass it on in the same way. This depends on language, and man is the only animal with any properly so-called language habit.

Among distinctive features of true language is a capacity to convey what is absent—distant in time and space and perhaps presently unobservable—including what the hearer or reader may never have seen, heard, tasted, or smelled, and what may not now exist and may never have existed, but may ensue upon something which is a "here-and-now" factuality. Animal cries and behavioral "gestures" are mainly of the "here-and-now," that portion of it which is capable of being sensed, and are characteristically emotive or instigational, rather than "ideational." This ability to "describe" and "understand," in the human sense, results in the capacity to warn of, predict or direct to, what the recipient may never have experienced, for example, to "educate" the immature and inexperienced about matters which they have never encountered and to enable them, accordingly, to orient themselves to what may now and as yet be unfamiliar. If this be a matter of degree as between ourselves and other creatures, it is a degree of it which makes all the difference. It also includes the capacity to convey and impart an understanding of things like atoms, which no human or other animal can ever sense but may be explanatory of what he observes and of importance to what he had better do, and perhaps do before long. A tradition is distinctively significant of what may be so informational and advisory of such matters to the otherwise inexperienced, to those who would otherwise be unprepared. What any man knows and grasps, or has found out about, the whole group may come to command. And no items of human learning need ever be lost and forgotten. Tradition represents some selective and cumulative body of the useful to impart, carried forward in the group memory. What is traditional and so carried forward is likely to include whatever has "a lesson," a reason to note and give heed to. It will bear upon occasions of choosing which those to whom it is imparted are likely to meet. That is the *raison d'être* of the traditional as such. Other animals, lacking language, have no tradition; they can't learn by being told; they must learn a little by imitation, or learn the hard way, each by his individual experience. Each generation of them begins at the same point the preceding one did. The only propagation of behavioral habits runs with the biological inheritances, and does not alter so long as such instincts and the general environment remains the same.

The human form of sociality is distinguished, for one thing, by having traditions, cumulative in character, being characterized in process by adding a bit, dropping a bit, according as those bits appear important for transmittal. As a continuing entity, a tradition is—and traditionally so after a while—both cumulative and selective according to the ascribed importance and value of the bits. Let us pause here, briefly, to remind ourselves of the contrasts, of which we are aware, merely in the West, between the period preceding the Industrial Revolution, the period of the Industrial Revolution, and that of our own time, that of the "Scientific Revolution," the effects of which are observable, and obvious, in every phase of our current civilization. These are products of something learned. Presently, too, we observe the necessity of a new international ethics.

It is unnecessary to spell out the consequences for human history of what is so newly learned. Having traditions is a tremendous economy. Largely, it accounts for human "progress" and for "civilization." What one generation learns the hard way, later ones may come by without the initial grief and frustrations incident to finding out. Having the same strictly biological inheritance as their stone-age ancestors, and perhaps being in an unaltered geographic environment, those of the new generation may nevertheless be, in virtue of a more effective contemporary social order, in almost every way that concerns them, much better off. They know better what to aim at, and how to get it at lower general cost. If that should not be the case, they must be less intelligent than their ancestors were—incapable of learning anything from history, and so wasting time and energy repeating it. And as we may observe, this kind of phenomenon must be reflected in laws and in any general rules or maxims directly applicable to our ways of behaving and held to be such as must be thus socially mandatory if a sufficient social amity is to be preserved, and if disastrous political and economic consequences are to be avoided, such as the intolerable social disruptions involved in moving from cottage to factory industry, or the demoralization of large numbers of youth who become delinquent because they are insufficiently educated to find a job in an increasingly more automated, more sophisticated economy.

But all the while the ethic of any social order—that part of its tradition which comprises the principles of general conduct and whose precepts will receive general approval and support, even to the extent of being enforced upon any who repudiate or contravene what they dictate—this ethic is the cement which holds society together. If these laws and precepts are *not* conformed to generally, disruptive and intolerable behavior among its members will dissipate or preclude any desirable effects of what is now newly learned and would otherwise work for a better life for society at large.

Every social order has, and must have, its ethic; otherwise disorder will become endemic and its civilization will at best be unprogressive and at worst the society itself may be wiped out. And this body of socially supported and even enforced precepts of conduct is of course what we shall recognize as the positive ethic of any society, anywhere and at any time. And that kind of social phenomenon is what we shall mean by 'the ethics of—'. What other term is appropriate for that? Comparative study of this topic in the case of various societies and those larger social groupings referred to as "cultures" is a highly desirable—necessary even—branch of learning, for the purposes of any society or any culture obliged to some self-criticism of its own ethic or wishing to obtain some advantage by observing the socially desirable or undesirable consequences of the ethics of other societies, societies which have, or do offer us, the findings of "social experiments," experiments in the way of an ethic or feature of an ethic which it would be costly and hazardous for us to come by the hard way, through our own adoption of like modes of directing and governing our own social institution. Such study and learning—comparative ethics—is a branch of cultural anthropology, and what it so seeks out and collates is a general body of fact as determinate and fixed as those collated by the scientists in any other branch of study. Not to be interested in such a study and in the collated results of the investigation of such historical and comparative facts must, for the members of any society at any time, and particularly when faced by problems of such self-criticism as now beset us, would argue them, and, if pertinent, us, to be more stupid than one need be, and more lacking in just that kind of capacity mainly responsible for human progress generally, the capacity to learn from the experience of others instead of repeating their experimentational, wasteful, costly, trial-and-error manner of finding out.

So what do we mean, "Ethics"?

One thing we mean is that body of general accepted doctrine which is to be found in any social group which ever lasted long enough to be singled out and named as a social order or a culture.

And one large lesson to be learned from "Ethics" in this sense, and one hardly needing mention, is that any such body of general accepted doctrine, any such particular "ethics," is relative. We are no longer naive enough to suppose our own such positive doctrine is *the* ethics, and that any departure from it must be an anomalism and a total misapprehension on the part of barbarians or primitive societies. There will be reasons for such an ethics, considerations explicative of it, considerations both specific and general, specific considerations particular to the time and place and the social circumstances, and the consequent such tradition of any time and place, and of any historic antecedents and other pertinent factualities, and considerations as general as those involving the outstanding necessities of any identifiable social order whatever. What it is morally right to do is, even in the most critical sense, always so relative, and always will be. What we might look for, and perhaps eventually find, is some higher order of generalization about "what it is thus right to do," in any time and place in any social order. If we can eventually discover some such generalities, that will be the moral to be drawn from such a study for our own society and the critical determination of our problems of a like kind.

But on the other hand, if there is nothing in the way of such a critical "moral" to be drawn, a useful lesson to be so learned, why study cultural anthropology? Do the specialists in that subject pursue it, and pursue information of the phenomena pertinent to it, for the same kind of reason that men risk their lives on Mt. Everest, because these facts "are there"? If so, the anthropologists might do well not to let the rest of us find that out. We might cross off their subject in any curriculum of learning. That any ethic is, and even must be, relative, that we should hardly need to be told. That there is no lesson having some significance for our own to-be-adopted attitudes of a like kind would be an equal stupidity and an even sillier "disillusionment" for any who should claim intelligence. There is a "good reason" for this relativity of positive ethics as an identifiable feature, and some "moral" to be drawn from that—some counsel applicable to the problems of our own mores, whatever our own time and place, and to our particular problems, those now confronting us and requiring to be met and resolved, those in our own positive and social ethics which are now in question or which would better be—some social confluence to judgment as to what we ought now socially to resolve upon for our own social guidance. But, beyond this, if there is any such thing as what we now ought generally to approve and conform to as directives of our own conduct as affecting others than ourselves only, then this whole business of cultural anthropology seems likely to be nugatory and a waste of time. If the only "lesson for life" to be obtained in that quarter is that any positive ethics is relative, then let us abandon such ethical relativists to their own ivory tower, there to amuse themselves in their own way, and not bother others about their special kind of occupation any longer. What we ought, here and now and in view of our present social circumstances and resultant social problems, to resolve upon as our own positive rules for the direction of our socially significant self-government may be as relative as those social circumstances and those social problems which characterize our social order. But so what? So nothing, if there is nothing which we would best to resolve upon, and promulgate and ourselves conform to. But there will be, and there will be something, in our tradition, pertinent to, or meeting, unanticipated problems of this general sort. If our social scientists have anything bearing on that to offer, then let them, whether as scientists or as citizens, advise us of it. And otherwise—? If they should tell us that that is not their own special kind of problem—well, they are still members of our own body politic. Let them now take off their anthropological hats, and take a hand in addressing themselves to our present and exigent problem, that of the to-be-approved moral view, here and now to be determined. There will be something in the body of the past experience of men in societies at large which will be relevant. And they are our social repository of this store of wisdom, gathered from social experience, from past experiments and the consequences of them. If so, this is the pat occasion for bringing it forward, and, if not, what is their special branch of learning good for? Is the comparative study of cultural anthropology something pursued just for fun—if you find it fun—or is it a serious and responsible vocation having a social function to exercise, and general social purposes to meet? If there be nothing in the way of such social utility of a branch of learning, then devotees of such a sport can form their own sport club and solicit funds for it amongst those who are taken that way. What good is *any* science? That question will answer itself. If it does not, why this waste of time at the general expense? As with philately, let those who are interested in it pursue it, and, as for the rest of us, let us take it or leave it, according to whether we find it a diverting recreation or a bore.

Cultural anthropology *is* a science, a highly important one, socially useful as perennially bearing on problems likely to be current at any time. But if, right now, with an exigent policy decision to be determined, there should be no answer nearer to right than alternatives, would this science have anything to say to us, or would there be any excuse for them to interrupt our earnest effort to meet this problem as it will later prove desirable to have met it, if what they have to tell us is that there is nothing in particular which will be appropriate and to be recommended, that questions of rightness and *justified* deciding are just questions of what you happen to be bent on approving and propagating, so let everybody just follow his nose, without critical comment? If that is the case, then let us tell those who so respond that we do not invite them to *persuade* us. Do they have on hand anything that will be *convincing*? If not, let them hold their peace; it is no time for idle chat; we have something at stake, and as of now. The next time any Bay of Pigs episode comes up, we shall know who not to summon to our aid.

If there be no lesson of critique, of the advisable or inadvisable, to be drawn, then the pursuit of cultural anthropology is a waste of time.

Any suppositious scientist who indulges in that kind of sophistry discredits himself and his vocation. Cultural anthropology is a branch of learning peculiarly apposite to meeting problems of social policy. Any such scientist should take note, and be a little careful in what he says about right or wrong mores—social policies which have sometime and somewhere been approved and followed, and the desirable or undesirable results of such social experiments, results which are a matter of experimental fact.

But our principal interest here and now, in this digression, is a quite small point: it concerns a common use of the word 'ethics', in reference to mores—ones which are actual or have been actual. Any such body of fact, and the finding out of it, is not itself a question of any rightness or wrongness of the referred-to mores—or is only a question of right or wrong in the reporting of such fact. We look to the cultural anthropologists to be responsible for *that* kind of rightness or wrongness in their science at least; and they recognize this and behave accordingly, with no persuasion from the rest of us. Let them take the moral of *that*, and not say things about the moral in general which will make them out to be silly or perverse in the pursuit of their own business, and which would belie the responsibility they accept for conclusions they publicly announce. We do not, of course, attribute this type of inconsistency to cultural anthropologists: it is would-be philosophers or dabblers in both anthropology and ethics who may exhibit this particular brand of unself-conscious foolery. There is a right and a wrong about everything to be decided and about every commitment taken. And 'right' is a synonym for 'that which it is imperative to be, so far as in you lies, in any decision taken'. Any who should speak in contravention of that surely can make no claim to be right in what he says. He must be a culprit or some kind of undiscerning blockhead. If he says anything worthy of deciding about, it must be overlooked as accidental. That kind of accident happens: "Out of the mouths of fools—." But, praise be, it does not happen too often.

But let us cease this digressive interlude. Our present point to which it is relevant is a quite small one: one respectable and common meaning of 'Ethics' is to refer to "ethic-s" in general, mores which sometime and somewhere have prevailed. And the question of anything to be so referred to involves a kind of fact, the determination of which is something to be found out, independently of any question of rightness in the content of any such ethics. But there *is* such a question about any such ethic and anything comprised in it—the question of actual rightness. This last question—the question of *actual* rightness—is not one included in the determination of the historical fact of any ethic, which is the peculiar vocational pursuit of cultural anthropology. That second sort of question, that pertaining to a second sort of fact—actual rightness, or such—falls under the peculiar business of ethics. Ethics is not the examination of historically factual ethic-s, other than in the sense of concerning itself with the actual rightness or wrongness of items contentual to such ethic-s.

But we hardly need so much warning concerning possible confusions over the uses of words. The point is obvious. We turn now to matters which call for a little more concern.

3. Some Hints as to Horizons to Come

Ethics proper concerns only questions which are normative in character. But not every question of the normative is one of ethics. We have so far suggested that ethics proper is confined to questions of the right *to do,* to bring about. But we have not, however, so far even asked the question, "Does ethics extend to what may be "right" in any and every sense of 'right'?" We have implicitly suggested the answer, "No, only to the right to do; the "right to think" is another kind of question and falls under logic." But is that answer—that ethics is limited to questions of the right *to do*—exactly right? As will have occurred to the reader, it is not, or at least the sufficiency of it is dubious. Better, ethics, as most strictly and commonly understood, namely, as a normative discipline, is limited to questions of what it is right to do toward others: right when others will be affected by what one decides to do. When nobody but the doer will be much affected, what is done may be prudent or not, but still fail to be of moral import. And what a carpenter does in his carpentering will be either right-carpentering or wrong-carpentering, and depending on whether it is his own house or somebody else's, it will be either morally right or prudentially right, and possibly both, but the question "right carpentering?" is not exactly a prudential question or a moral question, since the correct answer does not *ipso facto* imply "moral rightness" or "prudential rightness," though it must have some kind of "rightness-import" or it will not be a question of right doing at all; it would not even be a normative question. We can answer the question "right carpentering" without implying either moral or prudential rightness. And a piece of "right carpentering" could be prudentially right—such as will save the carpenter money—but morally wrong—such as will cost the owner money for repairs. How—according to prevailing usage—do "morally right," "prudentially right," and "carpentry-right" stand related?

We presently observe that common usage implies that moral rightness concerns only "right toward others." This is a quite obvious reason for our setting off "right to do to others" from "right to do because I shall find the results gratifying to me"— the "prudentially right to do." Smith and all the rest of us have a personal interest in what Jones puts in the class of "gratifying to do but to do merely"—the "prudentially right for Jones to do." What Jones does because it is prudent for him to do may or may not do us any harm. But what Jones puts in the class "right for Jones to do toward others," and does or does not do accordingly, is a matter of personal interest to the Smiths and all the rest: we may be the "others" in question. We all have a personal interest in Jones' precepts of morality; apart from that, we have no personal stake in his precepts of prudence. So there is this good reason for the two classifications, moral precepts and prudential precepts, even if almost any rule of doing, followed by anybody, is likely to be classifiable in both ways, and classifiable as moral and prudent, moral but not prudent, prudent but not moral, or neither prudent nor moral.

But this general fact being obvious, and our tentative decision being to apply 'moral' in the narrower sense of 'right to do toward others', there is another question, a semantic question which must interest us: In the case of acts which are, for any one of us, morally right but not prudent to do, or prudent but morally *wrong,* what do we do? We are generally agreed about that: What is finally right to do is what is morally right, whether it is also prudentially dictated or not. But do we really *accept* that, whether we act conformably to it or not? None of us conforms to it strictly, and occasionally when we fail to do so, we are not affected by any sense of sin.

It is, we agree, an important and sound and often pertinent moral precept that promises made should be kept. We accept that as being a moral rule. But if I promised yesterday to meet somebody today at eleven, and now I find myself in bed and my doctor tells me to stay there, I don't go. Nobody in his right mind would. And nobody who has good sense will think the worse of anyone on that account.

So what about that?

Do we abandon the notion that there are any moral rules universally imperative to follow? Or do we say about sound moral rules, as about other rules, "Every rule has its exceptions"? Or do we say, "Moral rules, as a rule, overrule prudential or any other kind of rules when rules of two different kinds apply, but that *that* rule also has its exceptions"? Or do we say there are, among rules properly called moral, little rules— "maxims"?—and more general rules which are rules for applying those lesser rules; and the overarching moral principle—or one such—is "Follow the big rule; that's the final arbitrament of the morally right to do."

It is not the case that the moral consideration always overrules any also pertinent prudential or otherwise nonmoral consideration. So the moral dictate allows or even requires working in the merely prudential dictate. But supposing that this is true, is there a "higher" general rule for such weighing of—? And, if so, then this higher rule is the moral rule which would apply and be the rule for the final arbitrament of the question, "right to do?"

So much for initial remarks.

Obviously a great many subtle and complex issues and problems are involved in these matters. To this point we have done little more than provide a hasty, abrupt, and crude summary of some of them. And one is observant, of course, that there are many further issues and problems involved, each of them deserving, and requiring, extended and judicious consideration. At this point we have done little more than recognize, or precipitate an awareness of, an entire "snaggle" of such issues and problems.

We now address ourselves to the process of sorting things out, examining them, and attempting to relate them, each to the other.

We begin with the consideration of something without which ethics would be inconsequential, if not impossible, a consideration of the good and bad in experience.

This is where making sense of ethics begins.

The Good and Bad in Experience

Prolegomena

In the root sense, good and bad are qualities with which experience is affected. We have, all of us, the native sense of reality as more than and beyond the experience in which it is manifested to us. To reduce the world we live in to the experience we have of it would be to belie this experience itself. Even if such subjectivism should be the final metaphysical truth, none of us would be able to believe it.

But there is one feature of this reality in which we find ourselves which would be different if we were not in it: whatever this world we live in might otherwise be like if we and other conscious beings did not exist, it would in that case lack any quality of good or bad. If the world existed before consciousness, there was then no character of good or bad ascribable to it—except by reference to conscious creatures destined to come later and be affected by the consequences of such antecedent states of it. And if the world is to go on after all conscious beings shall become extinct, there will then be no character of good or bad which it will have—in any other sense than that of striking with horror those who may foresee this debacle before it happens. Good and bad are in the world by relation to conscious life; out of that relationship, they have no being, and ascription of them has no meaning.

To repeat: good and bad are, in the root sense, qualities with which experience is affected. So taken, the good is that quality of a content or passage of experience by virtue of which one is satisfied to have it as it is and would be content to prolong it. And the bad is that quality of an experience to which we are averse, and by reason of which we would alter it or be rid of it. And in this root sense, experience is as you find it.

All other senses of 'good' and 'bad', and of those words as applied to other things than the experiential, are ultimately derivative from this basic one in which they signify the satisfying or dissatisfying character of experience which they may affect. We shall later have to consider various other senses—they are legion-in which 'good' and 'bad', and other value terms, are used. Broadly speaking, what other things than the experiential are said to be good or bad are so spoken of because of their actual or possible, or their expected, influence in conducing to the goodness, or the badness, of experiences affected by them. Whatever would—or may or might—in its direct or indirect effect upon experience contribute to the betterment of a conscious life is so far forth and in that respect good. And whatever would—or may or might—so operate as to make some conscious living worse is so far forth and in that respect bad.

By reason of its fundamental significance for all other modes in which goodness and badness are ascribed and may require to be assessed, this basic sense of the good and bad as qualities directly found in experience ought to be our first topic of examination. But in any attempt so to begin, we must inevitably be drawn into the consideration of other and collateral questions which also concern direct experience. And in view of that unavoidable involvement, we may do better if first we make a preliminary digression here—as briefly as we can and as inadequately as we must—endeavoring to set this topic of the good and bad as features or factors in experience into the frame of reference of direct experience at large, within which it must be viewed if we are to attain any measure of clarity about it. By so doing, we may hope to achieve some preliminary conspectus in the light of which we can thereafter pursue our more limited topic of the valuational without the necessity for the continual interruption of it for the interpolation of some sidewise explanation.

This order of procedure may also be appropriate to the fact that we must eventually face the fundamental question as to how our apprehensions of the good and bad in experience stand related to empirical knowledge in general. Any valid empirical knowing must similarly find its data in direct experience, as well as looking to further "such" experience for any possible corroboration of it. If we can, by preliminary considerations, put ourselves in a position to observe how the ultimate grounds of value assessments stand related to the first premises of empirical knowing generally, that will be notably to our advantage in the discussion of later topics, topics to which we must in any case proceed. We shall discover, however, that these other and preliminary considerations which concern direct experience as we find it are themselves various, and complex, and complexly related to one another. With the utmost brevity which we dare attempt, they will occupy us for the remainder of this essay.

On this whole topic of phenomenology—the description, classification, and analysis of the experiential as such—it is peculiarly evident that none of us is in a position to tell another anything which he could not ascertain for himself without being told. We are all of us equally conversant with experience. At most, we can only draw attention to something which might otherwise pass unnoticed, and hope to express what we so observe in language aptly indicative of what we would point out about it. But on the other hand, the attempt to tell the truth about matters relating to the experiential as such suffers from two difficulties peculiar to it which may well make any of us wary and reluctant to venture upon that kind of undertaking.

In the first place, if it is true—as it must be—that all of us are capable of determining the facts about matters of this kind—since it calls for nothing more than clear self-consciousness—still it is also true that to turn our thought in this direction is antipodal to that ordinary and practical bent of attention which must predominate in the case of any of us. We must focus primarily upon the external world, what goes on in our neighborhood, what we can do about it, and what is likely to happen if we do so intervene—or happen if we fail to take a hand. It is this world of external objects and environing states of affairs of which we must be pervasively aware and to which we must be ready to respond. And that enterprise requires us to look well beyond the end of our noses. Self-consciousness, otherwise than as attention to what we are doing, or may do, to affect outward circumstances, is a bit of a luxury, to be indulged in those interludes of practical living in which we may feel secure enough to take our eyes off what may harm us if we fail to be alert to it, or prejudice our welfare if we fail to seize the propitious opportunity.

Second, and largely in consequence of this first consideration, the findings of direct experience represent that kind of truth which ordinary language is least well fitted to express. By reason of the required and commonly prevailing intent, any words we may try to use merely for the report of experience, and any syntactic putting of such words together, come near to being copyrighted in advance for purposes of referring not to but beyond anything which might be assured merely by attentive self-observation.

The first difficulty is, thus, because the practical and pervasive interest is not in looking *at* experience but in looking *through* it to some external factuality of which it is a sign, we are normally inattentive to experience as such. And second, when we would—exceptionally—observe the experience directly and on its own account, instead of looking to what it further signifies in the way of objective things and facts, we find that this business of formulating the content of experience itself, as immediately realized, is left without any apt linguistic vehicle for the conveyance of it. Often we are reduced to locutions such as 'looks like', 'appears to be', 'feels as if', and the like, that is, to the attempt to formulate the immediate fact of experience itself by mention of the external circumstances in which this directly findable content on which we wish to report would be likely to arise. This linguistic predicament is a bit ironic, since it is only by reason of this content of direct awareness that we have any intimation of, or reason to believe in, these signified objective factualities we mention in our endeavor to report this content of experience which is our evidence of them.

We may call the use of language with the intent to convey a content and character of our experience its *phenomenological* or *expressive* usage. And we may call the use of language with the intent to communicate information of external things and factualities signified—whether these are intimated to us by present experience or not—its *objective* usage. But there is no well-marked expressive mood of syntax. And even so far as there are idioms of language used for signaling the expressive intent, these are easily open to perverse misconstruction by any objector who should be bent upon the denial that there is any such thing as immediate experience. Any such idiom we attempt to use is—as we have just acknowledged—open to such obtuse or perverse misinterpretation as a kind of metaphorical usage of "object language." It requires no more than the semantic dogma that all truth is to be told in the "object language" mood to capture the metaphysical thesis that we are no more than intricately organized physical objects behaving in physicochemical ways, and that conscious experience is a myth. On that point, it may as well be said at once that, to any who do not recognize conscious experience as a factuality which is over and above, and distinct from, those external factualities which are sensed and represented, we shall have nothing to say. Since it is experience of which we would here speak, the negative thesis of physicalism must represent a disagreement too fundamental to allow any hope for any common premises, as a basis for possible conclusions we shall be interested to consider here. We shall later observe certain commonplaces of our knowledge which—we take it—should be sufficient to compel an admission of our presumption in this matter, but we shall not argue the metaphysical point.

For the rest, abjuring any pretense to expertise, we can do no better than to proceed on the presumption which has been mentioned: that the general features of human experience are common to all of us and open to the determination of any who will attentively observe. If we go beyond, or qualify, what may be readily recognized as such "common sense," we do so with the full recognition that any reader will, of right and of necessity, function as his own critic, to whom we must appeal to remark the point and determine whether he finds it so or not.

There are four main aspects, features, factors, which may be distinguished in experience at large: the sense-presentational, the representational, affective feeling, and the volitional. Roughly at least, these represent what are commonly denominated sensing, thinking, feeling, and willing. Whether there are others, not to be accounted for as some complex of these, we need not for the present ask, but may postpone any such question until the relevance of it should appear, and confine ourselves, for the time being, to matters which may be plainer.

There are such plainer matters, more easily determinable, concerning the factors in that knowledge which must find its basis, eventually, in perceptual experience. And there may be also matters which are plainer concerning the question of the relationship between affective feelings, sure to have some relevance to our valuations, and those labeled sense-presentations, which must function as the basis for what we commonly and unquestioningly recognize as empirical knowing. Questions concerning the root of empirical knowing in perception, in comparison with our value assessments, and with normative judgments generally, are bound to be basically involved in any theory of ethics. If we should have any doubt of that, even a cursory observation of recent and current discussions must convince us of such a relevance. Let us make an attempt upon this question of comparison, of likeness and difference between those perceptual apprehensions we more ordinarily label those of "objective fact," and our basic value determinations, by looking to the root of them in common experience.

Perception may at first and unthinkingly be supposed to represent the simple apprehension of a datum, something which dawns or comes as a simple presentation to sense, and which we find to be as it is and not otherwise. Something which answers to that description must surely be involved; otherwise there would be no accounting for the fact that I presently see a desk and books, and do not see a potato or a rhinoceros. And as we say, seeing is believing. But on second thought, this simple identification of the seeing with the believing, or of the seen with the believed, cannot be altogether correct. Seeing is one thing, and believing is a different thing. The infant at an early stage—so we must surely be correct in supposing—sees something but believes nothing. And later, as generally with adults, though the believing may accompany the seeing more or less spontaneously, the seeing cannot be repudiated or set aside—there is the visual presentation—but the believing sometimes can and must be. Occasionally we make mistakes about what we are looking at and believe to be the objects there and seen. This morning I saw what I took to be a pencil on my desk and picked it up to write. But it left no marks on the paper, and, on second glance, I observed that what I had picked up was the wooden skewerlike instrument which I keep handy for scoring photo-mounts. When I picked it up, it was with a confident expectation which was promptly disappointed. And as this little episode should remind me—as one who would think about his thinking and doing—I omitted to remark two factors other than my seeing which are involved in my perception of an object. I not only "saw" something—found it visually presented—but I thought of, represented, something further in thinking "pencil." I thought of the manipulation of it as leaving marks on paper. Without that commitment of anticipatory belief, I might not have remarked my error. It was the believed-in representation of certain words to appear on the paper before me which was disappointed. What I so believed in and represented is that part of my "perceiving" which was proved mistaken. The "look" of this thing was "pencillike," but also "skewerlike." My hasty glance did not determine "will write"—essential to being a pencil—and the test of that showed it false in this instance. Indeed, I am a little lucky that my story can be told so simply. There is also another thing on my desk which I might have as easily picked up with an entirely similar result. I thought to myself "pencil," "will leave visible marks on this paper." But this other thing I now mention *is* a pencil but *will not* leave marks on this paper; it is a white pencil which will leave marks on brown photo-folders and the like, but none which are visible on white paper. As this reminds me, the thought I had in this matter—my interpretation of what I glanced at and picked up—was more specific than my words, and takes longer to express than to think: "ordinary pencil, which if manipulated appropriately will leave dark gray marks on white paper." But let us just say 'pencil' for short.

There are three discriminable factors in perception: the presentation; the element of the thought-of, some representing, which runs beyond the sense-apprehension; and a belief or confidence attaching to this "thinking of," as an expecting of something further, conditional upon a possible doing, a testing of this expectancy, a trial of the applicability of this representing to this content of the sensibly presented. These three have grown together, become associated, by reason of past experience. In my first glance, in the above example, they were all there at once and undiscriminated in the perceptual experience. But for any perspicuous account of my perceptual knowing, they have to be distinguished, by abstraction, within this full perceptual experience. This discrimination, in the example cited, was *ex post facto* to the experience of seeing. In a different case, it might not be.

Let us choose a slightly different example. In driving the parkway the other day, I saw what looked like a rock in the road and automatically swerved. I did not feel sure that it was a rock: it could be just a ball of dirt or a wrapper of burlap fallen from some truck. I didn't hit it, and I was past it too quickly to look again. But in any case I thought "rock in the road": otherwise I might not have swerved. If I had run into it and gotten a bad jolt—or gotten no jolt at all—I should have found out. But I was interested in safety, not in confirming or disconfirming my conjectural apprehension. My representational interpretation, classification, and cognitive expectancy remained, and still remain, a *dubitandum*. But I saw what I *saw*, some physical object anyway; it was no hallucination. That is to say, I still am confident that if I had gotten out and investigated, I should have observed some removable object lying in the road: "speck of something blown against the windshield" is an implausible interpretation of my momentary content of vision. But beyond that, what representational expectancy would have stood up under further investigation, I have no firm conviction at all.

To fill out the picture, perhaps we should add two further examples. Let the first one be of that ordinary and most frequent sort which passes almost without notice and with no retrospective consideration. When I observed my mistake about the supposed-to-be-pencil, I picked up another and similar-looking thing, glancing this time at the pointed end to make sure that it looked dark on this paper, and it did; and that was that. This exemplifies "usual perception," "normal perception," the kind which succeeds in its practical project, raises no doubt and calls for no reconsideration.

There is still another kind of perceptual occasion: the once or twice in a lifetime sort. I once saw a cow in an open meadow—or what I thought was a cow. But after I had walked a few steps further, it suddenly and inexplicably disappeared. I was still thinking "cow," but no further cowlike appearance appeared to me. I did not know what to think and believe about that, and I still don't. But I promptly repudiated any conviction that an actual cow had been there where I seemed to see one.

With these supplementations, perhaps such trivial examples are not too far off from typical of those experiential passages which fall under the head of perceptual knowing—or of misperceiving, of perceptual cognition anyway.

However, let us pause in passing to remark that, in reviewing the examples, we have still not depicted in full any actual perceptual experience very likely to arise. We have confined ourselves so far to the aspects which mark any occasion of experience as a perceptual cognition. And perhaps no full experience anybody ever had was *merely* cognitive. In almost any experience the content of which is attended to and in any wise "taken seriously" as signifying some factuality or object, there will also be some enterprise in mind, some possible doing thought of, to which this moment's experience may be relevant, and some desirable sequel of this occasion which we are bent upon furthering, or some undesirable eventuation of it which we would avoid. We visually apprehend and pick up pencils desiring to write something down, and swerve our automobiles to avoid being killed or injured. Considerations of desirability—and valuations made—govern our ways of acting adopted and are directive of what we look for, may perceive, and of what we think of when sense-presentations are given in experience, as also they serve to direct our activities in response to these presentations. The knowing serves to guide the doing, and the doing is governed by the valuing. Thus the valuing even governs, indirectly, what we think of, represent, on occasions of perceiving. That is the point to which we must return later on.

To leave these considerations out, and speak as if perceptual or other knowing contained its own significance wholly within itself, would be a gross misrepresentation of the facts of life.

But confining ourselves for the present to so much of any actual experience as is essential to its being called cognitive and perceptual, we must still remark the plurality of the features of it and the relations of them to one another. On any occasion of perception, there will be something in the way of each of the three factors mentioned above. First, there will be something in this experience which is a datum of presentation, disclosed with a certain specificity of appearing. This is willy-nilly, incorrigible, seen—or heard, smelled, tasted, felt—just in the way it is and not otherwise. If what presents itself looks yellow, we cannot make it appear blue; it if tastes bitter, we cannot taste it as sweet; if it smells acrid, we cannot smell it as fragrant. This specificity of the appearing is simply given in the experience—it is what William James called a "hard datum." With respect to this content of appearance, we are passive rather than active; its particular specificity is imposed upon our awareness.

Second, there is something thought of, represented, something which adds itself, or is added, to this content of appearing and does not itself so appear. In the case of what I saw on my desk and picked up, "pencil," "thing that will make marks on white paper," was so represented. It added itself, by habit of thought, relevant to a purpose. In the case of what was seen in the road ahead, not only "rock," "hard thing which will give a jolt," but also "lump of dirt" and "burlap" were thought of. The specificity of "yellow-brownish looking" and "appearing about so big" was given, but "will cause a jolt" or "will cause no jolt" was not given, not included in the presentational appearance. These added themselves somewhat spontaneously, but in this instance with more attention and with a question mark.

It is also in point, in both these examples, that what so accrued to the appearing reflected a purposive attitude which was contextual to the occasion. If I had found that thing I picked up from my desk in my pocket on a rainy day in camp, I might have thought of something different, "dry shavings to start a fire." In that case "pencil" or "skewer" would not have mattered—what would have mattered would have been "dry wood." And both "pencil" and "skewer" satisfy that added thought. And if the rock appearance had presented itself on a walk in the woods, it might have aroused no more than some idle question, "granite or shale, or anthill?"

This factor of the representation—the interpretation or conception, "pencil," or "skewer," or "dry wood"—is not incorrigible. It reflects an activity of thinking, and is amenable to purpose or interest. The specificity of *this* factor is governable, and amenable to purpose or interest. And if such representing has any character of deliberation, as in the case of the suppositious rock in the road, then so far from being willy-nilly, it may stand as a challenge to thinking, directed to the guidance of our doing. If I had represented "burlap" only, and given credence to that thought, it might have been just too bad.

And as this draws to our attention, there is also this factor of believing, crediting, having confidence in, whether the thinking be spontaneous and uncritical or a conclusion deliberately adopted. This credence attaches to the representing—the concept or interpretation—but the two factors have to be distinguished since we do not give credence to everything we think of, or even to everything we represent, given the instigation of what appears. We read fiction, for example, and think of what this story tells, but think of it merely as make-believe and with no credence. If everything we think of were to be actual and as we think of it, our world would become too cluttered up for any finding of our way about in it, and too full of incompatibles to be understood. We may do a bit of daydreaming while driving a clear road, but we don't mix up any daydream with what we see ahead. People who should be liable to confuse a merely thought-of rock with the representation of a rock as seen would be well advised not to drive, but also they should not drive if they do not have "imagination enough" to anticipate a possible jolt when the presentation of a possible rock in the road appears to them.

It is just there in the factor of extending credence to what is thought-of, represented, on occasions of perceptual appearing, that the significance of dubiety and possible deliberation, and the hazard of perceptual knowing come in. Also this constituent of a believing in what goes beyond the appearance and extends to what is further represented, and taken as signified, cannot be ruled out in any case of perceiving whatever. You can see no object at all without some representing and some credence extended to it. A cow in the meadow isn't a cow in the meadow unless it has another side you cannot presently see. You confidently expect another side to appear if the cow walks around you or you walk around the cow. If there isn't more to an object than can appear on any one perceptual occasion, it isn't the perception of any actual object but an illusion or hallucination. Also, that is where your trouble lies in any dubiety of perceiving—the "more" which you have to take on trust and can only represent and may give credence to. The factor of the represented—if you believe in it—is your cognitive *interpretation* of the given factor in perception.[1] Perceptual believing is, in any case, believing in something you *don't* see but is added to what you see—fortunate believing, we shall hope; justified believing if the evidence is sufficient for it; true believing or not, as we may later find out.

It is also important to observe that, in the case of any *error* of perception, the discovery of it requires us to "take back," to recant, the content of the representing and believing, but we should not, indeed, cannot, repudiate the content of the seeing, the hearing, or such—the given factor. If I had run over that suppositious rock but got no jolt, I should have recanted my interpretation, my dubitable expectation of its causing a jolt

---

1. Whether we should call a doubted representing an "interpretation" or not is merely a question of the appropriate use of words. Perhaps we should say that it is an interpretation—since it has to be in mind in order to be even doubted—but not an *adopted* interpretation.

   The word 'represent' is subject to a similar question of aptness, and we might have done better to stick to 'thought of'. Sometimes 'represent' is used as implying 'believed in' and sometimes not. But it is of some importance to indicate that "representing," "interpreting," and "conceiving of *what* appears" are here considered to be the same thing, and to be an "operation of thought."

and my dubious ascription "rock." But it looked to me just the way it looked to me, rock or not. And in the case of the thing I picked up from my desk, there was nothing about the given appearance to be taken back when I discovered that it will not write. The trouble was in my not looking at the point; there was nothing wrong with what I *did* see. Even in the case of the cow, I still saw what I *saw*. If I walk around any cow I see and see no other side, it may be that I would better consult a physician, but if I want any help from him, I should still do well to tell him the truth about that *appearance* which appeared to me.

Speaking more exactly, we shall confine the rightness or the error of perception to the believing in or crediting what is thought of. The representation or concept "pencil" was a wrong concept to apply, and "rock" may be a wrong interpretation of what was seen in looking ahead, but there will be no perceptual error—and no right perceiving either—if there is no conviction or crediting involved. And even in the example of the cow, any physician consulted might say, "You had an abnormal experience perhaps, but if you did not believe in this apparition after it disappeared, it is not medically to be classed as a hallucination."[2] That is, in the case of any appearing, a certain representation or conception may be erroneous to believe in, wrong to credit, but, strictly speaking, it is the believing or crediting which is right or wrong—just as, also, in the case of right or wrong doing, what is done will be right-to-do or

---

2. The three words we commonly apply to perceptual error—'misperception', 'illusion' and 'hallucination'—are all of them highly ambiguous, but it is the degree of seriousness of the possible mistake which more or less governs our choice of them. "Misperceptions" are "normal"—easily corrected errors which happen frequently. "Illusions" are a little more trouble to dispel, or a little more serious in their possible results. "Hallucinations" are quite bad, a matter calling for some kind of treatment perhaps. But every time my spectacles slip down my nose, I am likely to see my interlocutor with two heads, one above the other. The only reason that this visual appearance is not hallucinatory is that I am not ever tempted to believe that anything out of the ordinary has happened to my companion or to me. Otherwise I might be shocked out of my wits twenty times a day. It is what one may be convinced of as objective fact by means of an appearance which is the serious matter.

wrong-to-do, but it is the *doing* of it which is right or wrong. (Rightness or wrongness is always predicable of the activity, or the committing-ourselves-to.)

Quite similarly, in the activity of thinking, what we think may be right-to-think or wrong-to-think in the particular instance in question, but it is the thinking which is right or wrong. And the present point, precisely located, is that a conceptual representing, in the case of a particular given appearance, will *not* be a perceptual error if you merely think of it *but do not believe in or credit it*. However, *what* you so think of will *truly* have the character of right-to-apply or wrong-to-apply, right-to-believe-in or wrong-to-believe-in, in the particular instance. In the case of any misperception, the exact locus of the error is in the believing in or the crediting of a representation or conception in a way which, confronted by this appearance, is a wrong way to think of it, to believe in it or to credit it. In effect, one applies the wrong concept to the appearance. And there will be no *right* perceiving except as there is something thought of and believed in which, one being confronted by this appearance, is a right thing to be thought of and believed in—and as being factual. Here one, in effect, applies a correct concept to the appearance.

And let us add, lest we lose sight of a point already made: Confronted by a given appearance, there may be, and, indeed, there will always be, more than one such "right-thing-to-think-of-and-believe-in," *e.g.,* "pencil," "dry wood" or "cylinder with a point," as well as any number of things which would fall under the heading of "wrong-thing-to-think-of-and-believe-in," given what objectively presents itself to us. It lies in this multiplicity of right alternatives of conception, in particular instances, that, over and above the alternatives of being right or wrong in what we perceive, our perceiving may be determinable by reference to some particular *quaesitum,* determinable by relevance to some purpose or interest to be served by finding out. And as we shall all be aware, upon reflection, even this simplest and basic type of empirical knowing—perceiving—may be directed to, or almost we can say, "requires" to answer to, some further determination than merely the imperative to confine ourselves to the cognitively justified to believe—and requires some *relevance* to purpose, wish and will.[3]

And so we see, on the whole, on any circumstantial examination, even in this summary fashion, perception turns out to be a quite complex matter, and completely related to other aspects of our conscious living. The supposition that we look and see, or listen and hear, etc., and forthwith—bang!—a piece of reality is apprehended, is oversimple; as wide of the mark as supposing that the infant, first opening his eyes upon the world, promptly knows what he sees as well as we do. Even in that sense in which he might be said to know what he *sees,* he still has no idea *of what* he sees. And neither should we, without associative, representational, and directable thinking.

A sober metaphysics and epistemology, and ethics, will not essay any funny little intellectual games to play with our human predicament, and affront the common sense of the reality in which we find ourselves. Instead it will attempt to elicit the general features and structure of it, and our situation in it. If we do not share a common reality, and communities of our own nature, there will be nothing for us to speak about to one another, and no possibility of communicating anything. Basic common sense is our common and required postulate—if it be nothing more than that. To elicit this community, as faithfully and with such accuracy as we can, is the philosophic task.

Let us now proceed, on the basis of these remarks on the nature of perception, and, more generally, on the nature of human experience, to the next essay.

---

3. [An abrupt transition occurs at this point in the particular text under consideration. I have included two further paragraphs from the fragments, and a sentence, to form a transition to the next essay. In the particular text here under consideration, there is a plenitude of following materials which are omitted. These go into more detail than is helpful, or felicitous, in the context of the limited project in hand. –Ed.]

The Good and Bad in Experience

Good and bad are, in the root sense, qualities with which experiences, as they come to us, are imbued. And experiences as such are good or bad according as they are, or were or will be, or would be, found good by those whose experiences they are, or were or will, or would be. We can be mistaken about the goodness or badness of any kind of external actuality, even in the presence of it. But one who suffers the illusion of pain really suffers, and for one who should have the illusion of gratification, his experience would be actually gratifying, whatever mistake he might be making about the cause of it or the justification of his enjoying it. If, as some conceive, all physical ills are in fact disorders of our thinking and believing, the recipe for the cure of them may be different, but the badness of the experiences remains just what it seems to be. Otherwise no regimen for release from this illusionment would be in order. With respect to the good or bad quality of an experience, when and as experienced, there is no mistake which he whose experience it is can make, unless a merely verbal one in the language he uses in formulating it to himself. With respect to the good or bad quality of a present experience, there is no distinction of appearance and reality.

However, goodness and badness are ascribed to things—to all sorts of entities—in a variety of different modes, and they are ascribed even to experiences in different ways which it is necessary to distinguish. For example—and as we shall shortly have to remark—an experience which is found bad in the having may still be a good experience to have had, by reason of its salutary effect upon experience which comes later. And an experience which is gratifying within its own temporal boundaries may nevertheless be a bad experience to indulge in, because it will later prove bad to have indulged in it. Such verbal paradoxes are no practical puzzle to us, being merely statements of familiar fact, but we could not spell out what may be thus obvious without the possibility of predicating value in all the linguistic modes in which we also speak of other things—in the past tense, in the future tense, and in the mode of supposition ("if") and consequence ("then"), and of supposition as having the *same* consequences whether it be in accord with, or contrary to, fact.

In this connection, it may be well to remark that experiences are a kind of actuality, temporal if not spatial: they are events of consciousness which occur. And it must be possible, too, to speak of them in all the modes of predication which are significant in the case of occurrences in *general* even though they have their particularities as one species of events, the specific nature of which is a matter familiar to us but one the *statement* of which involves a longstanding metaphysical puzzle. This metaphysical puzzle we cannot undertake here to unravel, but must confine ourselves to such points concerning it as our familiarity with the experiential as such is sufficient to assure.

The value of any *actual* experience, in this root sense presently in question, is the value actually found by the experiencer of it *when* this experience is present to him. But we cannot fail to make assessments of value which *was* found in experience now past, since these are our only final bases for predictions of value to be found in like experiences in the future. The actual goodness or badness of any past experience, again in this root sense, is the goodness or badness which *was* found in it. But with respect to values, as with respect to other matters, our cognitive predicament obliges us to speak of this past factuality as it is remembered, or as it may be otherwise and indirectly assurable at present. And we may—and often do, and perhaps must sometimes—regard such past fact as assured by present remembering, neglecting the possible error of recall. Future predicted experiences are as they *will* be found when they later come—with respect to value qualities, as on other points. But we have to speak of them as we *expect* them to be, and with whatever measure and kind of assurance there may be for what is so anticipated. We cannot do better than to gauge the value of them in the sense of "if and when," though there may be uncertainty both about a future experience, as described in other than value terms, and about the value ascribed in case this experience, as otherwise described, should actually eventuate. Also, if we have any sense of empathy or feel any moral concern, we must ascribe goodness and badness to the experience of others, whatever the theoretical or practical hazards to be encountered in so doing.

A further point which already suggests itself, and which is one of prime importance, is that we cannot avoid the assessment of values *to be* found in experience and as these experiences will or *would be* found, without knowing whether the experience in question will or will not in fact occur. This necessity is involved in any deliberate decision of action if it is to be regarded as rational to make. There can be no such decision without consideration of the value consequences of the *alternatives* of action open to us and amongst which we must choose. Consideration of such different value consequences of the contemplated alternatives of doing is an indispensable, and the only possible, justifying ground for choosing what to do. If we cannot make justified judgments of the form, "If I should do A, the consequences (to somebody's experience, perhaps my own) would be good, but if I should do B, they would be better (or worse)," then we can make no rational decision at all. And unless judgments of this hypothetical form can have a truth which is independent of the truth of the "if-clause" in them, then there can be no nondelusive ground for the decision of any deliberate act. And this must hold despite the obvious fact, the fact compelling choice, that only one such "if" of action, one chosen alternative, can ever become the fact about this occasion of our doing.[1]

There are other such problems with which we may find ourselves involved, though they are not peculiar to ascriptions of value or other predications which are normative, but are instead general questions of epistemology, or of metaphysics,

---

1. Those who discuss "contrary-to-fact conditionals" often overlook this practical and vitally important bearing of their topic. The explanation of the cognitive validity of such "if —, then —" statements as *have* any cognitive validity is both simple and obvious. They express beliefs which are logically justified, either by deduction or induction, or by a combination of the two. 'If this is a potato, then it is a vegetable', 'If this is a match in good condition, then it will light when struck on the box'—these are analytic statements, true by the relation of concepts, by the definitive meaning of 'potato' or 'match in good condition'. If someone were to say, "This is a match in good condition but it will not light when struck on the box," that would imply some misconception in calling the thing a match in good condition. And if someone were to say, "This is a potato but poisonous," that would involve some misconception in calling the thing a potato. On the other hand, "If this is a potato, it will not poison you, but will be good to eat" and "If this is a match in good condition, it will not ignite by spontaneous combustion in your pocket" are inductively warranted statements, justified by past experience as highly probable in any particular instance. The problem concerning such statements is not semantic, though semantic accuracy may be required, and could be obtained if the "condition" were stated in the now-obsolescent subjective form, "if it *be*." The problem is rather nothing less than the problem of the validity of induction, of natural science, and of empirical knowledge at large. Strictly speaking, all such empirical generalities are theoretically no better than probable, though the degree of such probability may amount to "practical certainty."

   If we remember this fact, that what rests upon generalization from experience for its warrant of belief is no better than probable, then there is one "deduction of the categories of empirical knowledge" which is easily stated. To paraphrase Hans Reichenbach: "If thinking and acting according to the probabilities does not do you any good, then there is nothing you can do which will do you any good." That pragmatic justification is complete and final. If you believe, with the Sophists and Hume, that there are no such justified cognitive convictions, there is still nothing for it but to emulate Hume while playing draughts—and no better alternative while making general statements which you hope other people may agree with and act on. If there are no valid generalities, then philosophizing is as silly as any other pointless diversion.

or of logical theory. There are such questions concerning any knowledge of the past, or the prediction of any event in the future, or any claim to knowledge of other minds. Again, we may have questions concerning any relation of ground and consequence, and special doubts about any such relation between events of experience on the one side and external happenings on the other. And some solution of these metaphysical and epistemological questions may have to be presumed in discussions of the normative, as in any other branch of study.

So far as such problems are general philosophic problems, we cannot, of course, undertake them here. At most, we can only consider such as are peculiar to, or have a peculiar bearing on, questions of valuation and the normative. And perhaps the main point of what is peculiar to valuations in the root sense which we so far attempt to explicate is covered by the consideration that with respect to the content of experience, when and as experienced, there is no distinction between appearance and reality: the experience in question *is* the reality in question.

We may the more cheerfully resign such questions belonging under other branches of philosophy, if we observe that these are, in large measure at least, puzzles of the "how can we" type: how can we know the past, or the future; how can we, by taking thought, affect a future and external factuality; how can we justify the presumption of a consciousness other than our own with which we can communicate, and so on. And most if not all of these how-can-we questions are such as may be countered, even if not satisfied, by the consideration that the denial *that* we can must result in a kind of *reductio ad absurdum* of human life altogether. In part at least, they are like the question, "How can we wiggle our little finger?" *Unless* we can, there is nothing to be found out, and, *if* we can, it is not necessary to know how we do it in order to exercise this capacity. And any doubt *that* we can is resoluble by the *solvitur ambulando*. In further part these how-can-we questions may be such as it would be meaningless for us to *debate* if they do not admit of some positive solution. Without the presumptions which belong to our common sense of ourselves as human, both the practical questions of our doing and the intellectual questions of our knowing would dissolve into a kind of silliness, being an attempt to infer from premises we do not have in ways for whose justification we have neither a rule nor any other attesting criterion. Inquiry concerning ultimate questions might well take as its initial problem, "What must we recognize as the common sense of ourselves as human, in order that what we ask about, and would decide about, shall be meaningful and admit of any answer which we have some ground of attesting and can self-consciously and self-critically accept?" And, in philosophy, there are no antecedent first premises. Perhaps philosophy at large must consist in the progressive and self-critical clarification of the common sense of ourselves and of our common experience of life, or otherwise be baseless and senseless from the start and self-condemned to futility and frustration. To adhere to what such a criterion of the philosophically justified would dictate may be difficult and hazardous enough, but at least we might so relieve ourselves of those philosophical negativisms which it would be pointless to argue about if they were true.

In these matters, incidentally, we must occasionally go beyond "common ways of speaking." Such are often too ambiguous for precise distinctions which must be made. On the other hand, we shall still intend to rest upon the "common sense of ourselves and of human living," and abide by discernments which can so be substantiated.

In order to speak further of good and bad as qualities of experience when and as experienced, we must become clear as to what may contrast with good and bad in this root sense of value as immediately to be found. That other things than the contents and passages of experience are called 'good' and 'bad' is, as we have suggested, to be explained by the direct or indirect effects which such things have, or are believed to have, on some experience of some conscious creature. In our own living, we find no reason, no justifying consideration, for acting in a particular way except by reference to some experience which so acting may affect. What would have no eventual influence for experienced good or ill is a matter of complete indifference: there is no ground for rational concern with it. Good and bad are the "stop" and "go" signals of conscious life altogether.

To say that it is experience only which is good or bad in the root sense, from which all other usages of these words are derivative, and that all other things have whatever value or disvalue qualifies them only by their eventual relation to experienced good and bad is the same as to say that nothing other than contents and passages of experience are, strictly speaking, good or bad *for their own sake, intrinsically* good or bad. We shall accept that dictum. However, this usage of 'intrinsically good', and 'intrinsically bad', and 'intrinsic value', to which we shall adhere, is hardly the common one in English. More frequently, this qualification 'intrinsic' is used on the supposition, with which we must disagree, that other things than experience may be said to be "good in themselves," or "good *by* themselves," if not "good for their own sake." And 'intrinsically good' is, in consequence, applied to some objects, as well as to the gratifying experiences to which these objects may give rise. And it may not be evident just what criterion those who so speak of some *objects* as "intrinsically good" and other objects as "extrinsically good only" are using in making this distinction. Attention to that matter will make it clear without much doubt that the distinction which they have in mind lies between those objects which, like the products of art and things which satisfy some appetite, are such that this goodness ascribed to them and spoken of as an intrinsic goodness of them is one which is realized in experience, in the sense-presentation of these objects to us, and not by way of the effects these objects in question may have on other *objects*. The objects of art are such as are good to look at or good to hear or, in the case of literature, found good in the reading of them. And good food tastes good: "The proof of the pudding is in the eating." Such good things are good by reason of their *direct* effect upon the quality of experience. And this kind of goodness in objects contrasts with the goodness of tools and other "utilities," which are desirable by reason of some instrumentality of them in conducing to the production, possession or availability of *other objects* which may gratify us directly by their presence.

This is, of course, an important distinction, but we shall mark it here by other words. We shall say that those objects and other objective entities, and the objective properties of them, which gratify us directly by their presence are *inherently* good—instead of "intrinsically good"—and we shall say that those things whose existence, possession or availability is desirable because they are conducive to the possession or availability of *other objects,* which other objects may gratify us directly, are *instrumentally* good. But we shall recognize, as others do, that many objects have both some inherent goodness and some instrumental goodness, so that this distinction is really one between two different types of goodness which objects may have rather than a distinction between two classes of objects which it is desirable to have. Food, for example, may be good to the taste, and that goodness is inherent to foods which have it. But it is even more important in the case of food that it be instrumentally good, good for keeping us alive and healthy. Poor-tasting food is not inherently good to eat but may still be "good food"—good instrumentally. Also we shall recognize, as others do, that objects which are believed to have some instrumental value, some utility, tend by that fact to acquire some measure of inherent value for us, *i.e.,* tend to gratify us merely by their presence. To see that new saw in the tool chest tends to please us, because it will be there when we need it for putting up a shelf or framing a picture. And any one of us might be pleased by the sight of a good store of cash on hand, though to value it *more* for the seeing than for the things it will buy (its utility) is the miser's perversion.

We should also remark in passing that the instrumentality of an instrumentally good thing to an end which is inherently good may be an indirect or stepwise relationship. The nails that are good for nailing the lumber, which is good for building the house, which is comfortable and pleasant to live in, are, by that relationship, instrumentally good nails. And this house-that-Jack-built story may be as long as you please, provided it ends with something inherently good, without prejudice to the instrumental goodness of the thing it begins with. But some inherently good end result is essential to any genuine instrumental value of an object.[2]

---

2. The word 'utility' is sometimes used in the meager and dubious sense of "*thought* to be useful" or "considered useful by some people." But the attribution of utility in this sense plainly does not imply any real value at all.

We shall not hereafter use the phrase 'good in itself' because of the possible ambiguity of that as between 'good for its own sake' and 'directly gratifying by its presence to sense'. It is experience itself, and the experiential only, which is good for its own sake, *intrinsically* good. Objects are good only by their potentialities for conducing to experiences found good in the having of them. Objects can be extrinsically good only. We call them here inherently good if and insofar as they are such as gratify by their presence, instrumentally good if and insofar as they are such as are instrumental to the production, possession or availability of other and inherently good *objects*.

The parallel considerations concerning the intrinsically or extrinsically bad, and the inherently or instrumentally bad, will not need to be spelled out.

We must further observe, however, that experiences themselves are called good or bad in two different senses, the root sense of being *found* good or bad when and as experienced—*immediately* good or bad—and the different sense of being good or bad experiences to have in virtue of their influence upon other experience. For example, there are experiences which are gratifying within their own temporal boundaries but are nevertheless undesirable to indulge in because they will later prove undesirable to have indulged in, and there are experiences which are disgratifying in the having but still desirable to undergo because of their salutary effect upon further experience. This category of the value or disvalue ascribable to transient experiences by reason of their influence upon other experiences we shall call the *contributory* value of them.

Let us distinguish two senses in which one experience may contribute to the goodness or badness of another.

First, since what we may mark off as "one experience" may be included in another passage or larger whole of experience, one experience may be *"ingrediently contributory"* to another, may, by being included in it, affect the goodness or badness of this more comprehensive experience, as good table talk may enhance the goodness of attendance at a dinner, or a good day's fishing may contribute to the goodness of a vacation.

Second, having had an experience may contribute to the value quality of a later, and perhaps temporally disjoined, experience, as studying for an examination may contribute to happiness in receiving the report of it, or the trouble of planning may contribute to the experience of what is planned. In such a case, the earlier experience may be said to be *"causally contributory"* to the goodness or badness of the later one.[3]

Before going further, it may be well to pause here, and provide some explanation and defense for our procedure of attending first to the significance of value ascriptions to experiences, and then later explaining other assessments of value as derivative from this, from the root senses of 'good' and 'bad', instead of beginning with the generic meaning of 'good' and 'bad', and then later considering other and more specific kinds of value ascription, ascriptions derived by limitations imposed upon that general meaning. We have indicated our approach here by attention to the fact, sometimes obscured by idioms of language and by words used, that it is the qualities of experience—or experiences as having these qualities—which alone are valuable for their own sake, and should properly be called intrinsically valuable. And it is the goodness of what is valuable for its own sake which imparts value to anything which is valuable for the sake of something else. If A be valuable for the sake of B, it is the value of B from which the value of A derives, and what it signifies that A is said to be good is to be found out by looking to see what it means to say that B is good.

There is, of course, a generic meaning of 'good', a meaning included in what it means to say that anything is good in any sense. That meaning of 'good' is 'desirable'. And 'desirable' does *not* mean 'is desired' or 'is capable of being desired'; it means, as Ewing has pointed out, 'worthy of desire', 'worth desiring', and, as we may add, 'justified to desire'. The proof, or confirmation, that anything is desirable is *not* its being desired but its *satisfying,* or conducing to the satisfaction of, desire.

---

3. We do not, however, require to assume that one experience can literally cause another—if there be objection to that. All that we need to understand by 'Experience A causally contributes to the value quality of experience B' is that the occurrence of A is a valid premise for the predicted character of B as probable, and hence explains, or is a partial explanation of, the character of B, if or when experience B is later realized.

More exactly—because a thing may be found to be desirable even if nobody ever thought of it before the disclosure of it to experience—any proof that a thing is good requires the finding of satisfaction in it or by means of it, in virtue of which desire for this thing is or would be justified if anybody had thought of it correctly and desired it. That a thing *is* desired does not prove it desirable because desiring may be a mistake, and is subject to disillusionment, and that a thing is *not* desired does not prove it *not* to be desirable—for the same reason of a possible error in not desiring it or in desiring not to have it, as well as for the additional reason that the question of its desirability may not have arisen. And what we have just said applies to experiences as well as to objects. One who has never looked out from the peak of a high mountain, and cannot imagine it adequately, may be as deeply gratified by so doing as one who is familiar with such an experience and desires it.

By the meaning of the words, gratification and dissatisfaction are qualities ascribable exclusively to experiences. And it is for the sake of realizing experiences of the one sort, and avoiding those of the other, that anything other than some experience is reasonably to be desired, or not to be desired. The nearest that any object or external state of affairs can come to being desirable for its own sake is to be such as gratifies merely by its presentation in experience. And this character of objective things we have marked off as their inherent desirability, their inherent goodness, in order to preserve the distinction of that from the intrinsic desirability of what is desirable for its own sake, and for which we reserve the appellation 'intrinsically good'.

There are, however, those who wish to begin with the generic meaning, instead of this root meaning, that confined to the contents of passages of experience, and then proceed to the more specific senses of 'good' and 'bad' by the qualification of this generic sense—a procedure which would, of course, give the same results if there be no misidentification of the precise significance of terms. But in so doing, some of them have spoken of what is good "by itself," instead of what is good for its own sake, and in a sense in which they think of objects as capable of being good by themselves, and quite without reference to any actual or possible experience of these objects. Such goodness-by-itself contrasts only with the "good-for-ness" of objects, thus tending to coincide with what we call the inherent goodness of objects in contrast to the instrumental goodness of objective entities. Thus goodness and badness come to be thought of as if their *generic* meaning had reference to things (objects) only, and the question of the good *for its own sake* is forgotten about altogether. In this way, the category of the "good by itself" comes to displace our category of the intrinsically good as the quality of the conscious experience which, as we conceive of matters, is the ultimate concern by reference to which alone anything whatever can finally be either good or bad.[4]

It is a basic thesis of our conception that no object is either good or bad except by reference to some actual or possible effect of it upon conscious experience and the value quality of it. But, as has been indicated, the *most general meaning* of 'good' and 'bad' as applied to *objects* does have reference to a character of them which they *do* have, independently of the question whether their *potentialities* for having an effect upon conscious experience *are in fact exercised upon any conscious experience or not*. This independent nature of objects, which they have whether they are experienced or not, and whether they are even thought of or not, is something which common sense ascribes to them, in the same general manner in which it ascribes to them their size, or shape, or their hardness or color; it does not have to be experienced in order to be as it is and not otherwise, though the *proof,* or confirmation, of this character can come only by way of some effect it has upon some experience. And *in this most general mode of ascribing value or disvalue to objects,* the object is as good or as bad as it is, and

---

4. It appears to me that G. E. Moore so conceives of the "good by itself" in his *Principia Ethica*. I pretend to no certainty as to Moore's intended meaning of this phrase, and pursue the point for the sake of clarifying my own conceptions. I shall presume here that 'good by itself' at least implies 'good by virtue of its own nature, and without reference to any consideration beyond that'.

as experience *would* prove it to be, whether or not, in point of fact, any experience does prove it so or not. It is, so to say, there in the object waiting to be found out, and as adequate experience of it *would* prove it to be, regardless of the actuality or nonactuality of such experience of finding out and proving.

But the point is, *what* is it that this goodness or badness of the object consists in? And the answer to that question is: the potentialities of this object for affecting conscious life for better or for worse. Apart from that, no objective entity has any character of good or bad whatever. The potentialities of it for having such an effect upon conscious experience *constitute* its value or disvalue, in the only sense in which any goodness or badness is ascribable to an objective entity at all. It is this which we have had in mind in saying that, in a world without conscious beings, nothing would be good or bad. And we submit that to be judged by common sense, in accord with our common intentions in the use of language. That accords with what we *mean* in saying that any objective entity is good or bad. Any further question is a question of the metaphysical correctness of common-sense realism. That question we shall not discuss here. But we may speak of this most general mode of the assessment of the value of objects as the "metaphysical mode."

It is in accord with this manner of ascription of value and disvalue to objects that we say that a saw which is never used is still "just as good a saw" as it would, putatively, have proven to be if it had been utilized for its appropriate purpose. And in this mode we say that one of those "gems of purest ray serene which the dark unfathom'd caves of ocean bear," the sonata of Schubert which is known to have been written but was never found or publicly played, the oil buried under the Antarctic icecap too deep to be located, is just as beautiful a gem, or sonata, or just as good oil, as it *would* prove to be if anything ever *should* be proved about it. This, being understood as meant, is a *right* way to ascribe value or disvalue, or mere worthlessness, to objects. That is, it is *one* right mode of the value assessment of objects, and frequently the most important one to apply, though possibly it is to be explained by the frequency with which things which never *have* exercised any discoverable

effect upon a human life may, at a later date, and in some ear-
lier-unforeseeable way, come to do so. We "metaphisize" "for
all time."

However, we do have another and contrasting mode of
ascribing value or disvalue, or worthlessness, to objects, the
mode in which we say that a saw which rusts away without
ever being used proves to be of no value to anybody, and that
any gem which is destined never to gladden any seeing eye, any
sonata which is never to be heard, or oil which is beyond all
finding has no actual value. In the factual circumstances, such
things are worthless. This we call the "pragmatic" or practical
mode of assessing the value of objective things: it is a realistic
way of valuing—realistic as being mindful of all the pertinent
factualities of the matter. It is also what we are likely to call
"real value."

It would be foolish to argue which of these two ways of
speaking of the value of objects is correct. Either is correct
when taken as meant, and neither of them is correct if meant in
one of these senses but confused with the other. The determinable question is: In the case of objects that fall in this class—
being such as by their nature have some potentiality for the
betterment of experiences affected by them, but also such that
no experience *will* be affected by them—is it desirable that the
things in question exist? And presuming this hypothesis of their
lack of effect upon any conscious experience, the answer is
plainly that the existence of these things is a matter of complete
indifference. It is neither desirable nor undesirable. In the practical mode—the mode of actual or real value—they are valueless, neither good nor bad. In conclusion, we may decide that
no object which is beyond the possibility of affecting experience has any *real* value.[5]

---

5. If we wish to pursue such thoughts further, we may find that 'X is desirable' always implies 'It is desirable that X exist', but that, in many cases,
this does not exhaust or fully satisfy its intended meaning. It appears
often to imply further, 'It is desirable to *have* X'. In the case of an experience, A, what it means to have A—say, "having fun" or "having a head-
ache"—is simple: "having experience A" means simply the immediacy of
that content of experience to the experiencer in question. But the meaning

But if, so far, we correctly read our common sense of the good and bad in experience, and as affecting experience, it might still be possible to confuse this matter with a slightly different one. There are some satisfactions, as well as some dissatisfactions, which are to be realized merely in thinking about things which are not actual, and never have been, and never will be, actual. It is for the sake of such satisfactions of mere reverie that we read fiction, and indulge in daydreaming and other forms of imagining without believing.

---

of "having an object, X," is more variant and subtle. Having a cup of tea, having air to breathe, having money in the bank, and having debts, would each mean something a little different. On examining their differences, we may conclude that the most general meaning of "having X," when X is some *objective entity,* is that of being so related to the thing in question as to be in a position to obtain some advantage from some or all of its potentialities for good, at will, or to be put at some disadvantage, given its potentialities for bad, willy-nilly, or both. (That in the case of "goods," 'having' signifies "possession, availability or control," but, in the case of "bads," it signifies "being stuck with," so to speak, is due to the different relation of "goods" and "bads" to our will and purposes.) And whether it is desirable that X exist, or to have X, may in some cases, *e.g.,* in that of fissionable material, depend not merely upon its potentialities for good or bad, but on matters of possible control, such that its potentialities for good may be realized and its potentialities for bad precluded. But, in any case, no one can have X unless X exists. And, the crux of the matter discussed above, in the case of any object X which *ex hypothesi* exists, but in such wise that no one will ever be in a position to be either advantaged or disadvantaged by its potentialities, "having it" would be in contradiction to the hypothesis, and "experiencing it" would be so also. In the light of this, we may conclude that the *general* manner of assessing objects as good or bad, by reference to their potentialities for the realization of good and bad in experience, tacitly presumes that some effect of them is at least possible to realize in experience, and that when this possibility is precluded, this common mode of ascribing value to objects is tacitly understood to have no application. The tendency to ignore this tacit limitation may be connected with our reluctance, for obvious good reasons, to set empirical limits to human possibilities having to do with the experience of things.

Variant meanings of value ascriptions to objects are more fully discussed in the last chapters of *An Analysis of Knowledge and Valuation.*

> In Xanadu did Kubla Khan
> A stately pleasure-dome decree:
> Where Alph, the sacred river, ran
> Through caverns measureless to man
> Down to a sunless sea.

The bizarre and oriental character of this pleasure-dome, the heathenish connotation of 'sacred river', the slight shiver over 'measureless caverns' and 'sunless sea', these just add to the titillation of our fancying—so long as we are safely removed from any actual contact.

Children continue to find pleasure in fairy tales after they stop believing in fairies—but it is a different pleasure. We may enjoy or may not at all enjoy thinking of things not believed in as actual. It makes a difference, however, if we think of them as actualities. And it makes some difference whether they are believed in as past actualities, or as presently real, or as future, or even possibly future, actualities, particularly so if they are supposed to be things it is humanly possible to do something about. It is in our own experience of contemplation that we so enjoy or suffer, but the character and quality of this experience of contemplating is affected by the postulation of actuality, or of probability, or possibility even—and is different in the absence of any such posit. Also it makes a difference to our concern and the affective quality of this contemplative experience whether its content is postulated as past and beyond all possibility to affect, or as present, or as belonging to that future on which some possible doing may still have an effect. And we regard such differences of our concern and attitude as rational. We do not argue here, incidentally. We but seek to read our human nature on such points. We do not beg a question about "rationality" here, but merely ask it.

In the light of these multiple and complex considerations, it is difficult to offer any example which would be pertinent to our final point here: pertinent to the question whether an object such that there is no empirical possibility of its affecting the quality of any experience is, or is not, one to which any real value, which could be a matter of rational concern, is to be ascribed. But without an example to "bring it home" to us, the question is likely to seem too abstruse to decide, or might even appear to be purely verbal. Accordingly, let us essay one example, having some touch of realism, and submit it to our common sense of the *really desirable*.

There could be, let us suppose, a beautiful garden on some far planet, never to be seen by any eye, and never to exercise by its actuality any effect upon any conscious experience. Would such a garden be desirable, be good "by itself"?

It might be a good thing to think about, that is, thinking about it might be good. The thought of it—whether the thing thought of exists or not—could afford some gratification. So far, however, it is on all fours with Kubla Khan's pleasure-dome. But it might afford more gratification to those who so think of it if they can believe in it, especially if they have, or think to have, some justification for believing it actually exists. This matter seems to come perilously close to, if not to touch on, other matters, such as are implicit in our concern for our descendants, or the future of our society, or of humanity at large. That we cannot help, but on this point, as on others, let us strive to adhere to the "common sense" of things.

And now, brother, will you spare a dime for the Society for Planting Gardens on Far Planets—by rocketed vehicles, of course? Well, yes, a dime, just for the fun of it. But if your society will extend its project to include a later orbiting of some observing instrument for the verification that this garden is blooming, I will make it twenty-five cents. And if you can offer a reasonable assurance that my children or grandchildren will be able to view this garden on television, I will happily contribute twenty-five dollars. But on the other hand, if your confidence in this project is misplaced and no one will ever get anything out of it except by *thinking* about it, then I can think about it for nothing. As a matter of fact, I am not edified by the thought of a beautiful garden which will never, by its existence, exercise any effect upon the experience of any conscious being. I can identify with my grandchildren, and even with my great-grandchildren not yet born. Perhaps I can identify with some queer conscious beastie on another planet, if there is any reason to believe in any. But I am not enough of a panpsychist to identify with a rosebush or a patch of algae.

If it comes to that, I am in favor of letting the members of your society "visionize" on their own resources. I want some foundation in fact for believing in some effect of the existence of this garden on some consciousness a little like my own. Short of that, I will take Xanadu. Some people can enjoy delusions; some have. But most of us have to believe in them to order to enjoy them. Enjoying fiction is something different: it is not an enjoyment of what the fictive account depicts, but an enjoyment of one's own experience in imagining it. You may ask, "But what is the difference between that and enjoying the prospect of what your grandchildren may see on television?" Well, to me, twenty-five dollars worth of difference. I think that is the way we humans are. And I don't want to hear any more about beautiful gardens on far planets being "good by themselves." To me, that is just verbiage: I say, some conscious experience to be affected by the existence of this thing, or else no real desirability or undesirability of it whatever, no *reason* for desiring either the actuality or the nonactuality of it. And as for anybody's enjoying or not enjoying *it,* in distinction from the mere thought of it, that would be a contradiction in the supposition as framed.

So far we attempt to establish the point that it is only contents and passages of experience which are good or bad for their own sake, that it is only they which have intrinsic value or disvalue, and that objects, external events and states of affairs are to be interpreted as good or bad only extrinsically, in virtue of their potentialities for conducing to experiences which will be found good or bad. But the last half of this statement seems to imply a kind of exception to itself: even an actual objective entity which, so far as its own nature or character is concerned, has potentialities for contributing good or bad to experience will still have no *real* value under circumstances which preclude any effect of those potentialities resident in it upon any conscious life. A potentiality is a possibility and a possibility which is precluded from becoming realized is an impossible possibility—a contradiction in terms. That, we have suggested, is indeed the case, and accords with our common-sense ways of attributing value, or refusing to attribute value, to external things.

Suggestive as it may be, however, perhaps we should feel that the discussion so far is less than conclusive. There are too many other and collateral matters, likewise more or less involved in this same point, and until these also are clarified, we might wish to reserve judgment.

———•———

Two points might be added here.

In conceiving of value as a potentiality of an object for having a certain effect upon experience, rather as one might, analogously, think of "color" as a potentiality of an object for having a different sort of effect upon experience, it is common sense to note, in both sorts of cases, that the observer's *experience* has another condition, as well, in the one case, the capacity for seeing the color in question, in the other, the capacity for enjoying the object in question.

Second, with respect to the desirable and the good:

It is sometimes said that 'desirable' means 'ought to be desired'. That goes beyond saying, "worthy to be desired," since 'ought to —' implies that the "failure to —" is a fault, that such a failure is to be disapproved. It can hardly be correct to say that whatever is good or desirable is such that the failure to desire it is a fault. That would imply that something we never think of, and the question of whose goodness or worthlessness, or badness, never occurs to us, and hence we neither desire it nor desire not to have it, is either worthless or else our failure to desire it is a fault on our part. That could not be in accord with the facts. We do not lie under any imperative to assess the value of everything, since thinking of every single thing there is is impossible for us.

The correct word in replacement of 'ought' here is a little difficult to determine. But the reason why 'ought'—as in 'the good ought to be desired'—may suggest itself is fairly easy to detect. We are prone to think of "right" and "wrong" in terms of black and white, *i.e.*, to think that with respect to anything decidable, we ought to decide in favor of it or we ought to decide against it, that for each possible decision, the decision ought to be "yes" or ought to be "no."

But this is a mistaken supposition.

For every criticizable decision there are rules governing right and wrong, and "right or wrong" is an absolute dichotomy—everything criticizable is either right or wrong, but that does *not* mean that everything to which these rules apply is either commanded, that is it imperative to adopt, or that it is forbidden, that it is imperative to avoid it, that it must be rejected. The rules of any game, for example, chess, will illustrate the matter; some moves are "chess-permitted," and some are "chess-forbidden," but at almost every stage of the game, there will be permissible alternative moves; otherwise there is no game, the player having no freedom of choice. Something very similar is true, incidentally, in the "game of logic." Given a premise, or a set of premises, an unlimited number of conclusions are implied, any one of which would be rightly inferable from the premises. This is literally true, a proof of it being Poretsky's Law of Consequences. But we are under no obligation to infer any conclusion whatsoever.

ESSAY 4

Semantics of the Imperative

However we may think of ethics nowadays, it is evident enough that it first became articulate as something taught, and not taught as information merely but inculcated, preached. The topic is how to behave yourself, what is to be done and what not done, precepts of action, and particularly of those acts which, by affecting others than the doer, become matters of common concern amongst us. The content of ethics is something exhorted to or dictated: dictated by parents to children, by responsible leaders to obedient followers, by the elders of the tribe to the initiates, by those possessed of wisdom or learning to those who are ignorant or inexpert. Or it may be resolutions we make against the future, or recommendations we venture to our peers, or pledges we recite together in some ritualistic confirmation of our mutual intent.

This content is expressible, if not expressed, in the imperative mood. But every mood of language must be stretched to cover a considerable range and variety of our mental entertainments of the content to be conveyed. Just as our words must metonymically acquire second and third meanings, by reason of the insufficiency of the vocables we can shortly pronounce and recognize to the number of distinguishable kinds of things and characters of things which we discriminate, so also the syntactic inflections and constructions we can contrive for our putting

56

together of words must be insufficient to our ways of entertaining what our sentences make mention of. All sentences have it in common that they refer to some indicated state of affairs, representationally contemplated by the speaker and likewise to be thought of by any addressee. Perhaps other creatures command only one mood of communication—"Take notice"—and can convey nothing beyond the immediately observed and felt. But what humans speak of may be present or absent, here or there, or halfway around the world. It may be now or yesterday, or beyond the memory of any living man, tomorrow, next month, or to be expected by the year 2050. Or it may be something which never happened and never will. If we could not mention what never was, and without our action never will be—and mention it as having just that status—we could not cooperate to affect the future. In order to act together for a common purpose, we must be able to convey the actual as now actual, the expected as anticipated, or only as hoped or feared, or as contingent upon circumstances not now fixed, particularly as contingent on our doing. We must be able to speak of some things as certain, and of others as uncertain, of the doubtful as probable or improbable in measure. And we must also be able to refer to the suppositious without regard to any expectancy concerning it, as well as to consider what would have been on suppositions known to be false. Otherwise we should never learn from past mistakes. Without the capacity to represent the nonactual and think of it as being such, we could draw no valid inferences. We can recognize that B is deducible from A only by contemplating A-but-not-B as something which could neither exist nor happen. And we can establish P as probable on evidence E only as we contemplate the unlikelihood of E without this consequence P.[1]

---

1. There are some who make a hopeless puzzle of the contrary-to-fact condition. The, or *a*, significance of it is easily identified by attention to the manner in which we determine probabilities, including those high probabilities on which reasonably directed action depends. I have a match in my hand, purposing to light my pipe. If I scratch it on the strip provided on the matchbox, it will, in all probability, light. If I scratch it on my shoe sole, it, in all probability, won't light. I have plenty of evidence for these probability conclusions. This evidence is pertinent to *any* striking of a

Without such various moods and the complex interweaving of them in our representational thinking, the human type of intellection could not exist. And without the communication of the intended mood, as well as the content it qualifies, there would be no difference between human history and that of apes; there would be no continuing progress through learning from the experience of others; we would be without the achievement of civilized living.

Our interest here will relate to the linguistic imperative. But for comparison, some brief notice of the range and nuances of the indicative may be in order. Broadly speaking, the indicative is the mood of assertion as actual, the expression of belief. But already we have suggested the difference between asserting what is represented as necessarily the case, with the impossibility of its being otherwise, and asserting what is represented as contingent, what is merely factual, so to speak, what it would be consistent to deny, and what would require empirical evidence for its substantiation. These are quite different modes of cognition, and to entertain them without remarking the difference is an inadvertence if not an error. But the modal inflections required for marking this difference are so often left out that even logicians fall into error about the difference, and a few obtuse ones think to do without it. The related and equally fundamental distinction of the asserted as certain from

---

match of the type I have in my hand. The match I lost in the grass just now *would* have lighted if it *had been* scratched on the strip. This judgment has exactly the same validity, and on exactly the same ground, that my judgment that a match I hold in my hand *will* (or *will not*) light, if I now proceed to strike it.

If these were not valid judgments of the antecedent-consequent "causal" relation of acts and their consequences which hold regardless of the truth or falsity of the "if" of action, nobody would have a reason for action, for choosing to strike a match, or not to strike a match. The prediction of such consequences is essential to the possibility of rational choices to do or not to do.

Remembering that all predictions are theoretically no better than probable, there is no further problem of the contrary-to-fact conditional which is not a *general* problem of all possible empirical knowledge, affecting any cognitive judgment expressible by 'if —, then —' which is not an analytic judgment.

the asserted as probable can hardly fail of notice, but it is even more elided in customary speech. Indeed, the omission of it comes near to being linguistically inevitable, so much of what we assert as if certain being actually no better than probable. Life is too short for habitually, explicitly mentioning the hazards we accept. But 'It will rain within the hour' and 'Probably it will rain within the hour' are statements which are quite different in kind, and the latter may be true when the former is false. What is genuinely probable when spoken of can fail to be the case, but the assertion of it as probable, at the time this statement was made, if once true, will be, like any other true statement, eternally true. It *was* probable *then,* and that will remain a fact forever. The elision of the probability indicator in the common indicative sentence makes it oddly difficult, and quite so, to tell the truth about what we say we know, and even about what exactly we believe when we "assert" it.

We should also remark that the indicative regularly serves for the recital of the pretended. We sometimes have to look in the index of the magazine to determine whether what we are setting out to read is presented as fact or fiction. Indeed, statement, assertion, the indicative, is an all too likely form for any manner of communication, regardless of the mood of entertainment. The indicators and inflections of other moods tend to disappear, which "shortens" our speech but may also exacerbate our mental flabbiness. The indicative tends to displace, for example, the hortatory subjunctive—"Suppose that —," "Assume that —"—as well as the subjunctive of condition—"If it *be* —"—with the sole exception of the contrary-to-fact conditional. And even that will soon disappear: no teenager says, "If it *were* —." But if we are to semanticize—to say nothing of logicize or philosophize—in the vernacular, we must guard against the degeneracies of elided modalities.

However, we should also note, and a little emphasis here may not be out of place, that there is a regular and precise formula of syntax by recourse to which anything that can be said at all can be said exactly in the indicative, by the assertion of some *fact.* The requisite rule is: Express the intended mood of entertainment as the main clause, and introduce the representational content thought of in the manner of indirect discourse: "It is incontrovertible that —," "I believe that —," "It is probable that —," "It is to be presumed that —," "We may consider whether —," "It is doubtful that —," "I wish that —,""I direct that —," etc.

This formula, let us note, allows the content of the qualified representation to be introduced diversely, in a variety of "voices" or "persons."

We might, incidentally, separate out that which names the state of affairs spoken of in any whole sentence whose intention is fully expressed, and call this the "*proposition.*" For example, consider a sentence to the effect, 'John is making a fence'. The "state of affairs" involved here might be *named* as, say, 'John making a fence' or 'that John is making a fence', which naming locutions might be regarded as the "proposition" involved. The *statement* would then assert the state of affairs as actual, that John is making a fence; a question pertaining to this state of affairs would inquire about it, say, "Is John making a fence?"; an imperative pertaining to it would indicate that it is to be bought about, say, "John, make a fence," a hypothesis would indicate it as a condition, say, "If John is making a fence, then such-and-such would be the case," and so on. This approach would call to our attention the distinction between the *inflectors* which in common language remain as a *part* of the total expression, as, for example, inflections of time (past, present and future), addressee ("you," "we," etc.), condition ("if —, then —"), etc., and the basic element of representation, the *proposition naming the pertinent state of affairs.*

An important point might well be entered here.

One should be careful, in dealing with these issues, not to confuse linguistic with extralinguistic matters. One should keep such considerations separated.

Every pronouncement may provide *evidence* as to the attitude of a speaker, but that is a different matter from the mood in which he *intends to convey* what is to be thought of. For example, one who asks a question wants his addressee to understand what is in question with respect to a referred-to state of affairs and understand also that he presents the locution appropriate to his concern *as* a question. Now, that the locution is interrogative provides some *evidence* that the speaker is in doubt, rendering that at least probable. To evince by the use of words is to convey, or seem to convey, something or other by one's *act,* intentionally or not. But, in fact, the evidence may be misleading, and the speaker might *not* be in doubt. But the locution is still intended as a question, and is a question. Similarly, in a given case a speaker might wish an addressee to share a doubt, but not in another case. Again, the locution is still intended to be a question, and is a question. And similarly, any who should interpret "I approve —" as evincing the attitude "Do so as well" may attribute a bent to togetherness where one of mutual respect and interest only is intended. But in all cases, understanding a communication requires understanding the intended mood of it as well as its referred-to content. A description without a modal indication is not a complete unit of discourse.

Let us digress to suggest a small moral for those who semanticize in philosophy by hasty oversight.

Every pronouncement intended to communicate must indicate *some representational content* entertained by the speaker and to be similarly entertained by any addressee if communication is to be effected. And unless what is so spoken about is present and demonstrable by "pointing," the language which conveys it must be "descriptive," and such a description of the content of representation is, by itself, common to all moods of entertainment. By the same token, it is distinctive of none. No one can understand anything said without thinking *of* the content of *representation* to which what is said refers. But to suppose that this content must be actual, in all instances, if what is said about it is to be veridical, would be to reduce ourselves to the level of the apes, if not somewhat below that. One who could not *think of* without *believing that* could never become in any smallest degree inventive, and must wholly lack the prime requisite of intelligence. There *must* be differentiation of human moods of entertaining; the capacity so to differentiate is a prime requisite for being human. As follows from this, every human communication must, tacitly or explicitly, convey the speaker's intent with respect to his mood of entertaining the state of affairs represented and mentioned. It expresses, or in some contextual manner must convey, this intended mood of entertainment, and, as intended communication, bespeak an interpretation in the same mood of entertainment on the part of any understanding addressee. This manner of required empathy between communicator and addressee may have its significance for the moral, but to suppose it peculiar to discourse relevant to the moral would be to confuse understanding what is said with agreement concerning it.

We may also observe that communications generally could be put into the imperative, by a similar use of indirect discourse, by *instruction* of the addressee as to the mood in which they are to be understood: "Believe me that —," "Suppose that —," "Consider whether —," "Take it as probable that —," etc. But such renditions would not, of course, be generally and correctly interpretable as "commands."

We may still say that, divested of its metonymic extensions, and corrected for inexact elisions, the indicative is the mood of assignment to the representational content expressed the status of that which is actual, fixed, inalterably as it is and not otherwise. In a similarly general fashion, we may say that the basic sense of the imperative is the entertainment of the thought-of content of representation as future determinable and as a *commitment to be taken*. Some represented and referred-to state of affairs is to be brought about. But at once two semantic cautions are to be observed. First, though our main interest here is in doing, in physical bringing about, we must not forget that directable thinking is itself an activity and has its own critical directives, which constitute the topic of logic and epistemology—the ethics of believing. Such governable thinking may also and literally fall under the head of the future determinable, but in a somewhat different sense from that with which doing is concerned. Second, we must not confuse the communication of a content expressed in the imperative mood with the imposing of a requirement to do upon the addressee. Imparting to another the imperativeness of something to be done is not—or not universally—commanding the addressee to do it, or even urging or exhorting him to do it. For example, one who instructs another how something must be done if the doing of it is to succeed in its aim is not laying on him a command to do anything, or, even if he does something relevant, to do it as instructed. The instructor may have no desires with respect to what his advisee shall do or how he shall act, and might be better pleased if he would stop bothering a busy man and go make his own mistakes. But the discourse of such instruction will fall in the imperative mood. And, even if it is unlikely, one who is called upon to instruct another how to live a good life in harmony with his neighbors might be similarly irked. The supposition that discourse having to do with the moral is either commanding to do or persuading to do, whether for the sake of, or for some advantage to, or for any other purpose of, the communicator begs the question whether or not there is a *reason* in fact for the addressee, or for anyone, to conform to the directives imparted. Even if that is to be presumed, it is something which it is the privilege—the necessity even—for any addressee to determine for himself. If there is no such objective reason, then the imparting of directives as such—moral, or of any other sort—must either be arbitrary, or a misapprehension, or else no better than bullying or cozenry. One so addressed could justifiably respond, "If you think to command me, please be advised that you are not in a position to do so, and if you present a request, kindly phrase it as such." In any case, the interpretation of the imperative in general, and of moral imperatives in particular, on the pattern of arbitrary commanding must represent a misconception of the status of the moral among peers, as well as a semantic neglect of the variety of submoods comprehended under the imperative.

The nuances of the imperative are even more various than those of the linguistic indicative. And they are even more often left to be specified by idiom, or by the context of the pronouncement, or by tonality or gesture, or merely left to that empathic understanding which any human may be counted on to have in the case of another. What they all have in common is the sense of being directives of some sort, not that of a command addressed by a superior or a bully to one who must do as he is told. They cover laws, regulations, admonitions, warnings, recommendations, advice, instructions in case there is some manner of commitment to be taken, prescriptions of all kinds, rules of every sort, including, *e.g.,* those of games, as well as directions for carrying out whatever procedure may be essential or practicable for achieving any purpose in mind, whether of the speaker or the addressee, or both. They may be addressed to a particular person, to a group concerned with some common interest, or merely "to whom it may concern," as is the case in notices posted, the recipes in cookbooks, and the advisements printed on containers.

All such varieties of the imperative have one other notable feature, namely, that they are either valid or invalid. Whoever is responsible for the "skull and crossbones" or the word 'Poison' on a label should have a good reason for that labeling. And anyone who gives route directions to another should have a sufficient justification for the directions which he gives. And also, one who is deterred, or refuses to be deterred, from drinking by the label on the bottle, and one who accepts route directions or departs from them, is responsible for his own commitment in the matter and should have a ground for his decision. No one can literally innervate another's muscles, and no one can literally implant convictions in the mind of another. Directives given may be correct or incorrect, right directives or wrong directives. And we are not bees in a hive, automatically motivated by the behavior of others in the swarm. Or if we are thus fatally inclined, in belief and action, to togetherness, it is a failure to exercise one distinctive capacity of the human individual. We conform or refuse to conform to directives given on our own initiative and at our own peril. The first and universally relevant question concerning any directive must be for us: Is it correct and valid, and to be adhered to, or is it incorrect, invalid, and to be disregarded?

There is a commitment to be taken with respect to what is communicated to us in the indicative, and the same kind of commitment with respect to what we so communicate. That commitment is the decision to accept, or to reject or disregard, the commitment to believe or to refuse to believe, and to believe as certain or as probable. And the question to be so decided is whether belief is warranted, justified, or not. This question of validity is not directly and simply that of truth or falsity, of the relation between the content of this belief and the independent and objective fact represented. It concerns instead the relation of this conviction to the relevant evidence, to the "premises" afforded, in virtue of which this belief is to be assessed. The *justification* of believing is that rightness or wrongness of it which is to be assessed by the critique of logic.[2]

The question of the validity of directives, communicated in the imperative, is more complex but basically similar. There must be—or be lacking—a sufficient reason for any doing or refusing to do which is a matter to be deliberated, as there must be—or fail to be—a sufficient reason for committing ourselves, or refusing to commit ourselves, to a deliberated belief. Also, there will be premises—antecedent convictions—which will be relevant to any deliberate doing, just as there will be premises relevant to any deliberate commitment to believe. And, again in both cases, commitments to believe and commitments to do, there will be formulatable principles for the assessment of the validity of any deliberate commitment, a critique of believing and a critique of deliberate doing. (Whether or not one is in command of such a critique, articulately, and "bookwise," so to speak, is not the point; the point is the capacity to determine decisions in accord with what could be so formulated. And the formulation itself depends on the exercise of this capacity.)

At this point, there may be found, "just around the corner," many matters which are complex and difficult. For example, in the case of any imperative—any directive of doing—what are to figure as premises, and what may occupy

---

2. With respect to "conclusions" generally there is a similar question about premises—which are already accepted or believed. This matter is obvious in the case of induction, since "probability is relative to the data." Whether in deductive or inductive logic, the problem of "ultimate validity"—the validity of the data or the premises—is commonly ignored, and left for epistemology to consider. That this problem is one of theoretic difficulty and is elided in logic—by "assuming" the premises—will be patent. We could equally well say in connection with deduction that *inferring,* in the sense of *believing the conclusion,* depends on an "antecedent acceptance" of the premises. But deduction differs from induction on this point. When a conclusion is *deduced* from given premises, it must be, in any case, at least as probable as the premises. Additional information which does not show the premises invalid cannot invalidate the conclusion. In induction such additional information *can* invalidate the conclusion *without* invalidating the premises. Something probable on data D may be *improbable* or *less probable* on data D together with added information.

the position of principles? One must begin somewhere, and not everything which is relevant can be considered at one and the same time. It will be a help if we can, for the time being, confine ourselves to one main point: There must be a reason—or reasons—for any justified decision of believing; and there must be a reason—or reasons—for any justified decision of doing. That there must be differences in what figure as "reasons" in the two kinds of cases is implied in their being commitments of different kinds. That they must have points in common is implied by their both being species of commitments which are deliberatable and to be deliberately made. For the present we would consider these matters of their essential similarity. And we here suggest as one such, that what is communicated as to be believed, and normally expressed in the indicative, as well as what is communicated as to be done, and expressible by the use of the imperative, are both of them subject to the distinction of valid from invalid, justified or unjustified. The content conveyed, in the mood of its conveyance, is to be accepted or else rejected or disregarded by the addressee. The communicator is responsible for the validity of what he conveys; the addressee is responsible for accepting it—or rejecting or disregarding it. Validity is a matter of the relation between the content of what is communicated and some ground or reason essentially relevant to the acceptance or rejection of the content conveyed—in the mood of its conveyance. Such reasons, as we have suggested, divide into two sorts: premises and principles of critique. In both believing and doing we will have premises of antecedently accepted fact. On the other hand, with respect to the second sort of reasons, those expressible as principles of critique, we discover a difference; with respect to them, believing will differ from doing; different modes of critical consideration obtain in the two cases. In either case, whether of believing or doing, we might note, in passing, that it is possible to treat the principles involved, of whatever sort, as a certain kind of premises. If one should choose to take this approach, then the remaining question of the valid decision becomes exclusively one of valid concluding and believing—believing of the sort called "normative."

Convictions of the right and justified, or of the wrong and unjustified, as the case *may be,* govern our believing, or our doing, in ways these principles formulate. But if these principles are treated as a kind of premise, they are distinct from those of a different kind, those of empirical circumstance or sense-discoverable factuality, and are not themselves finally determinable in the manner in which the antecedent premises of empirical fact may, in turn, be called in question and be determined, in the course of a critical assessment of believing or doing.

Let us not run further forward in these matters, but confine ourselves to what more directly concerns this fact that both what is conveyed in the indicative as something to be credited as factual, and what is conveyed in the imperative as something to be done, are either valid and to be accepted, or invalid and to be rejected, or disregarded, and that in both cases there must be some ground or reason for decision, either for accepting, or refusing to accept, what is conveyed. And if no reason is given, that by itself is a sufficient ground for disregarding the matter, for refusing any commitments in the matter, whether of believing or doing. It is immediately suggested that it is in virtue of our capacity to determine, and necessity to determine, our own commitments of belief and doing by deliberation, and for what figure as reasons, that we call ourselves rational. The contrast, of course, is with creatures whose responses are automatically elicited and not subject to ratiocination. These strong suggestions of etymology are not, of course, to be accepted forthwith, without probing. But it will do no harm to observe at once certain general considerations which go with these suggestions. First, it is the capacity so to challenge what is conveyed to us, either in the indicative or the imperative, and attest it for ourselves before deciding our response that we are "self-governing." We are not, as earlier noted, like bees in a hive, automatically responsive to the behavior of others in the swarm. We are concerned, rather, with issues of truth and rightness, with issues of correctness, validity, and justification. And second, we should observe that it is not in virtue of some universal, fatally predetermined *exercise* of this capacity that we call ourselves rational, but rather in virtue of our possession of the *capacity* itself; it is only in virtue of the *possibility* of our challenging suggestions received and reaching our own determinations of belief and action that we regard ourselves as self-governing and rational beings.

It will be in point also to remark certain relationships of, and the interplay between, what is characteristically expressed and conveyed in the indicative and what is expressed and conveyed in the imperative, in their vital function as determinative of our deliberated and deliberatable determinations of believing and doing. Both modes of communication function as advisements. We often advise doing, and are advised to do, by the communication of some factuality which is the reason, or a part of the reason, for doing, rather than by a direction indicating what to do. In different localities, for example, automobile drivers are advised in different ways. The sign may be "SLOW" or it may be "|—" which we shall use as a hieroglyphic for "Road ahead entering from the right." The action advised is generically the same, though advises also "And look out on the right." "Slow" is in the imperative, directing what to do; "|—" is in the indicative, stating the reason for so conducting oneself. There is an unexpressed context in both cases, which will be understood by most of those to whom this communication is addressed. "Slow"—for a good reason, because of which you may be sorry if you don't; "|—"—so slow down and watch out, if you would avoid possible trouble. The imperative form may be more judicious if, amongst drivers generally, too many should be inexperienced or stupid. The indicative is more courteous, presuming intelligence and a rational government of doing. "Wash in lukewarm water only" is imperative, "Not guaranteed against shrinkage," indicative. "Poison" on the bottle is indicative, "External use only," imperative. "The stove is hot" is indicative, "Don't touch the stove," imperative. In a given context, either form may function both as an advisement of fact and as an advisement of doing, one appropriate to that fact, utilizing it as its reason. One who reads "Poison" on the label of a bottle will presumably know better than to drink the contents. And one who sees "External use only" on the label will presumably infer that the contents are such as would injuriously affect the internal organs. All directives imperatively conveyed require to have some rationale, some ground in fact in order to be valid. And all facts conveyed will have their implications of advice for the government of possible ways of acting. In the case of advisement in the imperative, the sanctioning reasons are left to be inferred; in the case of advisement of fact, the advisability of doings to which it is relevant is left to be inferred. A major difference of the two is that the advisements of action implicit in an advisement of fact, supposing it valid, will be inclusive and various, and will depend on contextual circumstances, including desires, purposes, and ends to be furthered. The indicative pronouncement does up in one bundle, so to speak, many advisements of action, conditional upon ends to be furthered and other contextual circumstances not mentioned in the advising. The imperative advisement to do may, more often than is the case for the indicative, be pertinent by reason of the immediate circumstances, and on the basis of some presumption pertaining to the desires or purposes of the doer, but imperative advisements which are general, such as rules and instructions on containers, though similarly hypothetical, having to do with something not mentioned, are likely to presume something common in the case of all those to whose notice they are likely to come. But broadly and loosely, one may still say that for every imperative there is, in the circumstances of it, and for those addressed, a presumption of some fact, indicatively expressible, by reason of which alone that directive will be valid. And for every indicative of empirical fact, there must be determinations of action to which it is relevant and concerning which it is advisory, if it is to be significant, and valid as information. What has no significance advisory of possible deliberate activity has no significance whatever. Such considerations have their basis in relationships between knowing and doing generally.

That the stove is hot has the status of empirical fact if and only if it is verifiable or confirmable, if and only if possible statements to that effect, that the stove is hot, implicitly assert expectable consequences of experimental ways of acting, for example, that if you draw near to the stove, you will feel warmer; that if you touch it, you are liable to be burned; that if you remove the lid, you will see glowing coals, etc.

There are some delicate, complex issues here, largely peripheral to this project, which might be noted in passing.

That a condition of activity is universally essential to predictable consequences could be challenged. Let us consider two points here, one trivial, one more serious. There are *some* predictable eventuations which do not depend on anybody's *action,* in the usual sense of 'action'. But even in such cases, as we may observe upon reflection, there will be no *observable* consequences independently of at least some *behavior* on the part of the observer. He may, for example, simply notice that the stove is hot. There can be no consequences *to* anybody independently of, at least, something of this sort. Similarly, and more seriously, we might consider the possibility of predictable eventuations which will *not* involve consequences *to* anybody *regardless of what he does,* eventuations which are not *experimentally* verifiable or confirmable. Such would have no pragmatic significance, no significance for anyone's choice of doing. Such would be beyond human control, in a sense, inevitable. It seems plain, in such a case, that foreknowing something which has absolutely no implication for any possible activity of anyone—even of preparing oneself to meet it—could hardly, even if it were possible, fall within the proper signification of the word 'knowledge'. Such "knowledge," if one wishes to use the term to refer to such possibilities, could, *ipso facto,* exercise no advisory function for anyone. Such "knowledge," *ex hypothesi,* would carry with it no power to affect anything in the world, even one's own future state of mind. At the least, such "knowledge," even if it could exist, would be utterly *useless.*

As these considerations must remind us, the vital function of knowledge is precisely the implications of it which are advisory of action, by being advisory of what will result, in view of what is so apprehended, in the case of various decidable activities it is possible for us to adopt. Even knowledge of the inevitable must—rationally—affect *decisions* of action, advising us not to waste our efforts in attempts to ward it off. Nothing we conceivably could know, in any familiar, standard form of knowledge, could conceivably be without *some* advisory significance for decisions of *voluntary* doing. We may, thus, sum up this whole matter in a more comprehensive way: Knowledge advises what will happen if we do; what will not happen if we do; what will happen if we don't and what will not happen if we don't, and any knowledge which implies no such advice for decisions of action could not conceivably be knowledge, in any normal sense, *of anything.*

However, if we should assume forthwith that the indicative as informational and the imperative as directive eventually coincide in their significance, we should certainly be charged with overlooking one difference between the two: the use of the indicative carries with it no sense of commanding or rec-ommending; the imperative is distinguished precisely by hav-ing just such a sense, that of hortation to the addressee. As a general observation, considering the motivations of what is said and how it is expressed, this is broadly true. But we have observed at least one type of exception, that in the case of the impatient instructor. And the moral of that example has a very broad range of application. If we are to psychologize about communication, it will be in point to remember that there are always two parties to it. In any case, the communicator intends to affect in some way the state of mind of the addressee. If he fails to do so, *nothing,* of any sort, is communicated. Whereas there may be cases in which a communicator does not wish the addressee to *accept* the content of a communication, but per-haps reject it, or view it with suspicion, and cases in which the communicator has no interest in whether the communication is accepted or not, it will be a correct supposition in the great majority of cases that one who speaks in the indicative wishes what he communicates *to be believed.* But that point, shortly, will call for careful examination. In what fashion, or on what grounds, does the communicator desire to secure this belief on the part of the addressee? For example, does the communica-tor wish to cajole the addressee into believing without being convinced?

But first let us briefly gather together certain salient points, rather synoptically, so to speak.

Normally the communicator wishes his addressee to accept the content of the communication. In the case of the indicative, he wishes the addressee to respond by believing. In the case of the imperative he wishes a response of doing as directed. But this marks no distinction which is more than verbal between the indicative and imperative. On that point, we could at once remark that the indicative has the general sense of "Believe you this," and is as much a hortation as any imperative. The difference, so far, would seem to be only that which lies between eliciting belief and eliciting physical action—though, of course, imperative pronouncements are not in fact confined to those acceptance of which would involve physical doing.

We are now going to *moralize* a little about communications.

There was once a party organ entitled *The Appeal to Reason,* and it carried on occasion, with this title, the quotation from Francis Bacon: "Read not to believe or to disbelieve, but to weigh and consider." The party lost out regularly in every election. It would appear that politicians need to be able to persuade more than they need to be able to convince—at least where some people are concerned. But if it was poor politics, it was quite good morals. One who would convince, in the indicative, should have, and be prepared to present, if called upon, good reasons, reasons of the sort called "evidence," for what he presents for our belief. What he asserts should be validly credible. And, too, one who would exhort to do, in the imperative, should have good reasons, of some sort of factuality, for the rightness of what he exhorts us to do. Also, and in either kind of case, we ought to respect the privilege—and the necessity even—of those whom we address to determine the validity of what we assert, and the validity of anything we may exhort them to do, to determine it for themselves, as, in turn, we look to others who would inform us, or exhort us, to respect our similar privilege, that of determining for ourselves the validity of what they communicate to us. Unless we are unfortunate in our social milieu, our being *told* that something is the case is, by itself, *some* evidence that what we are told is credible, and, likewise, our being advised to do is, by itself, *some* evidence that what is so advised has a sanction for the doing of it. But, in both cases, the weight of this evidence will bear weighing, and it will be different in different cases. It will be strongest in the case of communicators who take responsibility for what they say and are careful to communicate only what is valid, and weakest in the case of any who are known to be irresponsible on such points. It will be utterly weak in the case of any who are known to be motivated, in what they say to others, simply by their wish to be believed and to have their advisements followed. And if anyone should tell us that this wish to persuade, without having or offering any grounds for the validity of what one would persuade to, is the *moral* motive of communication, he would be too great a cynic, or too big a simpleton, to merit consideration on our part for anything he has to say. It is the *validity* of what is communicated, whether in the indicative, and to be believed, or in the imperative, and to be conformed to in action, which lies at the root of this matter. In the case of the indicative, it is plain enough what constitutes such validity; it is the evidence. Admittedly we do not as yet present any clear depiction of what it is which constitutes the validity of imperatives. It is our task to find that out. But the extensive parallelism between advisements of fact and advisements of doing, and the relations between these two, may hold some promise of throwing light upon that matter.

In closing, let us reiterate a consideration touched upon earlier, the distinction between the nature of a communication, for example, what is actually conveyed in it, and the attitude or motivation of the communicator. It would be well not to confuse these two matters, despite the fact that there is normally a congruence between them.

Recall our parable of the "unwilling instructor."

We are going to expand on that, just a little.

One who informs another that the stove is hot implies, "If you touch the stove, you are likely to be burned." And this carries with it the implied injunction, "If you wish to avoid being burned, do not touch the stove." But, although it is "normal" that one who conveys such a piece of advice wishes it to be heeded, there can be exceptions. And the state of mind of one who advises, "The stove is hot," may be such that, if he is rude enough to be candid, he might add, "But if you don't believe me, or don't choose to follow my advice, go ahead and put your hand on the stove—and see if I care!" And an "unwilling instructor" could be similarly minded in any other case: "I have done my duty by you. I have advised you of what I take to be the facts. I have advised you what to do. And, frankly speaking, that is my only interest in the matter. If you want to learn the hard way, that is your privilege, which I gladly respect. And I am, further, uncharitable enough to hope that, if you are not convinced of the facts in this matter or how you should sensibly conduct yourself, you will do exactly as you choose and find out for yourself whether I am right or not."

One may guess that philosophers, and others, who can suppose that the *universal* motivation of pronouncements in the imperative is the desire that the addressee should follow the directive given must be people of uncommonly good dispositions, who have no such uncharitable moments. If this is indeed their supposition, it is a little unfortunate that they lack certain evidence relevant to their conclusion, which a less universally benevolent social bent would have made familiar to them.

Ethics and the Logical

Integrity, in thought and in the deliberate action it may serve to guide, is the nonrepudiable imperative of the creature privileged to make his own decisions, and obliged to live with the consequences of them. Intelligence is the capacity to recognize the general in the particular, to subsume things under concepts. And rationality is the adherence to what is dictated for the preservation of consistency, consistency in believing and consistency in what we choose to do. Consistency in what we think is the avoidance of the self-contradictory and impossible in each and every conviction to which we commit ourselves, and the achievement of a mutual compatibility amongst all our believings. Consistency in what we do is the avoidance of a commitment to any aim which, by the nature of it, must be self-frustrative, and the maintenance of a compatibility amongst the purposes of all our deliberate undertakings.

Such overall consistency—in our thinking, in our doing, and between what we think and what we do—is that intended consonance which is the self-imposed imperative of the self-directing being, thinking and acting in the present, in the light of his acquired knowledge and experience, and in view of his possible future. Intellectual integrity is that command which intelligence cannot set aside, and the moral integrity of consistently maintained purposes is that command whose validity he who can do by choosing cannot rationally fail to acknowledge.

Consistency of thinking, in short, is the self-compatibility of each and every conviction to which we commit ourselves; and consistency in doing is the self-consistency of those purposes to which we commit ourselves. Together, these two consistencies, be self-consistent in thinking and be self-consistent in doing, constitute the autonomous rule of conscious self-direction; they constitute indispensable requirements for an integrated personality, and for any intelligent and rational living, and thinking and doing.

Adherence to consistency in thinking and believing is thus imperative because it is essential to correct understanding and to the possible truth of what we believe, and this, in turn, is essential for the guidance of our doing, so as to attain our purposes. Consistency alone will not guarantee the truth of belief; it is not a *sufficient* condition of truth, but it is a *necessary* condition because *in*consistency is a guarantee of *falsity*. What fails to be self-consistent is necessarily false, and any conjunction of beliefs which fails of consistency must be in at least some part false and, as a whole, must fail to represent the facts. Likewise, any self-inconsistent purpose is foredoomed to frustration, and any plan or other conjunction of purposes which is not consistent must, in so far forth, fail of achievement. Inconsistency of aims guarantees a failure to succeed. He who thinks or acts in contravention of consistency cannot, in the nature of the case, achieve what he intends. For he who must trust in his convictions and hopes for the realization of his purposes, adherence to the consistent is imperative, no matter how he feels about it. His affective feeling or his emotive inclination, or his wishful thinking, can in no wise save him from his fate; they must inevitably mislead him if they are not governed by a constraint to the imperative to be consistent. That, in brief, is the sanction of all imperatives of rationality, and that constraint must extend to all that we understand, all that we believe and all we undertake to bring about. The only alternative is some failure of expectation and some disappointment of intention. This is a law of nature, whatever nature should or could be; and it is a law of human nature, insofar as, and in whatever sense, human nature is rational, a law not of how we *do* think and behave, but of how we *must* conduct our thinking and our acting if we would serve any purpose in so doing. The validity of imperatives consists precisely in this fact of life, which would be a fact of life in any world which could be that in which we live. And this validity of rational imperatives could not possibly be gainsaid—unless perhaps merely verbally, or by the unreflective, the shallow or thoughtless. But let us repeat: It is not that consistency will guarantee the truth of what we believe or the success of what we attempt; it is only that inconsistency will guarantee some correlative falsity and failure. We cannot altogether and completely help ourselves in what we think and do, but we must adhere to the consistent insofar as we would help ourselves at all.

This, in sum, is the whole "deduction" of the "normative and self-critical." And so far forth it summarizes the connection between the logical and the moral.[1]

That logic as the basic rules of consistent thinking and morals as the rules of consistency in doing are intimately related is something which hardly could be otherwise. A failure to recognize this interconnection would seem to bespeak some strange supposition which would repudiate the pertinence of deliberate and criticized thinking to deliberated and critically considered doing.

We cannot undertake, within reasonable limits of space here, to set forth the interrelations of logic and ethics with an adequacy commensurate with the importance of the topic. But it will be the attempt of this essay to indicate certain salient points and to bring to our attention the extensive parallelism which obtains between them, and to remark certain consequences, important both for logic and for ethics, which follow

---

1. For any who may be interested, it likewise summarizes my animus in insisting upon a logic which turns upon consistency and inconsistency— "Strict Implication"—as opposed to a logic which turns upon truth values and relationships among truth values—"Material Implication."

from this interconnectedness of the two main branches of normative investigation.[2]

Conclusions once reached tend to persist; they are "stored up" against any future like occasion, and stand as ready-made intellectual responses—unless or until some impediment is encountered or some disappointment in our reliance upon them moves us to rethink the matter. On this point, that of persistence, or perseveration, beliefs are like habits formed, and like resolutions taken. If it were not for this tendency of beliefs to persist, or perseverate, this tendency for the perseveration of beliefs, we could hardly arrive at deliberate decisions in time to act—before the occasion calling for action passes the point which allows us to affect what otherwise will happen. And it is also on the assumption of this perseveration of beliefs that acts which are corrigible but not deliberated on the occasion of the doing are still called deliberate and attributed to the doer as his responsibility: They are presumed to be determined in the light of his past thinking and deciding.

Action governable by thinking stands in contrast to doing which is determined by impulse or inclination, by feeling only. So far as we, like other animals, do simply as we are moved or inclined to do by the way we feel, our behavior fails to be affected by what we call intelligence, fails to exhibit any modification attributable to thinking, to the envisagement of anything beyond the immediate and "now visited upon us."

Deliberate doing is, obviously, so designated on the supposition that it is doing which is subject to control by thinking, either present thinking, as in the deliberation summoned on the occasion of the commitment to do, or primarily past thinking, as when previously formed convictions are brought forward as relevant to the matter presently in hand.

It is not the modifiability of behavior by past experience which is the main point here. All creatures with a central

---

2. If, for the purposes of summary statement, what we should present for consideration is too dogmatically set down here, we shall hope for the reader's indulgence. That we shall pass over much which cries out for further explication, not here given, and for a substantiation not here offered, seems to be unavoidable, if we are to come to any end of the matter in these pages.

nervous system appear to be subject to some conditioning of their behavior, the behavioral modifications depending, obviously, on the nature of the experiences in question. Feelings as well as ideas are modified by conditioned associations. The animal which is attracted to a bait by smell and suffers in consequence will thereafter, if the opportunity presents itself, feel differently when he smells that odor, and will feel moved to do differently. Such conditioning does not necessarily go beyond doing which is governed by feeling and impulse. The distinction between intelligent and nonintelligent behavior turns upon the determination of doing; in intelligent behavior, doing is determined by thinking and believing; in nonintelligent behavior, doing is determined by an automatic response to present feelings and impulses.

Thinking is an envisagement of the nonpresented. All thinking is thinking *of*—is representational. This is what distinguishes it from mere feeling. The content of representation may be assigned a reference beyond the here-and-now; something not presented may be taken as so signified. "Thinking-of" without any specific reference beyond the present may be called 'imagining'.[3] Thinking-of, representing, with an assigned reference to the actual, is thinking *that*—believing. Representing which is referred to one's own past is remembering. Representing which is referred to one's own future is expecting. Any believing or knowing—empirical knowing—posits as actual something beyond the immediate and now presented, something present as entertained in mind but absent to sense.[4]

We can indeed think about the now presented. But it is of the essence of any manner of empirical cognition that something *not* now presented but identifiable if or when disclosed be added to the content of presentation and be believed in, be posited as actual. What we see is apprehended as a house on

---

3. We may also, we might note, use 'imagine' where there is a "reference beyond" and that reference is taken to be nonveridical or there is some doubt of its veridical character.

4. The animal which responds to a food-object, say, one detectable to him by vision only, so long as it is in sight, but loses interest when his vision of it is obstructed, is "less intelligent" than one which remains interested and persists in trying to get at it.

the supposition of its having other sides we do not now see but believe to be there and "seeable." And even the simplest and most fully observable thing, such as the period at the end of this sentence, is not the thing we believe it to be if it disappears while our eyes are focused on it or is readily brushed off with a handkerchief. Without some supplementation of the immediate content of presentation by some implicit expectancy, nothing immediately presented figures to us as any kind of object whatever. To be a thing of any kind, there must be some further required and anticipatable behavior of this apprehended thing in further possible experience, if the now seen, felt, heard, and so on, is to be posited as an actual existent. It takes, so to speak, both seeing and believing in something not now seen for the apprehension of an actuality. We see something and we believe in something more. And unless this believed-in is verifiable in further experience, there is no actual object there but only an illusory appearance—illusory because the seeing is supplemented by a believing which is mistaken and not verifiable. That the same kind of story holds for other modes of presentation than the visual will be evident without discussion.

Furthermore, it is only because seeing, or hearing, or smelling, or factually feeling, etc., leads us to believe in something specifiable but not now seen or otherwise experienced that this manner of empirical cognition called perception operates for the guidance of our doing. We see this side of the house. We are led to believe that if we walk around it we shall see the other sides. If we have some interest to be met by inspecting the house, we proceed accordingly. And if, having such a purpose and acting accordingly, we discover that what we saw was not what we believed it to be, but only a moving-picture-lot facade, we may fail of our purpose. Our seeing was misleading; it was a cognitive blunder. We do not, in such a case, retract the previous seeing; we do, however, retract the previous believing. And if the dot at the end of the sentence brushes off, we retract "period" and substitute, say, "speck of dust or something."

The pragmatic function of perception, and of the other modes of empirical knowing, is the guidance of our behavior, so as to realize what will satisfy some interest. If any behavior is essential to satisfying this interest, it is to be guided by some expectation of the results of behaving in certain ways, on the ground of present conviction as to relevant objective fact. The prediction is of the form, "If I do so and so, such and such will be realized in my experience." This prediction functions as an "advice of action," sanctioning some ways of doing, and prohibiting others. In view of the now presented, if you wish the eventuation of such and such in experience, then that may be attained by doing so and so. Hence, that being wished, do so and so. Or if, the wish being to avoid experience such and such, then, in view of the same prediction, based on observation, the imperative is, "Do *not* do so and so." We see the red-glowing stove top and feel the radiated heat. Not wishing to be burned, we must not touch the stove. Or, wishing hot water, we may put the teakettle on.

In passing, let us note that the implicit and *positive* directive is "permissive": there may be other ways of getting hot water. But the *negative* directive is categorical: one cannot touch the stove but avoid the burn.

It is the given appearances of the stove which are the basis of our cognitive conclusions as to what is further verifiable, realizable in further experience, depending on ways of acting. It is such predictive conclusions which function for the guidance of our well-directed doing. Anyone who should ignore the directives of deliberate doing, thusly implicit in cognitive experience, would be unlikely to live long and certain not to live well. Behavior not subject to the guidance of cognition is the behavior of the witless. And if intelligence did not function to improve one's deliberate doing and better serve one's interests, there would be no pragmatic sanction for it; the exercise of it would be nothing better than an aesthetic whim, if even that.

As we might put it, nature has two choices for creating conscious beings whose behavior may be adaptive, either the modes of automatism, whether native or conditioned, which approach the infallible, or the mode of intelligence, with its capacity for conscious learning. Intelligence must be, by and large, more fallible, in order that the creature's self-guidance may be more extensively corrigible. And perhaps nature awards intelligence only where the lessons to be learned are more far reaching, more complicated, and more difficult.

Autonomy (self-direction) or automatism: these are the alternative possibilities for behavior.

Some of our believings may be as spontaneous and ungoverned as the automatic promptings of any animal, and it would seem that the earliest of them must be such. But the ratification of them in any later and conscious consideration—their deliberate acceptance—must be an exercise of critical intelligence. Without intelligence there can be no deciding, and without deciding there can be no right or wrong. Conversely, where there is deciding, there is the rightness or the wrongness of it. Something is at stake, and may be missed: we may be disappointed in what we hazard, and our decision shown to be erroneous or untoward. Empirical cognition hazards some futurity which will verify or falsify, confirm or disconfirm. And doing hazards some futurity which is its end in view and which may be realized or not. That intelligent and directed doing must be guided by some cognizing, and that any wrongness of such directive thinking must be prejudicial to the aim it serves to guide, comes near to being axiomatic. This matter belongs to the general nature and economy of life, the way life is and how it must proceed. And there is one further simplicity to be observed here. The rightness of doing calls not only for intelligence but for conformity in action to what it dictates, that is, it calls for an adherence to what rationality dictates in deciding.

What the word 'rationality' means, in its application to ourselves, we who pride ourselves as human by claiming this capacity, may not be clear on the face of it.

It includes two things at least: first, it *presumes* intelligence as the capacity to subsume the particular under the general, or, otherwise put, to identify the general in the particular, and, second, it dictates as imperative the adherence to consistency. But the first of these is merely the counterpart, in terms of the occasional self-consciousness in thinking which intelligence calls for, of those spontaneous associations which presumably dominate any subhuman behavior which is conditioned by experience. Intelligence eventuates in conscious classifications, made with an eye to some purpose in view. But all conscious beings with a central nervous system behave *as if* they responded to classifications of that to which they react. So to say, subhumans *find* their classifying already done for them; but humans have alternatives in this matter. To be intelligent carries with it the possibility of recognizing the presented as an instance of A or of B, depending on whether it is A or B which has some recognized relevance to a matter in hand. But it is the other signification of 'rationality' which has peculiar relevance to right and wrong. Consistency is the *imperative* of reason. It concerns adherence to, or neglect, or repudiation, of the advices of intelligence. It concerns commitments to believe. And it includes any concluding, inferring, as well as any doing which such concluding may advise. The antithesis of rationality on this point is careless insouciance toward the expectable future or that perversity which flies in the face of what is to be expected, a silly obstinacy of inclination and a willful disregard of what is at stake in decision, and of what is vouchsafed to us as the advice of intelligence.

The capacity for moral discernment, like any other mode of the discrimination of right from wrong, is correlative with the capacity to be intelligent and rational. Pragmatically defined, that is, defined by reference to the interest-bound difference it can make, intelligence is the capacity for conscious and explicit foresight, as formulatable thinking and believing, and stands in contrast to that humbler capacity which approximates to it in its results, the response of behavior to premonitory feeling, either native or conditioned. And rationality is the capacity for self-constrained behavior, by reference to foresight, and hence the ability to act counter to impulse and felt inclination. Intelligence contrasts with premonitory feeling by the status of its eventuations in explicit and representational foresight and belief. And rationality contrasts with automatic impulsions of premonitory feeling by being *conscious self-constraint*—imperative—instead of an urge of feeling or emotive drive. Aristotle said that the function of reason is the government of the affective and emotive feelings. We agree. It is in that significance of it, the government of the affective and emotive feelings, that rationality functions—discriminating right from wrong and setting before us the imperative of right self-government.

So far we have only summarized matters which are familiar to all. We now approach considerations which, if still open to reflection on grounds of the familiar, are less exigent for attention in common practice, and are more subject to divergence in the way familiar facts may be read. But we must still proceed summarily, not expecting our brief notice to be adequate, but hoping to indicate the more salient points of what is relevant.[5]

Knowing and doing, for a creature capable of, and intent upon, self-government, are inextricably intertwined. And normative critique is applicable to both. We recur frequently to such points. But knowledge essentially involves not only the "empirical" but also what we may speak of as the *a priori.* Indeed, no adequate understanding of knowing and doing, and of life and ethics, is possible without an adequate understanding of the nature of the *a priori.* Yet this topic is seldom treated, at least with patience, in discussions of ethics.

Indeed, we ourselves, so far, have said nothing of the *a priori.*

We now embark upon a discussion which will doubtless, to some, seem tangential or digressive.

It is not.

That kind of knowledge which can afford specific advices of doing, on particular occasions, must be empirical and concern the actual. *A priori* knowledge concerns exclusively our concepts and conceptions. It can have no dependence on the actual for the warrant of its truth, upon what exists and what does not, on what presents itself to us in experience and what does not. Finding something to be actual may prove our persuasion of the *a priori* to be mistaken, but nothing so found can establish anything as *a priori* true or valid. Some would read the *a priori* as no more than the formulation of our intellectual habits in dealing with the content of sense. It is that— or it would be if our habits of thought were impeccable—but it is also something more, and more important. It formulates something to which, for safety and success, our intellectual

---

5. With respect to some of these points, more lengthy examinations may be found in *Mind and the World-Order, An Analysis of Knowledge and Valuation,* and *Symbolic Logic,* the latter with Cooper Harold Langford.

procedures *must* conform. The breach of it must hazard intellectual self-frustration and practical disaster. The bearing of it upon the content of the actual, and our dealing with what is encountered in experience, lies in the consideration that what should contravene the *a priori* could not possibly exist or be the case, whatever the findings of sense experience may be. In adhering to it, we may be free of any wariness of an encounter with some negative instance, and we may divest ourselves of any vain hope of realizing what it rules out. But this same thought can as well, perhaps better, be read in the opposite away. The *a priori* is no law imposed on nature, or imposed on us by nature—unless by our own nature as intelligent. It neither precludes any natural fact which, without it, could be the case, nor secures anything which otherwise might fail to happen. As Leibniz would remind us, neither nature nor omnipotence could create a three-legged biped—but that is no limitation on what nature or omnipotence might create. It is merely a limitation on our own consistent classifying. It may so be imposed on the child who would draw a three-legged bird, or one who, having already eaten two drumsticks, asks for another. But this indicates only a free-working imagination, one not yet linguistically disciplined, one not yet aware of the intensions of certain terms, intensions which are socially accepted and sanctioned. The *a priori* precludes nothing which could be observed or imagined. That which it governs and for which it legislates is our own thinking, classifying and inferring. These conscious activities of ours may violate the edicts of the *a priori*, and such lapses, if we fail to correct them, may lead to self-frustration in deliberate acts. It is no miracle that what is square is never round, and that a square peg cannot fit a round hole. The point is that some individuals, and not all of them witless, may not understand such things, and may even try quite hard to come up with exceptions to them. The Pythagoreans, and doubtless others, tried quite hard to find two whole numbers, x and y, such that $(x/y)^2 = 2$. They desisted, with dismay, upon discovering that if there were any such two numbers, one of them would have to be both odd and even. Incidentally, no procedure of empirical trial and error, however extended, could ever have established this fact; nothing but *a priori* thinking, proceeding to draw out

the consequences of conceptions adhered to, could have proved
it. With respect to the validity of any *application* of empirical
concepts, and with respect to empirical knowledge at large, of
course, the case is different. The empirical must exceed the *a
priori,* which lies ingredient within it. It requires the *a priori*
but must transcend it.

It is indeed a kind of miracle—something for which there
can never be any scientific explanation—that in this world in
which we find ourselves, it is so often the case that the look,
or feel, or smell, or taste, which we encounter in experience
will afford us a prediction of what is to ensue, or of what will
ensue if we do thus and so, that, in Berkeley's terms, one idea is
a sign of another which is to come. Just possibly, however, we
usually look in the wrong direction for an explanation of this
miracle—that what happens in experience makes sense to us.

It may be that we give our attention only to those aspects
of the presentational which hold some significance for us, and
dismiss without attention those features of the presentational
which have only the "so-what-so-nothing" character. And when
we find our deepest commitments of expectation violated, we
dismiss the presentational as illusory. That would be one way
of saving the world for intelligence: what totally resists understanding by way of subsumption under *some* concept or other,
or by way of inclusion under *some* category of the actual, and
thus resists all attempts to find any clue to valid expectancy
in it, is just an item "seen" or "felt" but nothing there in the
actual world. The *totally* unintelligible just is no kind of existent thing whatever. But if this thought is too unmanageable,
at least it is clear that what thwarts all attempts to find some
verifiable significance in it is rejected as illusory. That which
thwarts all signification of the verifiable must be rejected as no
real thing at all.[6]

---

6. A presentation, in one dimension or another, of course, may not readily
reveal its significance. Those who discover a valid expectancy signified
in the presented where no one has ever found any such clue to the verifiable before are those who supplant necromancy by science. They enlarge
the scope of the intelligible real, and that of the "nonmiraculous," in our
experience.

It would be a new deduction of the categories to say that what is not understandable under some category or other is not a *Ding an sich,* but no real *Ding* at all—unless the kind that dreams are made of. If seeing is to be believing, we must not include our nightmares.[7]

But let us excuse ourselves from coming any closer to the cosmic chaos of nonbeing. In the world as we find it—or, perhaps better said, as we are bound to understand it—our concepts are, at one and the same time, our rules of classification and our *paradigms of verification and confirmation.* What looks like a potato is likely to be classified as a potato. But if it should rise off the plate and burst into song, we stick to our concept and rule it out as not a potato. Or if too many potatoish-looking things behave that way, we shall become a little more discriminating in our observations of them, and entertain a new concept for the subsumption of such potatoish-looking nonpotatoes—as we have had to do in the case of mushroom-looking toadstools, which poison us if we eat them. We *can* make our classifications as we will. But we do so at our peril. And we shall *intend* to choose them in such wise that the way things so identified *appear* will hold some assurance for a prediction of what will ensue upon the occasion of such appearances—or will ensue if we do thus and so on the occasion of such appearances. The endeavor to arrive at concepts which will exercise this pragmatic function of correctly predicting on the grounds of present observation is the continuing effort of intelligence and the driving force behind all science.

There is a plain conclusion dictated by these considerations: any concept capable of application must be, at one and the same time, a rule for classification by reference to the observable characters of what is to be classified and a rule for expectation—intelligent expectation—in the case of what falls under this concept. The humbler concepts of common sense are such as are relatively susceptible of application by common inspection, but they tend to be less trustworthy as bases for

---

7. A Kantian "experience," as spoken of in the Deduction, is an experience of *objects.* Any who do not read Kant so should read again. Perhaps he forgot to add that the experience of dreams and illusions are understood by being categorized as visions of the nonactual and unverifiable.

expectation. The more ambitious concepts of science are comparatively difficult to apply with assurance, but they are notably more reliable in providing grounds for prediction.[8] But *any* concept which can be applied must function in both ways, and find in certain characteristics, identifiable in direct inspection, a ground for predicting something which will be verifiable in the future. And any recognition of a thing, as belonging under any classification of real objects, hazards some prediction as to what the future experience of it will disclose. To look red is not, *ipso facto,* to be a really red thing, and to feel sharp is not, forthwith, to be an object suitable for cutting. Substantiation in further experience is essential to the correctness of a subsumption under any concept for which we should have a use; and a concept which should find no clue to its application in direct experience could never be applied at all. Every applicable concept must serve as a bridge between given appearances and predictions signalizing something or other as being verifiable in the future. This is the basic character of all empirical knowing. The function of it as guidance for well-directed action, by found reliable expectancies to which the appearances afford a clue, is its most obvious significance.

Empirically to know is not merely to see but to understand. To understand is to bring under a concept. And to subsume under a concept is to believe, to hazard predictions as to what will be verifiable in the future. It takes both seeing and believing to constitute that simplest mode of empirical knowing, which is the recognition of the presented as a kind of real object.

If we would move in the direction of what pertains to rightness or wrongness in knowing and believing, we should next observe that while the seeing, so to say, is never questionable—we see what we *see* if we raise no question of what real thing it is we so observe—the predictive believing so signalized is always at some hazard. To overlook the necessity for the application of *concepts*, and that they involve predictive reference to the as-yet unverified, to overlook these concepts with their ingredient predictions, predictions which in the nature

---

8. I think to find here some parallel to Whitehead's distinction between "knowledge by *adjective*" and "knowledge by *relation*."

of the case must *go beyond* what is present at a given time—to overlook the essential importance of concepts and prediction for any understanding or any empirical knowing—is a fallacy of a too naive empiricism and realism. To overlook, on the other hand, that no conceiving can dragoon that denouement which alone can verify what conception hazards is a fallacy of a too naive rationalism and idealism.

Descartes proposed a neat resolution of the problem of the responsibilities inherent in thinking and acting which is guided by observation: what we *see* is an act of God, but anything we add to it in the way of belief, on the grounds of what we directly observe, is our own doing, for which God has no responsibility. Our empirical expectancies are our own hazard. As we have observed, Berkeley enlarges the scope of that which is attributable to the goodness of God, and includes the fact of a world in which our expectant beliefs so often turn out well. But he forgets to observe the theological problem—that of cognitive evil—which is implied: God becomes responsible when our most judicious of expectant believings turn out badly. Descartes had the better of it on that point, but forgot to mention that if we do not hazard such believings, sometimes to our detriment, we are reduced, in our active attitudes, to saying, "Here I am, Fate, now what are you going to do to me?"

We shall not pursue this theological problem, but, also, shall not quite agree either with Descartes or Berkeley. Errors of expectant belief are corrigible, some of them before the fact, and some of them only after the fact which our expectant believing hazarded. We can attribute those of the former sort to our own incogency, but there will be some of the latter sort left over which we cannot attribute to any escapable wrongness on our part. Some hazard of empirical knowing is inescapable if we are to hold empirical beliefs at all. And here, as elsewhere, to hazard nothing will be to achieve nothing. The point is that the best we can do in the way of empirical believings which are prompted by present observations will sometimes not be good enough. And by virtue of that inescapable fact, *any rightness of empirical believing will not coincide with the truth of it. Justified empirical beliefs, if there are any which are justified, will sometimes turn out false.* The *truth* of expectant beliefs depends on verification, but the *validity* of them depends only on the relevant premises available to us and the *cogency* of our decisions of believing in the light of them. Empirical *truth* is at the mercy of the future; the *validity* of empirical believing depends only on something past or present and the character of our concluding with respect to what is possible in the future.

And, as we shall find, this distinction between the *validity* of decision and the verification (or falsification) of what the decision inescapably hazards extends to the distinction between right and wrong in deliberate doing also. Rightness or wrongness of any kind can never depend on anything which is in the future and not open to observation at the time and under the circumstances in which the decision as to the commitment to be taken must be made. It is by reason of that simple consideration that the rightness of a commitment taken, whether of believing or of doing, cannot simply coincide with the satisfactoriness of the results of taking it. We cannot take responsibility for the unforeseeable. And on this point, the connection between the rightness of empirical believing and the rightness of deliberate action is inescapably clear. Where there can be no foresight of results there can be no blame for what is done. Both the rightness of believing and the rightness of doing turn upon what is predictable to cogent thinking, upon the *validity* of the commitment deliberately taken on grounds of what is open to our apprehension at the time of decision. Without knowing what is right and justified, or wrong and invalid, there could be no right or wrong doing.

Self-government is open to intelligent beings only: self-direction without reference to intelligence would be a contradiction in terms. There could be no right or wrong of any kind—though plainly there is good or bad—beyond the jurisdiction of intelligence. Rightness or wrongness of doing as deliberate, and corrigible to deliberation, is inseparably conjoined with cognitive foresight, which itself is right in the sense of valid and cogent on the grounds of antecedent and present apprehension, or is wrong in the sense of invalid and incogent. And the limits of responsible, that is, right or wrong, doing are set by the limits of responsibility for our thinking and believing as determinably cogent and valid, or incogent and invalid, on the grounds of what lies open to our cognitive apprehension. That the critique of deliberate doing either coincides with, or is included in, the critique of knowing in no sense follows. But any critique of right doing must either presume or include the critique of that deliberation which is the *sine qua non* for governable and responsible decisions to do.

Let us briefly consider the position in ethics known as "noncognitivism."

That position, in the light of considerations such as the preceding, must either be misnamed or commit the absurdity of attributing acts to agents who are incapable of directing them to results which are in any sense or measure foreseeable to them. The ethical critique is not the cognitive critique; its criteria of the morally right are other than those for the logical or epistemological right; but the logical and epistemological critiques are ingredient within any rational approach to moral action; a practical moral critique could not exist without them; significant elements of morality lie within the jurisdiction of epistemic criticism. If there were nothing which it is cognitively justified to expect when action is taken, there could be no justification and no contravention of the just—no right or wrong. Nothing which lies beyond the limits of criticizable knowing could fall within the limits of criticizable doing. This is a commonplace, but perhaps one it is well to have in mind.

If we seem to have gone off on a tangent here, and forgotten the topic we set out to discuss, we hope it will be found excusable, first, by some necessity to be clear as to what we would speak of in speaking of concepts, before proceeding to a consideration of *a priori* knowledge as knowledge of the relations of concepts; and, second, because it seems desirable to suggest, even if somewhat vaguely, the bearing of these epistemic topics, which might seem to carry us so far afield, upon the considerations essential for ethics. Let us add to this the suggestion that we must eventually consider how, or whether, or in what sense, the fundamental principles of ethics may themselves be *a priori*. And with these thoughts in mind, let us now return to an examination of the cognitively *a priori*.

A priori knowledge is free of the hazards of empirical knowing because it is independent of existential facts, and of the question whether any actuality, which is as it is and not otherwise regardless of thinking of it, satisfies this concept or not. Truth which is *a priori* is determinable by reference to concepts alone. We can only know any actuality by subsuming it under concepts. That is the nature of any possible *understanding* of what greets us in experience. But the actuality we confront— real things in a real world—exists independently of any concept applied to appearances in understanding what they signify as real, and the concepts are as they are independently of their applicability or nonapplicability to anything which exists. To be sure, our concepts as entertained may be in some part indeterminate, fuzzy around the edges: There is such a thing as mental indecisiveness. But as we intend these concepts and intend to apply them, they must be definitely bounded, fixed, Cartesian "clear and distinct ideas," such that whatever is apprehended, *so far* as it is apprehended, must be definitely subsumable under any concept in question or it must be definitely *not* subsumable under that concept—"Everything is either A or not A," for any concept A. So far as we are unable to determine whether or not this thing in question is subsumable under a concept in question, either we do not know what manner of object this thing is, or we fail to know what question about it is the question which we seek to answer. Our concepts entertained must function as our *criteria* of things apprehended, so far as they are apprehended or are apprehensible to us. In order to so function, the concept itself must be antecedently clear and fixed, and inalterably just that concept which it is. Insofar as that should fail to be the case, it cannot function as the criterion of anything. We cannot determine length with a rubber measure. And let us remark in passing that, as follows immediately, what is often spoken of as the "modification" of a concept must, for the sake of accuracy, be recognized to be the *displacement* of a concept, earlier entertained for application, by another and later adopted one which overlaps with it but does not coincide with it. If the old expression continues to be used for the new meaning, that may obscure the substitution, but cannot alter the fact that the substitution has taken place. Concepts may be utilized or not, and may continue in use or be abandoned, but the fixity of concepts as criteria of classification is indispensably dictated if they are to serve for purposes of understanding. Indeterminacy of what a concept requires in order to apply must, *pari passu,* defeat the possibility of understanding, and so far forth foreclose the project of knowing the real.[9]

We explicate our concepts, to ourselves or to others, by reference to what any application of them requires, for the correctness of it, concerning that to which such application is intended. To explicate is to unfold, to make explicit, what is implied. Any concept is bounded and fixed by what it does and what it does not imply, what the expression used to convey this concept implies as being the case about anything in order that it be correctly applicable, that is, by what is *inferable,* concerning anything, from the fact, or the supposition, that this thing is subsumable under this concept and is, so far forth, rightly understood.[10]

There are two ways in which we may explicate our concepts, two modes or dimensions in which the implicit meaning which is the concept can be unfolded, that of sense meaning and that of linguistic meaning.

We shall first discuss the explication of sense meaning, which is fundamental.

Consider the direction in which we must move in thought, in order to follow through in proceeding to apply or not apply the concept in question. This is that mode of explication which we have attempted to suggest earlier, that which would provide an answer to the question as to what we require of a thing apprehended, in deciding whether or not it is one to which a given concept applies. What findings in experience will substantiate,

---

9. It is to be recognized that our concepts, as entertained, are, in some measure, personal and private. If I talk with a chemist about free radicals, it is that area in which our two concepts coincide which constitutes our "common concept." Outside of that, we fail to understand each other, a consideration he will have in mind and which, perhaps, may prompt him to instruct me as to the nature of this scientific concept.

10. It is essential to observe that the word 'implies' is here used in its time-honored meaning in which "A implies B" has the same meaning as "B is inferable, deducible, from A." This matter will be further explicated as we proceed. However, in what follows, we must be in the highest degree terse, and correspondingly dogmatic in statement.

verify or confirm that this thing apprehended is one correctly to be subsumed under this concept, and what findings would falsify or disconfirm the applicability of this concept to this apprehended thing? This type of implication, comprehended in our concept, is the "sense meaning" in question, the implications of the concept in terms of "sense findings" determinative of its applicability. Briefly put, this sense meaning of any concept, or expression conveying it, is the answer to the question, "What sense findings will attest the applicability of this concept?" Rather obviously, it is this sense meaning of our own concepts that we must be clear about in order to determine whether or not, in the case of anything presented, they apply, in order to use them for the purposes of understanding what we encounter in experience.[11]

However, although this sense meaning of a concept represents precisely the function it must exercise in cognition, we do not commonly try to tell this kind of story in any attempt to convey to others the concept which we have in mind. Yet, this

---

11. I have endeavored to set forth what is involved in such sense meanings in *An Analysis of Knowledge and Valuation*. Schematically it may be expressed if we remark that any single confirmation of a concept as applying to a thing will be expressible as a prediction that some presentation being given, acting in a certain way, a certain experimental way, will, in all probability, lead to some specifiable denouement in experience. Any set of such, expressing the predictable and confirming consequences of the experimental substantiation of an object-statement, *e.g.,* 'This thing I am looking at is a red apple', will constitute what I have called "a congruent set." A congruent set is a set of predictions so related that finding any one of them true by putting it to the test will increase the probability of all of them being true, and so will increase the probability of the object-statement itself. The qualification 'in all probability', above, is required in order to cover the point that any single sense observation can be illusory, *e.g.,* if too many such tests of the object-statement, 'What I am looking at is a red apple', should have a negative result, I shall have to repudiate my present seeing as mistaken or illusory, though it will remain a fact that I *had* this misleading *experience* even if there was no red apple there to see. At any moment, the user of a concept implies some not yet exhausted meaning, some *further* test which will still further corroborate, or disconfirm, the application. These further tests may be repetitious in nature, activities in the *same mode* of attesting the application, or different in nature, involving a test, or tests, of a *different kind*.

sense meaning is precisely what we want to convey to another, at least eventually, and by some means; indeed, it is what we must attempt to convey to another in order to evoke in his mind what is in ours. Let us suppose that we wish to convey to some ignorant but highly intelligent savage what is in our mind, if we should say to him, "This is a dynamo." But surely we shall despair of achieving success in this endeavor until he acquires a much wider comprehension of many other things, ones familiar to us but not yet to him. Drawing out the implications of any concept, in any way which would do ample justice to the experiential richness of our own sense meanings, is much too long a story to be adequately put into words, even amongst those whose spread of experience may be widely similar to ours. Instead of attempting that, we customarily explicate any concept in question by way of certain other concepts which may be already comprehended. The relations so utilizable are—must be—confined to those such that, the concepts themselves being fixed, these relations of them are thereby fixed—their "necessary" and implicative relations to one another. For example, an apple must be fruit, must grow on a tree, must have an outside skin, must be pulpy inside, must have a core, etc.

This approach involves us in the second modality of explicating concepts, the first having been the attempt to explicate in terms of sense meaning, in virtue, for example, of appearances, anticipations, and activity. This second approach, in which we are concerned with the relations among concepts themselves, is much simpler and, for purposes of communication, more practical. Here we explicate concepts largely in terms of contained, or otherwise related, concepts. This must be done, of course, as a matter of communicational necessity, in terms of language and common meanings. In that sense then, this second modality of the explication of a concept may be thought of as the explication of the concept in terms of its linguistic meaning.

The most expeditious way in which to indicate the total implications of a concept is to define the expression which conveys the concept in terms of other expressions which are equivalent to it, in the sense that the definiens and the definiendum have precisely the same implications. But let us remark in passing that the totality of the implications so comprehended in a linguistic meaning is, as is also the case in that of a sense meaning, inexhaustible—except as it may be limited by vocabulary, and even that kind of limitation will turn out to be specious on close examination.[12]

As will be obvious, the sense meaning and the linguistic meaning of any concept must be correlative; any two expressions which, such as the definiens and the definiendum, have the same linguistic meaning must apply in precisely the same cases, and answer to the same sense meaning. And any sense meaning conveyed by one of two linguistically equivalent expressions must likewise be conveyed by the other. Any failure on that point is simply a failure to think consistently, a failure to be logical.

We must speak briefly here of the main types of concepts, with a view to indicating that the basic type is that of concepts of attributes—concepts of properties, characters, features, aspects of mentionable entities which are classifiable in various ways. The main types of entities which are referred to, mentioned, and are, or could be, ingredient in a total reality or "world" are individuals, events and states of affairs. An event is a happening, something that takes place within certain continuous and closed space-time boundaries. We must not think of this space-time locus as *being* the event, but specifying the locus "uniquely determines" any actual event referred to. But in another sense, specifying the locus does not determine *what* event it is which happens then and there. Specifying the locus, let us say, indicates the event, but does not *imply* any otherwise further cognizable character, or characters, of it. The locus is one feature of the event which, being determined, affords us some instruction with respect to finding out further empirical characters of it. An event is, let us say, what falls within some specifiable and closed space-time boundary. Any referred-to event will include other events which could be referred to, and

---

12. We know the totality of such implications to be unlimited in the same way that we know the whole numbers to be inexhaustible: we know logical rules by the use of which we can always add a new one, not already cited. Poretsky's "Law of Consequences," for example, provides the basis for such a rule.

will, in turn, be included in other and larger events. Two events may overlap, or may be separated and mutually exclusive.[13]

Any mentionable and actual individual will coincide with some actual event—that of its lifetime endurance, its existing in the time and space boundaries within which it exists. And any thought-of individual can only be consistently thought of conformably to what we have just said. We are prone to think of individuals as totally exclusive one of another. But every dog has hair, and any hair it loses will continue to endure for a time outside the dog. The space-time loci of the dog and the hair overlap but do not coincide.

We know or apprehend any individual only by knowing or apprehending that it has certain characters, features, attributes, and that it does not have certain other attributes. An individual can only be known insofar as it satisfies some possible recital of attributes—only by some description. By the accidental limitations of what is actual and what is not actual, we may, with luck, command a description specific enough to exclude, by our description, every individual but one.

For human individuals, the name and the present address represents a useful description for the purposes of distinguishing one individual from another, but one who knows only the name and address of an individual does not know that individual very well.

The individuality of an individual—that individuality in all its fullness—defies complete knowledge. That such remarkable individuality exists, in this strong sense, is a posit. The posit is a natural one, however, even coercive, and is consequent upon, and in a sense is expressed by, the Law of Excluded Middle, that any individual is either A or not-A, for every attribution, A. Consonantly, to know any individual completely would be to know the totality of its attributes, an impossible task, as these attributes would be infinite in number.

But, of course, any knowledge of an individual which we can have will be coincident with our knowing some subset of these attributes.

---

13. We take advantage here of much which Whitehead has said with the utmost precision.

Attributive *words or phrases* are adjectival as referent to an individual, adverbial as referent to an event. Adverbs are adjectives expressive of characters of being or "going on."

With respect to attributes, individuals have no essences, that is, no essential attributes, or, as it will be more precise to say, all attributes which any individual has are essential to its being just the individual that it is. If Socrates had had, on a certain date, a different number of eyelashes, he would not have been just the individual that he was. Given attributes of things are not essential to things *per se,* but are essential or not to the thing's being *classifiable* in any specific way. Also, they may be "essential" to any *interest* we may have in any individual thing. We do not care about Socrates' eyelashes, but we do care about where he went and what he said. From the point of view of our interest, he would have been the same person, or "as good as the same," regardless of eyelashes but not regardless of sayings. Certain properties of an individual, thus, may be essential to its being *what interests us,* and others not. The difference between adjectival and substantival expressions is semantic, not logical. Adjectives mention attributes and apply to things. Nouns, and such expressions, mention classifications, but likewise apply to things, entities. Neither a substantival expression nor an adjectival expression can be *determined* to apply or not, except by reference to what attributes are *implied* in applying the expression to a thing.

"Proper names" function for cognition as abbreviations of some description, such as "the so and so." They have, however, the peculiarity that what they imply, or connote, to an individual acquainted with its referent may be in large part private to that individual and would not commonly be conveyed to others by that individual's use of the proper name. For example, should one refer to "Taxco," only a small part of what one might have in mind would be likely to be communicated to someone else.

A state of affairs is not identical with an event nor with an individual, except in that unique, wholistic case of that individual, that totalistic state of affairs, that total event, which constitutes the world or universe. Taking note of this remarkable exception, but putting it to one side in the interests of general exposition, we reiterate that, at least for most practical purposes, no state of affairs is identical with either an event or an individual. To put this more clearly, a state of affairs is an "assertable," something which can be asserted, a "*being*" or a formulatable "*not-being*." The existence or nonexistence of a thing, the happening or nonhappening of an event, these are included in, but not exhaustive of, states of affairs.

Individuals exist or do not exist. Attributes exist only in the sense of *inexisting*. They inexist in their actual instances, if any. There is no other question, having any meaning, about the existence or nonexistence of attributes—of universals. Any further question about, say, universals, is either flatly verbal and altogether insignificant, it being no real question about reality, for example, there being no way to resolve it, or it is a question of semantics only, having to do with ways of speaking and the choices of words.

Expressions which mention states of affairs are propositions, for example, "Red being a color" or "That red is a color," "Today being Monday" or "That today is Monday," "My dog running fast" or "That my dog runs fast," and so on.

One point we might mention in these terse and inadequately developed pronouncements, a point alluded to earlier, is the fact that states of affairs are attributes of a total state of affairs which is that individual thing, that total event, we call "the world" or the universe. All true propositions name attributes, characters, features, of this one actual world. But what world this actual world is, we shall never know. I do not know, for example, where my brother is now. Consistently with all I know, he may be in any one of a number of places. "Ed being in Boston now" is consistent with everything I know, but so are many other such propositions, incompatible with that. No two of these could be true of the same world. And so far forth, there are many possible worlds, and which one of them is the one we live in, I do not know. But I do know where I am now; any possible world that is this actual one must be consistent with all that I know. The states of affairs which I know to be actual are features, attributes, of this existent world. To *assert* a proposition, make a statement, is to attribute such an attribute—some state of affairs—to this actual world.

The point of these odd remarks is that the logic of propositions is a special case of the logic of attributes, of predicates. Propositions are predicates of reality—of this actual world. "That so and so" is a proposition, where 'so and so' is a *statement,* asserting that the proposition "so and so" applies to this actual world. "Today being Monday" or "That today is Monday" is the name of a state of affairs, which the statement 'Today is Monday' applies to this actual world, and asserts to be an attribute of it. The logic of attributes is, thus, the basic branch of logic altogether.

The subject of logic is that truth which must be true of any possible world. Any truth of logic is certifiable by the fact that it must be true of any possible world because the negation of any logical truth implies some self-inconsistency which could not be the case in any possible—any consistently conceivable—world. Hence it must be true of this actual world—whatever this world is. This is the peculiarity and the importance of the truths of logic. Any presentation of logic, or of the logical as such, which fails to observe it, is so far forth defective. It fails to observe the distinguishing character of the imperative as characterizing the intelligent and rational in thinking and concluding. And this defect may conceal something which should be obvious concerning what is imperative also for any deliberate doing, subject to the critique and guidance of rationality in thinking and concluding, namely, the preservation of, and limitation to, what is self-consistent and consistent with all that we know and believe. Self-consistency is the overarching imperative of rationality. And consistency with what we know and believe is the altogether universal imperative of intelligence. We can repudiate what is thus imperative, but we can only do so perversely and by doing violence to the demand of intelligence and rationality. Beyond these, there can be no further appeal, and against deliberate and obstinate repudiation of these imperatives no argument. The force of argument rests upon the presumption of the capacity for, and the recognition of the imperativeness of, rational and intelligent thinking and doing. A basic question for ethics is the question whether anything beyond these requirements is requisite to the validity of moral principles. It is that question which we have had in mind as the eventual point of the preceding discussion.

Let us observe some major parallels between the basic imperative of the logical and basic imperatives of rational doing. A basic imperative of logic, almost, one could say, *the* basic imperative of rational believing, is "Do not believe the self-inconsistent, that which implies its own negation." This is the sanction of the *a priori* at large, and logic asserts nothing which is not sanctioned by the fact that to deny it is to assert a self-contradiction. "*P* implies *Q*" *means* "That *P* is true but *Q* is false is a self-contradiction, a self-inconsistent statement." For example, that today is Monday implies that tomorrow is Tuesday, because, remembering that 'Tuesday' is definable as 'the day following Monday', and 'tomorrow' as 'the day following today', the assertion that today is Monday but tomorrow is not Tuesday is self-inconsistent. By substitutions of expressions which have the same definitional meaning, that assertion would commit one to believe that the day following today is not the day following today. It commits one to believe the logically impossible. The logically impossible is precisely the self-inconsistent, the self-contradictory, or any thing the believing of which would include believing something self-inconsistent, self-contradictory. And the negation of the self-contradictory is the *a priori* true.

Any deductively right concluding is sanctioned by the fact that to believe the premises but deny the conclusion would involve a self-contradiction. The premises of our concluding may not be true. And we may be responsible for having accepted the premises. But the critique of just this concluding, by itself, the *validity* of the concluding, does not concern that fact. What it concerns is the fact that to affirm the premises but deny the conclusion would be a self-inconsistency, precluded by the dictate of rational believing. Having accepted the premises, the conclusion could not be repudiated without a contradiction.[14] Any who should repudiate the imperative to maintain

---

14. This is precisely the point on which "truth-value logic," is a pseudo-logic. In "truth-value logic" a false proposition "implies," in the sense of materially "implies," anything and everything, and a true proposition is "implied," in the sense of materially "implied," by anything and everything. No logic which intends to comport with rationality can dissociate implication from consistency.

consistency could draw any conclusion he pleased from any premises he happened to believe. Without responsiveness to the logical imperative to consistency, logic would be nonsignificant. It has significance only for creatures committed to preserve consistency in thinking and believing. For them, the dictates of logic, deductive logic, are *a priori* and nonrepudiable.

So far as the *principles of logic* go, its paradigms as attesting the validity of deductive *inference,* what logic certifies as rightness in drawing the conclusion from the premises is that the acceptance of the conclusion, when the premises are given, is required for the avoidance of a self-contradiction, that it is required for the preservation of consistency. And this is the *rightness* of deducing—its *validity.*

And if we look to the *principle of deduction* itself, the validity of *it* is attestable directly by the fact that *to deny it is a self-contradiction.* Hence, *to accept that principle* is rationally imperative. This same criterion—the avoidance of self-contradiction, the preservation of consistency—is the general, universal, necessary and *sufficient* justification of any piece of deductive inference, or any stretch of deduction, however lengthy. Any step of deductive inference is valid, if it is valid, because to accept its premises obliges the acceptance of the conclusion or the incurring of a contradiction. And the *rules,* criteria, of logic itself are imperative to accept because to deny them is *self-contradictory.*

A point to observe here is that for what is *a priori,* truth and validity coincide; the assurance of its validity assures its *a priori* truth. The consideration in point is very simple: what is self-contradictory could not be true of anything whatever. What *denies* the self-contradictory must, by that fact alone and without reference to any premise for it, be true. The *a priori* is self-attested as true by being rationally nonrepudiable, valid, right. It is consonant with this that what is *a priori* is deducible from any premise whatever.[15]

It seems a bit silly to say these things: they are self-evident to any thinking rational mind. Unfortunately, there are many

---

15. See *Symbolic Logic,* Second Edition, Appendix III.

"logicians" today who fail to observe this distinctive character of logic, its imperativeness, and fail to acknowledge it in their pronouncements about logic. Perhaps, just because they are confining their attention to *a priori* truth, they forget to observe and be faithful to what *distinguishes* that kind of truth, the necessity of its acceptance, its imperativeness, and *fails to hold* about the inferring of non-*a priori* conclusions from non-*a priori* premises. In the latter case, one is under no rational obligation to infer conclusions from premises which imply them. Too, of course, given Poretsky's Law of Consequences, every premise or set of premises implies an infinite number of conclusions.[16]

Let us keep in mind these facts: first, for the *a priori*, truth and validity coincide; second, the validity of the *inferring* of a non-*a priori* deductive conclusion resides in the relationship of the conclusion to its premises, its being so related to its premises that to assert them but deny it would be to commit a self-contradiction, to be inconsistent. And, third, the validity of the *conclusion itself* similarly, is the logical rightness of it, its conditional justification, in virtue of its relation to its premises. In short, an *a priori* truth is, so to speak, self-certifying and independent; a non-*a priori* conclusion, on the other hand, is not self-certifying and independent. It depends on premises and inference. In the case of such a conclusion, validity is twice involved. Validity may or may not characterize the *inference* of which the conclusion is the product, and the *conclusion* itself may be regarded as valid or invalid, relative to its premises and the inference involved.

The justification of believing turns upon what is already accepted, antecedent to the concluding. And this justification—*validity*—depends on nothing which is to be, or could be, found out later. The truth of the conclusion, however, is something different, and can depend on what is to happen later—verification or falsification. However, there are logical implications of empirical facts, and also of empirical suppositions, whether

---

16. [I have done a little more editing than usual at this point, in the interest, if not of clarifying, at least of reinforcing, what I take to be Professor Lewis' point. —Ed.]

they are factual or not. And the deductive implications of any-thing supposable are the same, whether these suppositions are in fact true or in fact false. The usefulness of deductive logic, and of the criteria of validity in thinking, are not limited to their significant application to what is assurable *a priori*.

It is another and basically significant consideration, hav-ing its applicability beyond the logical, that there is no peculiar logic of imperatives. Logic is itself a set of principles impera-tive to heed. But it is not confined in application to what is formulatable in indicative sentences. What it applies to is the supposable, to the consideration of any thinkable states of affairs whatever, states of affairs formulatable by *unasserted* propositions, or propositions regardless of those being asserted. Logic is certifiable truth about *anything whatever* which could be supposed—any states of affairs, regardless of the mood in which they are entertained.[17]

Linguistic syntax distinguishes certain major moods of our entertainment of states of affairs. And what a proposition for-mulates, some state of affairs, is the same whether that state of affairs is asserted, doubted, inquired into, wished to be, wished not to be, viewed with dismay, greeted with acclamation, com-manded to be realized, commanded to be prevented, or viewed as permissible to neglect altogether, and so on.

Logical inconsistency bespeaks the impossibility of an entertained state of affairs, or the incompossibility of two or more thought-of states of affairs. And the imperativeness of adherence to the logically dictated is the futility, or worse, of committing oneself to a belief in what could not possibly be the case. That is what logic forbids; and there is nothing it dic-tates except the avoidance of a commitment to the impossible or incompossible.

And what it so dictates extends at once to any purposes of doing which might be entertained. Do not try to bring about what could not possibly be the case, or two things which are

---

17. What logic asserts is not *a priori* truth about words merely, but about the concepts these words convey, and *a priori* truth also about any-thing and everything to which these concepts correctly apply.

incompossible. Do not wish for the impossible, or any state of affairs involving incompossible constituents. If two comprehensive states of affairs, such as A and not-A, exhaust the possibilities, do not try to avoid both A and not-A; do not wish that they should neither of them be—it is futile. Do not question that one or the other of them is the case, but only which. Do not believe the inconsistent; do not try to bring it about; do not expect it; do not wish for it; and do not repudiate that which, since it exhausts the possibilities, limits what could be, will be and must be. Logic has dictates referential not only to what is, and can be, but to what is rationally to be purposed, expected, willed, wished and accepted. It is the nonrepudiable guide for any rational being, in every wishing, willing, expecting and doing, in every considered attitude, in every considered decision, in every anticipation.

The principles of logic have their application to every phase of possible self-government or self-direction of any creature capable of rationality and able to decide anything factual or decide any belief, or hope or expectation or, indeed, decide anything which is in any sense decidable. Deductive logic leaves a great deal undecided—rationally permissible to, and rationally permissible not to. Within that scope lies everything which is contingent. But so far as logic legislates, its imperative extends to everything which is in any way to be considered by creatures capable, first, of such consideration, and, secondly, of ruling themselves in accordance with it.[18]

Also, the logic of moral matters, *e.g.,* moral commandings and forbiddings, is completely uniform with the logic of assertions, the logic of believing and concluding. The logic of thinking and believing is formally identical with a certain portion of the logic of deliberate doing, that which concerns the preservation of consistency with reference to the discoverable particularities of empirical fact. And the rest of the logic of thinking and believing falls under inductive logic, which

---

18. So far as I know, this insight was first formulated by H. M. Sheffer, who for many years expounded it to his students at Harvard University.

concerns empirically founded generalities attested as probable on the grounds of facts which can only be learned by empirical observation.

This logic of believing "according to the probabilities" is likewise essential to any rational self-direction, and by that fact essential to consider in ethics, considered as the rational government of doing. That this part of the logic of believing is essential to ethics, and must be presupposed, if not included in, any set of maxims of conduct which should function for any guidance of deliberate doing generally, ought to be recognized as axiomatic. We cannot even recognize what it is that we do except by predicting the results of our initiations of doing. It would not be even theoretically possible to attest any specific rule of doing as prudent to follow, or as promotive of any aim whatever, prudential, moral, aesthetic or of any other kind, without a prediction of the consequences of the acts to which we commit ourselves. What is so to be predicted *is* the act we do; the two cannot be separated, except as we separate what we *intend* to do from what happens as anticipated. And if we could anticipate nothing, we could do nothing. But if there be any who would maintain that *some* anticipations of the results of our deliberate initiatives can be certain, at least all of us with any experience of life will admit that, in general, the instances in which those results of our initiative can be predicted with complete certainty, those results which it is exigent to foresee in doing, are comparatively few. Practical certainty, Yes, for some of them; but that these practical certainties extend to a sufficiently large proportion of the consequences of what we do, enough to obviate any necessity for "acting on the probabilities," No. The practical certainties of life, omitting all consideration of those recognized as no better than probable, quite surely would not suffice for reasonably deciding all those actions which we have to decide—those which we must either do now or, by failing to do them now, hazard something worse. Indeed, we are concerned with probabilities and not theoretic certainties, as soon as we go beyond concepts and their relations, themselves, and seek to *apply* them. That a particular concept, together with its relations and such, applies to a

particular thing is a matter of empirical knowledge, and theoretically subject to some uncertainty in each and every instance.

The logic of probable beliefs—beliefs as to the probabilities—is peculiarly essential to any guidance of self-directed
doing. And ethics, or any other set of normative rules of doing,
must be pervasively concerned with probabilities, tacitly if not
explicitly.

First, let us observe that interplay of deduction and induction which is involved as soon as the *premises* of deduction
are less than certain. The important consideration here is that
any valid deductive conclusion will be at least as probable as
the premise or premises, *i. e.*, the conjoint statement of the
premises. And it is equally important to observe that where
the inference is purely deductive, *no addition* to the premises
can render the deductive conclusion *less probable than it is on
these deductive premises of it.* If a thing is red, it is, by deduction, colored. Add anything else you please to this premise of
its redness. Add, say, "This is red, but it is of a kind the color
of which often fades." It would still remain the case that so
long as the premise holds, the thing will be colored, and the
probability that it is colored cannot be less than the probability
that it is red. But now consider an instance in which the inference is inductive. If the barometer keeps falling, rain will be
highly probable. But now word comes by radio that in the low-
pressure area which is moving in on us there has not been and
still is not any precipitation. The *added* premise *reduces* the
antecedent probability of rain, even though it does *not* reduce
the antecedent probability of the premise of the falling barometer. Where the conclusion is deductive, added information can
have the effect of increasing the antecedent probability of the
premise but can in no case decrease it. Where the conclusion
is inductive, added information can either increase or decrease
the antecedent probability, that is, the probability of the antecedent premise of the conclusion. Otherwise put, the deductively valid conclusion is at least as near to certainty as the
premise or premises from which it is deducible. The inductive
conclusion can become *less* probable as well as more probable,
by adding to the information, the premises, from which it is

inductively drawn. Otherwise put, when the premises given are insufficient for imparting certainty to a conclusion, the degree of uncertainty may be increased or decreased by the addition of premises which are relevant.[19]

Another way to say the same thing is to observe that there is no such thing as a probability except relatively, as relative to premises. Before we listened to the radio, there was one probability of rain; after the added premise of the radio message, there was another. It remains a fact, however, that *on one set of premises*, there is just one determinable degree of probability.[20] The probability on just those premises is such and such—no more, no less, and nothing different—just that. But if further relevant premises be added, the probability may change—becoming higher or lower, depending on these new premises. This is what is intended to be conveyed by the adage, "Probability is relative to our ignorance." There are *no* probabilities except such as are, explicitly or implicitly, of the form, "*On the basis of data D, H has the probability p.*" And for the same *quaesitum*, or conclusion, H, the probability of H on the basis of different data, say, D supplemented by D', may be either greater *or less* than on the basis of D alone.

The same character of probability conclusions is sometimes suggested by saying that there is no probability of a particular event; the probability is of events in a certain class of cases. But that statement is injudicious: it overlooks something which judicious people intend when they speak of the probability of an event such as rain today. What may be thus judiciously meant by saying "Probably it will rain today" is "On all the relevant data we have—or on all the relevant data here and now available—there is a probability greater than 1/2 that it will rain today."

---

19. The added phrase 'which are relevant' is here a pleonasm, added only for clearness. Premises are "relevant" to a conclusion if and only if knowing them, as against being ignorant of them, will affect the determinable probability of the conclusion.

20. It might be noted that often, as in this instance, the degree of probability is not precisely determinable as an exact fraction. [I have here relocated, and adapted, an aside in the text. —Ed.]

There is a moral to be drawn from this: For anyone who is rationally concerned to determine a probability, it is as imperative to determine this probability on *all the available and relevant data* as it is to concern oneself about this probable or improbable happening, or *quaesitum*. That we may justly say is a condition of the *validity* of a probability assigned to any eventuality to be predicted. By itself, it is not of course a *sufficient* condition for the validity of a probability assessment, but it is a *necessary* condition. Also, even in the case of a purely hypothetical probability, such as might be involved in an exercise for students of the subject, this requirement is to be observed. For example, the student, presented with such an exercise, will not be out of order if he inquires, "Is this all we are supposed to know?" And he will be posing for the instructor a more troublesome question than he is likely to understand, because, as printed or announced, most statements of probability problems do not satisfy this requirement, but, in fact, suppose much which is relevant but left unstated. One of the major difficulties connected with probability theory is negligence on this point. Broadly put, one is supposed to know whatever is included in "common knowledge" which is relevant, though the full statement of all such pertinent items would usually be too long for any recital.

It is a question which lies nearer to the considerations in our foreground here, just what the nature of a probability judgment is, what constitutes the truth of it, and in what its validity consists.[21]

As we have already seen, no statement of a probability assessment is complete without the tacit or explicit preface, "On the basis of data such and such," or, say, "On the basis of all the relevant data we have or can in the circumstances ascertain," that preface being, in ordinary statements, relevant to a present question of practical concern. There is no such thing as *the* probability of any *quaesitum* on any other terms. And for any practical question which continues to be the topic of investigation, "the" probability is likely to alter with

---

21. This question has been discussed, at more length, in *An Analysis of Knowledge and Valuation.*

its investigation, as more and more pertinent facts are revealed. But, on the assumption above mentioned, and on any data at any time, there is just one correctly determined probability. Two persons who arrive at incompatible determinations either do not make their assessments on precisely the same data, or one or both of them is wrong. It may be objected here that, for a given problem, there may be *different methods,* giving different results. We shall not argue this question: it is too complex. But we suggest the observation that such different methods are like methods of approximation elsewhere, or else two methods giving divergent results, or one or both is incorrect, or—a third and different kind of alternative—they are to be taken as assigning a different meaning to "is probable in degree m/n." The accepted rules of probability determination *define the meaning of* 'is probable in degree m/n', just as the rules of deduction define the meaning of 'is deducible from', which correctly applies to the relation of a conclusion arrived at from premises by the application of these rules.[22]

Whatever one means—or is *entitled* to mean—by 'P is probable in degree m/n' is found to be determined by the rules of procedure for arriving at this determination from whatever are the premises of the derivation.

One thing which is immediately obvious is that we do not mean, by any probability statement, 'On data D, P is probable in degree m/n', that when data D are unexceptionably factual, 'P' is true. And it *should* be promptly obvious that we do *not* mean 'The frequency of the occurrence of the *quaesitum*

---

22. This is the conception which became current in reference to Peano's *Formulaire de mathématiques,* and called "definition by postulate." It obviously applies to *any* procedure for arriving at results from what is given: the rules of operation by which you get results determine the significance of the relation between those results and what is given as the initial ground from which they are derived. The general character of any *logical* derivation is—as we take for granted—such that, under *no possible circumstances,* could the initial assumptions be true and the results false. But, even so, and given the pertinence of such a consideration, one must then face questions of the following sort: "What is the *meaning* of 'P is probable in degree m/n'?" Or, say, "What is the *meaning* of 'On data D, P is probable in degree m/n'?"

character (indicated in 'P') in the class of cases indicated by 'D' is m/n'. And we cannot judiciously mean that as more and more samples of a class indicated by 'D' ('D' indicating the reference class) are examined, the cumulative fraction of cases in which 'P' holds ('P' indicating the *quaesitum* property) approaches m/n as a limit. We cannot well mean that because that would give us a specious and untestable criterion: there is no way of determining that a series of such *empirically* determined ratios approaches a limit. It may "look as if it would," but what is so asserted is not finitely attestable. (For attestation, the series must be determinable by some *mathematical rule*. It is series specified by mathematical rules and series limited, as well, to mathematically determined entities, and those alone, which determinably approach limits. Mathematical series are *generated* by a rule. No empirically determined series of results for which there is a question of probability is so generated. The applicability of a mathematical rule of series generation to any series of empirical findings is precisely the theoretical problem of probability.)

But let us retreat from the complexities of this problem "What is a probability?" to certain dogmatisms which will—we hope—recommend themselves to the reader. *Whatever* 'On data D, P is probable in degree m/n' may reasonably be taken to mean, it *must* answer to the requirement that this result is derivable from data D, by the right rules of probability determination—if there are any such right rules. And if there are *no* right rules for probability determination, then the assignment of probabilities is meaningless. To escape skepticism in science, let us presume there are such right rules—even if nobody as yet knows exactly and fully how to formulate them. (There was a time when nobody knew just how to formulate the right rules of deductive inference; and many "logicians" still do not know how.)

Unsatisfactory as this may be, it covers a point of first importance concerning the rightness and the truth of any particular probability assessment. Such an assessment *does not require to be verified* in order to be true. The correct determination is one *derivable from the data* according to the rules. The data, if factual, are *past* or *presently determined facts*. If those data give, by the rules, the result, 'P has the probability m/n on these data', this result, 'P is probable in degree m/n' is *true*. It does not matter what happens afterward or is found out afterward; *if this probability determination is valid, then it is true*. Strange as it may seem, a probability statement, 'On data D, P is probable in degree m/n', is, by the rules definitive of 'probable in degree m/n', determinable *a priori*; in short, if it is valid, it is true, true regardless of what may happen afterward, and, indeed, true regardless of the factuality or nonfactuality of data D. Like deductive logic, and anything deductive logic can certify, probability statements are either incogent and invalid, or they are *true*. The remaining question, the remaining theoretical question, is the epistemological question of the validity of induction, or the metaphysical question of the relation between the way the world wags and human ways of expecting. No empirical happening, nor any set of such, can disprove a probability determination; if it is valid when made, on the ground on which it was made, it is eternally true.

The remaining question is, as already suggested, "What is the good of making judgments of probability, and what is the use of conforming our deliberate acts to the expectations so determined?" We must not pause to say more than a few words concerning that. One such is to remind ourselves of the kind of answer Reichenbach, who pursued this kind of question more relentlessly than any other investigator has ever done, gave to it. If acting according to the probabilities does not do you any good, then nothing you can do will do you any good. Another consideration is that if the habit of acting according to the ways which associated ideas and feelings incline us animals did not do us good, those that now inherit the earth would not be here. And a third and perhaps more philosophically respectable suggestion is that the validity of induction is the postulate of all intelligence. In a world in which induction did not hold, there would be no identifiable objects the look and feel and taste of which would afford any ground for an expectation of what they will do next, and what will happen in our further experience of them, or what the result of any activity directed upon them would be. The complete skeptic will then be correct, though he has no valid grounds for thinking that conclusion correct; he doesn't know anything anyway, any more than "us dogmatists," even if he happens to be telling the truth. The validity of induction is the postulate of an intelligible world. And about that, Reichenbach has said the last word; if the principle of induction isn't true, you still have no alternative to it which holds any promise whatever. This *argumentum in extremis* is the pragmatic "deduction of the categories." There are either some determinable empirical probabilities, including the probable subsumption of things under concepts, or there is nothing to talk about, or think about or determine deliberate action by. And the right, in thinking, and in believing and in acting, in this world, is either determinably right when the decision is taken, and bespeaks some rules valid *a priori*, or there is no such thing as right and wrong of any kind. The right is the *valid*, and whatever decision is valid is knowably valid at the time when it must be decided, and on the premises of decision then open to the decider. What good being right will do you is, in each particular instance, something to be found out—something which is verifiable. But whoever is *inconsistent* acts on a presumption involving a contradiction, and nothing in the world or even thinkable outside it, could conform to the contradictory.

ESSAY 6

Deliberate Acts

There are three concepts which are peculiarly fundamental for ethics, as the subject which concerns the valid directives for the final determination of what we do: the concepts of the deliberate act, the right, and the good. Presumably there will be others which also are essential, but these three, at least, will be required at the beginning. First, we require the concept of the deliberate act because it is only to such acts which can be done deliberately that any directive of doing can find application. Second, we require the concept of the right because the rightness of such acts is that character which is correlative with the conformity of them to directives which are valid. And let us note, at this point, in passing, that this will hold whether we suppose that it is the rightness of the acts which is first determinable, and the validity of directives which is to be assured by their being generalities of such right doing, or suppose, conversely, that the valid rules come first, and that the rightness of action is to be determined by conformity to them. Thirdly, we shall require the concept of the good, if for no other reason, because without a reference to some goodness which acting may achieve, or some badness which may be so avoided, any doing and any direction of doing would be altogether pointless and of no concern to anybody.

The discussion of any one of these concepts must inevitably lead into a consideration of the others, and of further matters as well. It is difficult to find a way into any such large subject which will not involve discussing everything at once, and we must be content, at the outset, with such approximations to accuracy and clarity as can be managed in terms of common sense, leaving any further precisioning and elucidation of what can be so said until such time as some conspectus of the whole topic is before us. Perhaps in this fashion what is said in one place may be sufficiently guarded by what is said in some other, and retrospective qualifications will be understood without reconsideration.

Let us begin with deliberate acts. What we require as the concept to be conveyed by this phrase is the same as would also be commonly intended by 'willed act', 'voluntary act', and 'responsible act', as well as by 'doing by choosing'. The words here are not crucially important, because what we here intend to denote is something utterly familiar to any of us, the ordinary sense of doings which we wittingly initiate. Any of these synonymous expressions, or nearly synonymous expressions, might do, and none of them is completely appropriate. 'Deliberate act', for example, could too strongly suggest a pause for deliberation before the doing, and most of the acts in question are not, in fact, deliberated on the occasion of the commitment to action. 'Willed act' could suggest a firm determination and perhaps the overcoming of some disinclination. And that often fails to be the case, for many of the things we willingly do are not initiated at the expense of thwarting inclination but, quite the contrary, because they accord with our wishes. One might here correct 'willed act' by 'willing act' or 'voluntary act', suggesting 'uncompelled'. But 'uncompelled' is not quite strong enough. A good many of our performances are not subject to duress, but are perhaps not deliberate doings either, being hardly decided upon at all. 'Responsible act' will have the right connotation if we think of it in the context of legalities, or the law—what the doer can be held responsible for—but it will be too narrow if it should confine the class of acts in question to those having some social animus or satisfying some responsibility to other

persons. The most accurate term of all would be the least frequently used: 'corrigible act'. What is "done deliberately" may
not be deliberated at all, but we must be aware of this initiation
of it as something which would not come about if we should
will it to be otherwise: we could avoid this doing simply by so
deciding, by refusing to adopt this initiative. But we choose the
term 'deliberate act' instead, both because it is the commonest
term used and because some relation between this doing and
some deliberation by the doer of what is so done, or intended
to be done, appears to be of the essence.

Most of our behavior "does itself" in any case, through
some combination of native impulses, the conditioning of experience, and acquired facilities and habits. I write these words on
paper. Ask me how they get there, and I shall not be able to tell
you, except that if they had not been deliberated they would
not be there. And this business goes better if I pay no attention
to my hand movements. I am quite sure that they will happen according to my will and not otherwise, though not always
according to my wish. But—praise be—no one else can set
them off: my intervention in this matter, though superficial and
somewhat episodic, is nevertheless the condition *sine qua non*
of its happening, and I take full responsibility for the results.
I am sure of what I just now say on the basis of a large body
of experimental evidence. Tell me something that I cannot put
down here, or something that I cannot help getting down here,
and I will prove you wrong. Also you know quite well what
I mean here by attributing these words on paper to my own
choosing. One who would invent any puzzle over it must have
too much time on his hands, or his interest is in some other
matter than the distinction between voluntary and involuntary,
corrigible and incorrigible behavior.

The excuse for the customary extension of the name 'deliberate act' to any behavior which is corrigible to the doer is
the presumption just suggested that such acts which may not
be subject to any deliberation at the time of doing are such
as must have been deliberated antecedent to this occasion, and
reflect decisions then made. It is characteristic of the human
animal not only to acquire habits of response to occasions on
the basis of his favoring as against disfavoring the consequences

of such ways of acting, but also to store up decisions arrived at by deliberation in the form of convictions as to what he should and should not thereafter do. He meets any new occasion of doing in the light of his whole past history of thinking and deciding, in the light of the dispositions developed by the learned consequences of his active attitudes taken and in the light of the progressive alteration, amendment, and confirmation of general decisions about his own ways of doing. And on any occasion of challenge or hesitancy, he may think again: such hesitancy or challenge signifies the corrigibility of his present impulses or inclinations.

We can even make a distinction, in reference to any present and conscious doing, between what may be called 'corrigible at the moment' and what, though not thus corrigible at the moment, is nevertheless corrigible in a sense which allows of holding the doer responsible for what he at this moment does. This significance of 'responsibility' is of much importance for courts, charged with deciding what is and what is not the responsibility of doers, and the legal exigencies of that kind of matter must impress us with the similar importance of the point for assigning moral accountability.

As it happens, there is a legal precedent, now established, which may illustrate the point. It used to be that many steel bridges were built in such wise that small boys were moved to climb an upward-slanting span on which protruding rivet heads afforded footholds. Suits were brought against those who erected such structures, the nature of which tended to result in accidents to venturesome juveniles, and the courts came to award damages on the grounds of "maintaining an attractive nuisance." In plain terms, the planners were held accountable for not having used their imagination in such a way as to foresee the likely results of what they had done. A better example is, perhaps, a "bad habit." If one has the bad habit of speaking abruptly when his work is interrupted, and has come to do so without noticing that he does it, he is not, not morally at least, responsible for that until it comes to his notice. And if he continues to do so, for a period thereafter, it may still be that this doing is not "corrigible at the moment." But after a certain time, at least, his continuing so to do will be something for which he is accountable, even if it is done without thinking—just because he has failed to think about it and exercise a constraint which could have been, and should have been, developed. The good or bad habits of automobile drivers make an even better illustration, such habits having implications which are both legal and moral. One such implication is the obvious one that we may be responsible for *not* doing as much as for doing. And another is that we cannot always repudiate responsibility for what is not corrigible at the moment, if we are ourselves responsible for its failure to be thus corrigible at the moment. Quite plainly then we may be accountable for the failure to do as we should, as well as for doing what we should not. And similarly we are responsible for what at the moment we could not help wrongly doing, or wrongly failing to do, if we could, earlier, have so behaved as to have fronted this occasion of wrong doing, or wrong failing to do, better equipped to do the right, if we had behaved as we should have at that earlier time. Not only do our deliberated decisions have cumulative aftereffects, but we hold ourselves, and each other, accountable for what we do in a manner which definitely capitalizes upon that fact. And one who would urge any conception of responsible decisions and responsible acts which would limit the scope of right or wrong doing more narrowly would best give heed to the social and practical consequences of narrowing the category of the morally right or wrong in the manner he would propose. By practical standards, we are not only responsible for doing wrong, with a full awareness of what we do bring about, but for not doing what we should when we are aware of our nondoing, and aware that what we so fail to do should be done. Further, we are responsible for our thinking about what it is that we so bring about, and also of what will come about if we fail to do what we could to prevent any such coming about, if that foreseeable outcome of failing to do be undesirable. And if our doing or failing to do be incorrigible at the moment, because we "do not think," we may still be responsible for what happens, if its happening is due to our "thoughtlessness," if that be traceable to some antecedent wrong decision to do or not to do. Indeed, the bounds of responsible doing and not doing are hard to set, and we may be tempted to consider them, or their setting, a matter of degree. The courts also illustrate the same problem in its legal aspect, reflected in distinctions of culpability, as between willful doing and neglect, and between "negligence," unqualified, and "willful negligence." There are legal and strict rules "up to a point," but beyond that point a wide latitude is deliberately left to judicial discretion. We shall not here attempt any pedantic fixing of the boundaries of moral responsibility which would override the patent flexibility of common sense touching that point, in view of the social assignment of "responsibilities," "duties," "obligations," and "circumstances affecting action." We would emphasize only that 'deliberate acts' covers a category as wide as behavior amenable to deliberation, and that such an amenability is the essence of the matter. Recourse to this term also, of course, has linguistic advantages. It has the justification of being a term in common usage.

Two brief points might be made in passing. Both, it seems, are obvious: First, deliberate acts are not always morally significant. Second, the paradigm for deliberate acts is that manner of acting which is *deliberately decided*.

Let us now consider, in some detail, the concept of the deliberated act.

With respect to deliberated acts, a first and obvious point is that they begin with thinking, and include thinking about their consequences, actual and possible. Without a prediction of consequences, an expectation which is cognitive, and either cognitively valid or cognitively invalid, there could be no choosing to do.[1] A cognitive and predictive belief that certain consequences,

---

1. The capacity to foresee the consequences of an act is a longstanding criterion of legal responsibility which the court is charged to apply in the case of any defendant tried for committing a crime. And this essential requirement of cognitive foresight for the attribution of responsibility for bringing about is, of itself, the only disproof needed for any "noncognitivist" theory of ethics. That issue is not even arguable—to common sense. And we shall not trouble to argue it. [The qualification 'to common sense' is, I think, important here. First, Lewis is concerned, largely, with analyzing, and defending, what he takes to be a common-sense morality. Secondly,

and not others, will eventuate from the doer's chosen initiative of action is obviously a prerequisite for anything that ethics can be about. Where anything is done by deliberation, the terminus of the thinking part of this activity is in the decision to do. And a decision to do is wrong just in case it is wrong to bring about the consequences of it which are to be expected.

We must not, however, confuse the decision to do with the doing—the act itself. There are occasions on which we think and come to a decision to do but what is so decided upon is not done. Most obviously, we may decide to do something tomorrow but in the meantime change our minds or merely forget about it, or meet with unanticipated circumstances rendering what we decided upon inadvisable or even impossible. No matter when the decision to do may have been taken, the act is not *done* until it is executed, until it has been, so to speak, "committed." It is, for that kind of reason, the willed *initiation* which is "the act itself." Until that takes place, no act takes place; after that, the consequences are out of the doer's hands

---

it seems clear that "noncognitivism in ethics" would indeed be likely to seem a bit strange, if not suspect, to the great majority of the human race. It would probably be dismissed by most people without a second thought. On the other hand, clearly, too, at this point, it would be surprising if noncognitivists would fold up their tents and disappear into the night. Lewis is presupposing something here, it seems with considerable justification, that cognitivity, and thus normativity, is indissolubly interrelated with action, and action with life. Noncognitivism then would seem to him a sort of aberration. On the other hand, Lewis certainly, in other contexts, and as we shall see, is ready to "argue" with his noncognitivist brethren. If neither strikes his tent, and if armed advances are made, and repelled, etc. on both sides, that is pretty much what one has come to expect in the no man's land of philosophy. Perhaps, as Nietzsche suggested, it is the good war which hallows the cause. In a sense, of course, this whole book might be seen to constitute an attempted refutation of noncognitivism. For example, one way to convince a fellow that raccoons exist is to show him a raccoon. One way to show the noncognitivist that a cognitivist ethics is possible is to show him one. That is pretty much what Lewis is trying to do here, show us that a cognitivist ethics exists, that thus that at least one ethics is cognitive, and that this ethics, in effect, is our familiar one, one worked out over thousands of years of human thought and experience. —Ed.]

and the act cannot be retracted, even if, as sometimes is the case, some of its consequences can be counteracted or canceled by a further doing. The date of any doing is the date of its initiation. However, what is done only begins there. *What* act it is that is done is determinable, or knowable or assignable, only in terms of the consequences of this willed initiation. Sometimes—though not usually—one may take such a willed initiative but nothing of what is expected happens. One may will to get up and walk, for example, but find oneself too weak to do so. It is by reason of such exceptional happenings that we learn to distinguish between the fiat of the will—the commitment or initiative—and the act as an observable physical doing. This commitment is still a mental fact; it is not itself physical. Neurologists tell us that it cannot be identified with innervation of the motor nerves. That, the innervation of the motor nerves, can be induced, in the case of brain operations, by the application of an electrode. But the conscious patient can never be deceived into thinking that the consequent muscle contraction is something he, the patient, did. In any case, each of us always knows what it is that he wills to do; his failure to know that he wills it is proof positive that he does not will it. And whatever he wills he knows that he wills it, even in those unusual circumstances in which an expected movement of the body fails to follow. However, what he thus knows as being what he wills, in such instances, is some expected consequence of his willed initiative. He notices it as being contentual to his willing when it fails to occur as anticipated, and when some—and perhaps the same—movement of the voluntary muscles occurs without, or perhaps in spite of, his willing, he notices that. But there is nothing in terms of which an act, either contemplated or done, can be specified and recognized, even by the doer himself, except some anticipated consequence, or consequences, or some consequence or consequences further eventuating upon that, or those, which can be so attributed and recognized as eventuating from this willed commitment to do, or, if we be amateur or professional psychologists, perhaps some accompanying feeling of conation. If there is, as Wundt suggested, a "feeling of innervation," most of us are incapable of identifying it as such, and it would be extremely difficult to establish any criterion in terms of which such an identification could be made.[2]

The willed initiative is, so to say, the bridge between the thinking part of voluntary doing and the physical part. What first takes place overtly is some movement of the doer's *body*. It is only by such a movement of his own body—even if it be only tongue and lip movements—that any doer can bring about any difference that he makes in the external world. But we are frequently inattentive to this bodily intermediation, as one takes no thought of finger movements in writing—unless the fingers write something not intended. What we are likely to recite if asked what we are doing is likely to be some consequence or consequences for the sake of which we initiated the train of physical events, some purpose, some end in view. And a reply such as "I am making marks on paper" would be justly labeled "nonresponsive" to that kind of question.

Exactly at this point, however, we must begin to be careful—because we here arrive at certain matters of plain fact with respect to which common ways of speaking are ambiguous and can eventually become confusing. We have two different ways—at least two—of attributing voluntary acts to agents. And ambiguities so arising can involve us, eventually, in questions of ethical theory which can be quite serious. Some of these at least can be obviated by noticing our ambiguous ways of speaking about our voluntarily initiated doing. The

---

2. It may be suspected that what Wundt meant to identify is just this ability to discriminate between a willed movement of a muscle and an unwilled convulsive contraction of the same muscle. But even so, it remains problematic whether the capacity to make the discrimination with which we are concerned, that between voluntary and involuntary, really depends on differences of "feeling," at all, say, such as those between "expecting" or "having a feeling of ownership," or being "surprised" or "having a feeling of alienation." There would appear to be none but a dubious distinction, at least for our purposes, between feelings such as that of "ownership" or "alienation," or, on the other hand, between those of confirmed "expectation" and "being surprised." We shall not psychologize here, or, at least, not to an extent beyond what is open to common sense; rather, we shall think it sufficient to identify as voluntarily done the anticipatable sequents of the conscious commitment to do. [Wilhelm Wundt, a noted German physiologist, psychologist and philosopher (1832–1920). —Ed.]

acts are discriminated from other behavior, largely at least, by the presumption of their being initiated with the expectation of producing certain physical results, in contrast to other—and perhaps overtly indistinguishable—overt behavior which comes about without voluntary initiation, and without an anticipation of physical results. This is the root distinction between doings attributable to us as agents and other things which happen to us willy-nilly. But the overt and physical part of any voluntary act is also an event in the physical world, some train of physical events beginning with voluntary bodily behavior. At the moment of such an initiation, nature takes over, and the consequences are then beyond recall. It is not only what we intended and expected which will happen. The consequences go on and on until they become so merged with the consequences of other contemporary circumstances that we can no longer distinguish between what depends on our initiation and what would have taken place without it. Even at the start, what we intended may not happen, and something we neither wished nor expected may take place instead. All this is quite clear to us. We know in part, and with some measure of assurance, what we do in the sense of its being something which occurs and would not have occurred without our initiation. But among such consequences attributable to our doing, we may distinguish some which accord with our expectation and intention, some which may be contrary to our intention, and some which lay altogether outside our expectation and may also be a matter of indifference to us. Nobody ever knows, either at the time of doing or later, the totality of what he brings about when he commits himself to a voluntary act. The train of further circumstances dependent on it always runs beyond his power to discriminate it and finally beyond his ken altogether. But a historian, for example, may speculate no end about what might have happened if, say, Caesar had not crossed the Rubicon. Perhaps Caesar did sometimes. By and large, we have a high degree of assured discrimination with respect to what happens as a consequence, or consequences, of a volition in the earlier phases of the sequence or sequences only; and, in general, such discrimination becomes more dubious as the events in question become more remote in time and place. Nevertheless, it is only by such discrimination that we can ever find out what we do, or ever learn what to do and what not to do. This manner of our learning is essentially no different from that by which we learn to attribute other effects to other kinds of causes. And that is involved in almost everything that we can in any wise learn from experience.

As a consequence of these clear and well-understood facts, we have two ways of speaking about what we do deliberately and two senses of the word 'act' applicable to our doing. One way is by attributing to ourselves and to our voluntary initiations whatever we expected when we took the initiative of doing. This is the intention of an act. Whatever so happens in accord with that expectation, we intended when we took the commitment. Whatever we did not so anticipate but happens as a consequence, we did not intend to do, and did not *do* intentionally. The other way of telling what we "did" is to attribute to the act and to ourselves as agents anything which we can, either at the time of initiation or later, discern as being something which happened because this initiative was taken and would not have happened if the initiative had not been taken. This—these consequences—we say, speaking in this second manner, is what we actually *did*. "Johnny broke the window." But, as Johnny will explain, all he did (intended) was toss his ball and hit it with his bat (hoping it would go in another direction). It was the ball that broke the window. Or perhaps the window just broke: a really good window wouldn't fly all to pieces from a little tap like that. (Johnny may grow up to be a scientist: it is the scientific ideal to speak of all events in the middle voice; at bottom, all events just do themselves; they just happen—in place-time relationships to one another. The rest is a hangover from primitive animism. Scientists accept responsibility only for what they send to print.)

Correlative with this second manner of speaking of what we "set off," or initiate, by deliberate inclination, we have also a third mode of attributing consequences to doings. "I fell off the ladder and barked my shin." I didn't expect to. I did not voluntarily or even consciously move my feet in the way they must have moved. They just moved: it happened to me. But my feet are subject to my own control. Still, falling off the ladder was nothing I am responsible for doing unless—we never get rid of this horrid kind of complication—I should have been more careful about my feet! But let us forget about this third sense in which we may "do," bodily, something we did not think about and were not even conscious of as a piece of controllable behavior. It approximates to the sense in which we speak, animistically, of what the ball did and the window "does." Plainly we have little concern with such "doings" in ethics, unless—that horrid complexity again—we should have, say, learned to pay better attention to our feet when climbing ladders.

First and foremost, we deliberately do and are responsible for what we do by intention. The intention of the act, as we should remark, always includes any purpose of the doing. But it includes not only such purposed results, for the sake of which the commitment was taken, but also all that was expected as a result, even if, in some part, we regretted the necessity of bringing this about in order to achieve our purpose. We must also observe that the intention includes whatever the doer expected to result, even if it does not in fact ensue. It is a bit anomalous to say that one is "responsible" for something which does not happen. But the complexities of the law touching that point can be enlightening. Broadly speaking, the court does not assign responsibility when nothing interdicted happens. But a criminal intent may nevertheless be legally taken into account in assigning responsibility for whatever does happen. Although no crime can be committed without a criminal intent, a provable criminal intent may qualify "responsibility" for something which does happen. There is, for example, the legal category of assault with intent to kill. Also, one who intended to rob but not to kill may be indicted for manslaughter if the victim dies as a result of the action involved. And one who intended to kill A but not B may be charged with murder if his shot kills B. On such points we can hardly argue from law to morals: the law is hampered by the impracticalities of dealing with intentions which are not rather clearly inferable from overt behavior, and that kind of inference, though necessary to any practical law enforcement, is so parlous as to be hedged about with legal safeguards. Considerations of morals—being something we address to ourselves as well as to others—need not be so limited. But there is one aspect of moral assessment to which such an attribution of intentions, as distinct from a consideration of consequences, is peculiarly relevant. Incident to social relationships and social institutions generally, it becomes necessary for us to take cognizance of the intentions of others in their deliberate doing, and that aside from questions of what that deliberate doing actually brings about, and in some measure and in so far as the intentions of others can be judged, to judge their deserts according to their purposes and intentions, rather than by the actual consequences of that doing simply. There are social rewards and punishments outside the law. And by and large these extend far more widely, functioning as instigations for, and deterrences of, individual conduct, than those of the law, and are, on the whole, much more effective. Without them it is doubtful if legal institutions could be established or maintained. It is a part of our responsibility to others and to society at large to make the punishment fit the crime and the social rewards accord with what is deserved. And in large measure we are spontaneously minded so to do. But there is a justice about it to be observed, in doing to others in virtue of what they do to us—us individually or us at large. In so governing ourselves in our attitudes and acts toward others, we shall take it as a first broad principle that others are to be dealt with according to their intentions and not according to any unintended consequences of their acts. And that may stand unqualifiedly as the assessment we make of them as moral agents. Only so do we judge them and their doing justly. But this principle cannot well stand as anything more than a practical, unattainable ideal: not only because we are subject to the same limitations as the court in inferring intentions from overt behavior, but for a different reason also. As we are peculiarly conscious of in the case of children, circumstances do not allow us to deal with others in virtue of what they do completely and simply by reference to their intentions in doing. We are obliged to weigh the necessity of inducing deterrence on their part from acts which affect ourselves and others adversely, from whatever motive they may have been done. It is open to God alone to mete out ideal justice, but it is open to us to assign moral merit and demerit on precisely this ground of right or wrong intentions, insofar as we are able to judge the intentions and motives of others. And it is also open to us, and necessary for any approximation to just dealing with others, in virtue of what they do, that we aim to allow no departure from such an ideal justice except by reference to what is practically necessary for the attainment of some end which outweighs the ill of failing to visit no ill on any for well-intended but "bad" doing, in short, to allow no departure from the principles of such an ideal justice unless for the sake of some greater or more indispensable good—perhaps his own good as well as the good of those whom his further doing may affect.

The importance of these considerations lies in the fact that although we shall come to the conclusion that the "subjective rightness" of acts, which consists in the intention of the doer to do what is right, is not that rightness of doing about which ethics inquires, it is still necessary as a subordinate type of assessment, one subordinate to the determination of "objective rightness," which is the topic of ethics. Or to put it another way: it is both unjust and relatively useless to punish those who intend to do what is right but fail because, say, of intellectual incapacity, but in some measure and manner it may be necessary to deter them and protect ourselves and others from their rightly meant but wrongly directed doing. Historically considered, this has its counterpart in the necessity that those who achieve the better life by a higher civilization must protect it from those cultures which are still in the Dark Ages or the Stone Age. And an ethics which should be too sentimental to protect itself forgets that *right* doing must be intelligently directed doing for the betterment of human living. If that point be lost, the higher cultures will be buried and civilization will be destroyed, or at least the clock of history will be set back. The significance of ethics lies in the possible human attainment of the good life. Without that point, it has no sanction. Dealing with others in virtue of what they do, according to the subjective rightness of their doing, would be according an ideal justice to them if it were not that we—who judge them—have an equal obligation to all others as well, and must defend these others from the consequences of their stupidity. If we forget this obligation to third parties, our morality becomes "sentimental" and fails of its necessarily practical aim. For the sake of posterity if for no other reason, we cannot resign ourselves to the domination of intransigent fools.

Right Acts and Good Acts[1]

The concepts of the right and the good are interconnected. Or rather, the right and the good are themselves and by their nature interrelated, and the two concepts reflect that fact. They represent two aspects or two modes of the appraisable in general: what is good, or bad, in any sense is, in that same sense, to be appraised, to be evaluated; and what is right, or wrong, in any sense, is also in that same sense to be appraised, to be subject to critique. The good appeals, and to the bad we are averse: the right constrains, and the wrong it is imperative to avoid. Commonly the right and the good are bracketed together under one head and labeled "the normative," because the assessment of either one of them is likely to be made by reference to some standard, some rule, or to some ideal or paradigm. And too frequently both good and right, whether in the abstract, as goodness or rightness, or in the concrete, as that which is good and that which is right, are lumped together under the one designation 'values'. That procedure, however, invites confusion. The good and the right are essentially related but distinct. And until they are clearly distinguished, it is not possible even to discuss, with any hope of clarity, the manner of their relationship.

---

1. [The original title here seems to have been "The Normative," but there is some suggestion that this title may have been replaced with "Right Acts and Good Acts," which title I have used above. –Ed.]

Distinguishing between the good and the right is made even more difficult by the fact that, in common parlance, it is often idiomatic to apply the expressions 'good' and 'right' indifferently: "good intentions" are "right intentions," for example, and "right acts" are "good acts." And it easily appears from this that such predicates, for example, 'good' and 'right', are essentially synonymous and that, accordingly, the distinction between the good and the right is basically unimportant, that it is superficial, that it depends on an accident of idiom or something similarly trivial. But this appearance is not only deceiving, but deceitful, and if, in any connection, the expressions 'good' and 'right' are *used* as if they were synonymous, this is a lax use of language, and capable of being displaced by a more discerning and precise manner of speaking which may reveal the necessity of the distinction. A right act, for example, may be also a good act—*most* right acts *are* good acts—but *some* right acts are not good, and some good acts are not right. And even when an act is both right and good, the rightness of it is not the goodness of it, nor the goodness the rightness of it; and when an act is both wrong and bad, its wrongness is not its badness, nor is its badness its wrongness.[2] Thus while common usage is oftentimes undiscriminating and imprecise, there are, underneath such idiomatic but lax usages which may suggest an equipollence of 'right' and 'good', 'wrong' and 'bad', more precise senses of these terms which can be elicited and made clear, without an appeal to anything beyond a discriminating common sense and more judicious usages of common terms.

We shall not, however, be content to be governed here by what can be elicited merely by semantic and syntactic considerations, though it may be helpful on occasion to refer to such linguistic considerations. Our analysis of the concepts in question must be addressed to the reader's own discernment of the matters in hand rather than to the more complex and often doubtful questions of "ordinary language." Any language we can command will still be subject to the ambiguity of words

---

2. These facts must, of course, be explained later on, but we are not yet ready for that. [The passage preceding this note has been amended slightly for clarity. –Ed.]

and the ambivalence of syntactic constructions. But the very fact that such ambiguity and ambivalence pervade all "natural" languages bespeaks more specific meanings which are common and which, with one's best efforts and good luck, can perhaps be communicated. Our common understanding is more articulated and precise than our common speech can easily be made. And this common understanding can also be sharpened and clarified. It is to such insights that we must appeal.

Our primary interest is, of course, in the right: the rightness or wrongness of voluntary acts is the topic of ethics. But it must suggest itself to anyone who addresses this matter that if it were not for the difference between good and bad, there could be no distinction between right and wrong. In a world in which nothing was better than anything else, and nothing worse than anything else, seeking this and avoiding that would make no sense, and to speak of the rightness of bringing this about, and the wrongness of bringing that about, would be meaningless jargon. It will also and further suggest itself that it is the distinction of good from bad which must be primitive and antecedent, and the discrimination of right from wrong which must be secondary and derived. There can be the disclosure of good and bad without any recognition of the right and wrong; there could *not* be any recognition of right and wrong without the discrimination of good from bad. Animal life—and perhaps all conscious life—is affected by good and bad and is differentially responsive to them. But right and wrong represent a kind of distinction which is recognizable only by creatures who not only feel and respond but are capable of considered judgment and deliberately governed conduct. We might say that the *basis* for the distinction between right and wrong is already there in animal life: we, looking on, can observe their doing what we would call the right thing for them to do—or occasionally what we would call the wrong thing for them to do! But they do these things—so we suppose—by instinct or as a result of the conditioning of their feelings and impulses by their past experiences. In other words—again, as we suppose—the animal's behavior is wholly governed by his feelings, which may include inhibitory or constraining feelings due to its individual past experience. But the animal is incapable of marking or recognizing the right-wrong distinction for the same reason that it is incapable of self-direction by deliberate thinking instead of conditioned feeling.[3]

Looking to such basic considerations, it will likewise appear that the distinction of good from bad is, in all the various senses of these words, finally rooted in feeling and relates to the quality of experience as passive, as something encountered or imposed upon us, something which happens to us and, in the early and literal sense, is "suffered." By contrast, right and wrong relate to our activity, and to such activity as self-governable and directable. It will also suggest itself that, in such fundamental terms, acts and responsive attitudes are right or wrong depending on whether they lead to good or bad, and are thus gauged by reference to the common bent of all conscious life to seek the good and avoid or remove the bad. To be sure, discernment and further probing of the complex facts which are relevant here must soon convince us that such a formulation of the matter is overly simple, and, in particular, that it would inaccurately represent, and would be inadequate to cover, the wide range of different senses in which we use the terms 'good' and 'bad', as well as 'right' and 'wrong'. Nevertheless, a failure to recognize the plausibility of it as a first approximation to the truth of the matter would appear to argue some insensitivity to the obvious, or some antecedent prejudice. These basic suggestions lie on the surface of the matter.

This conviction that good and bad come first, and that right and wrong are to be explained, finally, by reference to good and bad, characterizes that general persuasion in ethical theory

---

3. Whether, in such suppositions, we misjudge the behavior of some of the higher animals is a question of animal psychology which makes no difference here; the point is one which wholly concerns *ourselves*. We should be aware by the general observation of *our own experience*—including the remembered experiences of childhood—that there could be, and is, the good and bad in experience independently of, and antecedent to, any distinction of right and wrong. And as we should also be capable of observing, this will still remain true even though it may be also true that our apprehensions of right and wrong serve, on occasion, to *modify* our apprehensions and even our feelings of the good and bad.

which is labeled 'naturalism'. And the opposite tendency, called 'perfectionism', characteristically regards right and wrong as the ruling category of the normative, and good and bad as incapable of a correct determination without reference to right and wrong, these understood as antecedent and as reflecting dictates which have some other and independent ground. Sometimes the issue which lies between these two parties is phrased as the question whether right and wrong are to be *defined* in terms of good and bad, *or, per contra,* good and bad are to be defined in terms of right and wrong, *e.g.,* the good is that which is *worthy* of being made the aim of seeking and of action. But that manner of formulating the issue is hardly judicious—for one reason, because the logical relation of *definiens* to *definiendum* is symmetrical, and thus independent of any question of priority between the two. Given the supposed symmetricality, what either of them would imply the other must imply, and whatever either of them would refer to the other must refer to, as well. On this approach the allegation of priority, of one to the other, cannot, on logical grounds, be sustained. So let us say, instead, that naturalism maintains that until you know what is good and what is bad you cannot determine what is right and what is wrong, whereas perfectionism maintains that until you know what is right and what is wrong you cannot determine—or cannot determine correctly and universally at least—what is good and what is bad.

The considerations affecting this issue are many and complex, and no adequate discussion of them could be hoped for until we have more clearly in mind the various senses in which all the normative terms are used. But, on the other hand, without some provisional clarity concerning points which affect this issue, it would prove difficult to get forward with this other matter of the different senses of 'right' and 'wrong', 'good' and 'bad'. We can only hope to unravel the tangle of questions, all of which are pertinent here, a little at a time. And we may as well begin with this one, that concerning the basic issue between naturalism and perfectionism, hoping that what can be said provisionally at this point will be held subject to review, and to a more precise and clear statement when a wider range of relevant considerations can be brought into the picture. Too, we shall not approach this issue with the intent to argue it. Instead, we shall seek to see what accounts for it, what underlies it.

It can, of course, be questioned whether or not we have rightly identified the basic issue of the naturalistic-perfectionistic controversy, in taking it to concern the question of priority, whether priority is to be assigned to our determination of what is good or to our determination of what is right. Let us acknowledge this, like the limits we have imposed on our discussion, and our unwillingness, in this context, to attempt to resolve these issues in favor of either the naturalist or perfectionist in any extensive and conclusive manner, as *another* moot point, observing only that if the issue as we have phrased it is *not* the root of the matter, at least it has sometimes been debated as if it *were,* and that it, the matter of the priorities involved, is, in any case, a question of fact, and perhaps a question of fact whose answer can be determined, and one which seems likely to have some relevance to our major concerns.

We are, accordingly, subject to the general limitations we have imposed on our discussion, choosing to limit ourselves to only so much of the naturalistic-perfectionistic controversy as pertains to one of its apparent issues, but seemingly a basic one, that of priority, as between the good and the right.

This issue is important in the pursuit of our central project, the analysis of the normative.[4]

At once, however, we are obliged to admit that *this* question of priority, as between the good and the right, has, historically, been almost hopelessly prejudiced by confusing it with another and quite different question, with the question, namely, whether or not the desirable is to be correctly conceived as that which *is* desired. And on *that* point, it is the naturalists—or some naturalists—who are responsible for allowing this confusion, not the perfectionists. There is no clearer or more striking example of this than the celebrated blunder of John Stuart Mill, who manages to convey the impression that he would so

---

4. [I have inserted this paragraph, and the preceding short paragraph, for transitional purposes.–Ed.]

identify the desirable with what is desired, although he does not quite say that, and the whole sequel to the passage in question could be interpreted as an attempt to correct this impression.

Here is the passage in question:

> The only proof capable of being given that an object is visible, is that people actually see it. The only proof that a sound is audible, is that people hear it: and so of the other sources of our experience. In like manner, I apprehend, the sole evidence it is possible to produce that anything is desirable, is that people do actually desire it.

It occurs in *Utilitarianism,* as the first portion of the third paragraph in Chapter IV.[5]

We shall have occasion to return to this matter of Mill's strategic error, and to the issue which he actually had in mind, at a later point. But it will be sufficient to observe here that, in some contrast to 'visible' and 'audible', 'desirable' does *not* mean either *'is* desired' or 'is *capable* of being desired'—'is *possible* to desire'. Instead, to say that a thing is desirable is a manner of marking it as something the attainment of which could be a reasonable or justified aim. Indeed, we might say that to call a thing desirable is ordinarily to *recommend* it as something to be aimed at. And the least implication of 'X is desirable' which Mill intends to identify is 'X is capable of *satisfying* some desire'.[6] We might also say that the maximal or strongest sense of 'X is desirable' is 'X *ought* to be desired; not to desire X would be unjustified and wrong'. It is this commendatory sense of 'desirable' which gives leverage to the perfectionist interpretation of this broadest of normative terms, as signifying an antecedent sense of the correct and criticized, and of some kind of "ought" or imperative.

---

5. I conceive that a somewhat similar inadvertence can be found elsewhere in the literature of ethical naturalism, e.g., in Ralph Barton Perry's apparent identification of the valuable with that which is the object of any interest.

6. We could not even add the qualification 'some *actual* desire': it is conceivable that although no one has yet desired to prolong the life of a neutrino, some scientific interest would be served if that could possibly be done.

As a matter of fact, the thesis that it is actual desiring which establishes desirability would be as disastrous to naturalism as to perfectionism, and is compatible only with a subjectivistic conception of both the good and the right, which, in turn, must inevitably lead to a cynical rejection of the normative in general, as having no import of any manner of objective and determinable fact. Unless 'desirable' implies *some* critique of actual desiring and some character of what is to be desired, by virtue of which the desire of it is justified, correct, and in virtue of which the attitude toward it is at least permissible—not wrong—no critique of acts and of intentions could have any manner of justifying ground, and no normative judgment could be more than an expression of feeling or emotion, or an implicit hortation—with no validity—just as our recent skeptics of the moral and of the normative in general have claimed.

The simple and obvious point is that desiring is subject to *mistake*. Desiring implies a prediction that the object of it, if attained, would gratify or satisfy. And such expectant attitudes are subject to corroboration or disappointment. One who desires believes something to be the case. And to assert that anything is desirable has precisely this significance, that of implying that the attainment of it will prove satisfying and not a disappointment. Otherwise such a recommendation would have no force of persuasion to seek or pursue, unless that of a senseless or malicious cozening of the addressee to an inculcated or induced orientation of his aims which at best would be pointless and at worst might prove disastrous.

There are, to be sure, ambiguities of the verb 'desire' which affect the matter. Some things are desired for their own sake, and some are desired only as being means to something else and not as being themselves intrinsically desirable, and directly satisfying. Also one may desire something with no expectation of attaining it and hence with no alteration of his active attitudes on this account. And again, there are different classifications of the "objects" of desire; it is one thing to desire to be happy, a quite different kind of thing to desire a cup of coffee. And there are accordingly correlative differences, and more specific differences, with respect to the sense of 'desire' depending on its being one or another type of "object" to which the desiring is addressed. But with respect to one and all of these modalities of desire, and associated variations in the sense of 'desire', it will be true to say that whoever desires *anything* believes that if what he desires should be attained, such an attainment would produce, or conduce to, satisfaction, or, at the least, that such a result is probable. Any failure of accord with that would argue a perversity or foolishness of attitude having no condonation, unless that of mental or volitional incompetence, or some disability of self-direction. We must always, incidentally, come in the end to some proviso of that sort—that to any who lack, or are deprived of, the attributes of our common humanity, we do not address ourselves. And that must include, to repair to the philosophical tradition, even famed Cynics who might refuse to turn out for a cart—unless indeed their object is suicide or some gratifying exhibitionism.

A desire is not a belief, but what is desirable is a matter of belief. Desiring, if rational instead of baseless or absurd, implies a conviction about that which is desired, belief in just that character of the object of the desiring which constitutes that manner of *desirability* which the desire of it implies. And by the same token, any *desirability* of anything must be capable of corroboration or disproof. And consonantly, the desire of that which truly is desirable—in whatever sense is in question—is a desiring which is correct and the desire of that which is not truly desirable is a desiring which is mistaken, ill-judged, and attributes to the object of desire some character which it does not truly have. And this character of the object, upon which well-judged desiring is predicated, must be one which the object has, or does not have, independently of the question whether anyone actually desires it or not, even though this character of it is its potentiality or capacity for satisfying, or failing to satisfy, particular desires or desires of a certain class, some goodness, or lack of it, which those who entertain such desires seek out for the purpose of satisfying them. One who is hungry and desires food seeks out the edible, but he will be disappointed if he eats sawdust. And one who desires the gratification which good music can afford will be satisfied or disappointed when he turns on the radio. The characters of things, events, states of affairs, by reason of which they satisfy or do not satisfy specific desires, are properties which they have, or lack, regardless of anybody's desiring or not desiring them. And any desiring of a thing predicated upon its having a potentiality for satisfying which in fact it does not have is a desire for what is, in the sense in question, not desirable, and a desiring which calls for a correction of its aim.

Any actual desiring is, consonantly, subject to criticism, as the implicit belief in the desirability of its object is something to be attested and something capable of proof or disproof, corroboration or disconfirmation. And the thesis that desirability can be established by the fact that the thing in question is actually desired is as faulty as the thesis that the truth of a prediction can be established by the actuality of the expectation. It is the verification or confirmation of the expectant belief, that so and so will or would satisfy desire, which alone can establish the desirability of a thing desired. No naturalistic theory of the normative, nor any other—excepting only the skeptical repudiation of any validity of normative judgment—could afford to entertain any conception contrary to that.

Furthermore, no naturalistic theory nor any other which could claim validity for normative assessments could consistently say, without qualification, that the *satisfaction* of a desire is, by itself, sufficient to establish the desirability of what is so desired.[7] The satisfying of a desire may prove it justified, correct, well-judged, "so far forth," but the satisfaction of some desires militates against the satisfaction of other desires; and there is, within the purview of any judicious theory of the normative, naturalistic or otherwise, this further kind of critique of desiring which reflects the "economy of our desires" and the "composing of our interests." One cannot here, of course, deal with the complications of this topic.

One need only look to the history of ethical naturalism to observe that no theory which is judicious can equate 'desirable' with 'desired', or fail to recognize that the validity of any normative judgment presumes criteria which are objective—in the

---

7. It is on this point that the various senses of 'desirable' or 'good' must be pertinent, and the complex relation of what is good in one sense to what is good in another.

same sense that predictive knowledge must be objective, in contrast to subjective belief—and that only such desires as are validated or validatable by means of such a critical examination have standing as determinative of either the good or the right.[8]

A desire is not a belief, but what is desirable is a matter of belief.

Let that point be reiterated.

And it is imperative for the attainment of what will satisfy when attained that such beliefs should be correct. What will satisfy our desires and purposes is precisely what we think about in choosing our aims, and such thinking and the conclusions so reached require to be correct if we are to avoid being at cross-purposes with ourselves and self-frustrating in the choices of what to aim at. Unless the determination of what is desirable in the sense of deliberately to be chosen should be subject to criticism, there would be no point in the deliberation of our purposive action.

What both naturalists and perfectionists may overlook is that the real issue which lies between them concerns *ultimate* aims only, *final* purposes, that which is the last and comprehensive aim accord with which stands as the criterion of all lesser and subsidiary aims and purposes, all rational choosing and desiring—the *summum bonum*. That particular choosings and desirings are subject to critique lies in the fact that what is now chosen and becomes the aim of particular action will have its effect upon the future—upon the rest of life, so far as life altogether is capable of being affected by anything we can and must now decide upon and seek to bring about. Without this concern for what lies beyond the present moment and is within our power presently to influence, there would be no

---

8. In the matter of recognizing the importance of, and attending to, this economy of desires, and the composition of interests, we might recall Bentham. He is a good example of this sort of thing, and is particularly clear on such points. Whatever is to be otherwise said about his "hedonic calculus," his discussion of the dimensions of, and the methods of, assessing pleasure and pain well evidences his concern with, and his sensitivity to, certain of the points mentioned above. Indeed, his calculus is intended to be a tool for adjudicating questions of this sort, purporting to *be* precisely a set of rules for the critique of desiring, a set of rules to which our choosing must conform to be rational.

point in thinking before we do, and no significance in possible self-government, the setting aside of immediate inclinations and promptings to do in favor of considered action. Any difference of our conduct from the unconsidered behavior of the lower animals would be a bootless capacity to bother ourselves about nothing. Whatever we do *deliberately* and from consideration, instead of impulsively and because of a prompting to immediate gratification, is done in virtue of the subordination of any immediate desiring to the *further desirable*—the rest of life which may so be affected, other and future occasions than this moment's satisfaction or dissatisfaction. If we modify our present aiming for the sake of other interests, incident to other moments, and weigh the desirability of a now-to-be-felt gratification or dissatisfaction by reference to what may further ensue, at other moments, what is it about such further experience and further living which may move us to be concerned about it? Obviously there is nothing in terms of which such a question is to be answered which does not itself involve a question of *desirability*. If, similarly, we desire *some* things not because the possession of them or the attainment of them is desirable for its own sake, but because it is desirable as a means to something else, something further, then again what is it about this something else, or further, which justifies the aim to attain what is a means to it? It lies in the nature of any self-government, any adjudication of our aimings and of what we aim at and desire to achieve, and any modification of immediate promptings and inclination, that what lies further and beyond, and is the topic of any concern, must have the character of the *desirable* in order to justify any modification of behavior by reference to what is not immediate feeling and immediate inclination. And we must, by such considerations, those of the rationale of the deliberate choosing and deciding of our doing, be led on to the question of the *finally desirable,* of the most comprehensive concern, which is to operate as the criterion in the governing of all lesser and included concerns. Thus our choosing and desiring on *this* occasion and for *this* presently entertained aim of achievement, and for every particular choosing and aiming at any concrete objective, is subject not only to what may be called the *cognitive* critique of choosing and desiring—*if* this is achieved, will it satisfy this present aim, and in general *"if*-what-*then*-what"—but every such choosing and aiming, and desiring, calls for concern, eventually, for the totality of what may be affected by any aim, and for the determination of the overall character by reference to which an overall objective of our aims and choosings, and our desirings, in general, may be justified—the touchstone of aiming and choosing, and desiring, at large. And this is the question of the *summum bonum.*

It is really this Ultimate Good which Mill and other naturalists have in mind—or at least *should* have in mind—if they are tempted to say that there is no criterion of the desirable except finally that it *is desired.* But if they so put it, they are still at fault, and injudicious: it still is not the *desiring* which is in question but the *desirable—what would, if attained, satisfy desire.* But it is concerning this *summum bonum* that there is a real issue between naturalists and perfectionists, if indeed there is any decidable issue at all.

I must confess myself hampered in the discussion of this topic by the conviction that there is no such issue dividing these two parties which is decidable, the conviction that their difference is not with respect to the final criterion of the intrinsically desirable, but largely a difference of preferred vocabulary, and of what they choose, differently, to emphasize in their attempted characterization of the good life. But I shall do my best to read their intentions accurately on this point.

First, let us characterize their difference loosely and crudely. The naturalists wish to emphasize that it needs no conversion, no spiritual rebirth, no modification of the natural bent of mind in order to envisage the final and comprehensive good. The *summum bonum* is that which if a man could possess it or attain it, he would ask for nothing more. There is paradox enough in that formulation itself: we cannot envisage the complete attainment of the completely satisfying, and, if we could, we should not be *satisfied* with it, because life in human terms would then be terminated—there would be nothing more to live for, nothing more to do. But we can perhaps take the intended point of the matter, in spite of the paradox. The naturalist would emphasize that he speaks of *this* life, as it is naturally lived, and that a good life is the life which he whose life it is will, or would, *find* good in the living of it. This is one import of his insistence upon the "natural," human nature as it is, and operating in this natural world, not a human nature as it might be viewed from some other world, the whole business then being somehow projected into an edifying empyrean. The final criticism of wrong desirings is only of those aims which are frustrative of themselves, or of *other* aims, and so of the fullest satisfaction of our aims and wants, and needs, in general, and in their complex interdependence and effects on one another. He suspects any who would differ from him in this viewing of the nature of the ultimately and comprehensively desirable as simply that which would most fully satisfy the natural bent of the natural man of bias due to some *supernaturalism,* some imposition of a critique which is not immanent to, or in, man as he is made and in this world in which he finds himself.

It is presumably this point which betrays Mill into his claim that there is no proof that anything is desirable except that it is desired. He is thinking of the pervasive aim of happiness, of being throughout a lifetime as fully satisfied as it is possible to be, and emphasizing that no superimposed modification of this natural bent to find happiness in one's living can have any justification.[9] Anything different would, on his view, be some sort of enslavement to purposes intrinsically alien to the human, not something in accord with what is immanent in human nature.

It may be well at this point to digress briefly, in order to answer a pointless kind of objection—one which would be as adverse to perfectionism as to naturalism, though it is commonly urged against the naturalistic portrayal of the *summum bonum* expressed in terms of pleasure or in terms of happiness. The objection in question is to the effect that we *do* not—or perhaps that we *cannot*—want happiness, that what we want

---

9. It may be observed that, throughout Mill's writings, 'happiness' is his preferred word for the character of the *summum bonum.* Too, we note that he admits difference of *quality* as one dimension of the intrinsically desirable, over and above Bentham's intensity and duration of pleasures and pains, and hence that some pleasures are better than other pleasures *as found,* apart from anything appropriately called the degree or the lastingness of them. In fact, he more often than not avoids the words 'pleasure' and 'pain' in characterizing the humanly pervasive or ultimate aim.

is *this* thing or *that* event, or state of affairs, to which it may be added that one who should want pleasure or being happy would be sure to lose it by aiming at it, that the way to find pleasure or happiness is to forget about it, and be intent upon something else, something in particular. Happiness must be a by-product, a superadded blessing of the aim which is forgetful of it and otherwise addressed.

This objection is as pointless as to say that we cannot want food, or would better not make obtaining food our aim, because we can only attain food by seeking beefsteak and potatoes, or a lamb chop, or *this* or *that* lamb chop. One can, to be sure, only obtain food by obtaining a steak or a lamb chop, or some other particular thing classifiable under "food." And it is quite true that wanting food is not identical with wanting steak, and that wanting steak is not identical with wanting this steak on the platter. One may also be permitted to want food but to add, "And I don't mean spinach." But the common sense of the matter concerns two points, and two points only. First, to want food is to want something or other subsumed in the class of food. And one who should want food will obtain it only by accepting something in this class. The *ground* of such an acceptance will be that the accepted item has the essential character of food, and perhaps of good food, or of some subclass of foods acceptable to him. He accepts this *because* it is good food, and will satisfy his need or want for something edible and sustaining. The point of his aiming—whether he settles for beefsteak or for lamb—is the satisfaction of his want or need. Similarly it is possible to want, and want pervasively, to be happy—to want something—or whatever—will most conduce to being happy, and to accept or specifically choose particular things or events, or states of affairs, on the ground of the supposition that the attainment of *these* items will conduce to happiness. One could be, and may be, minded to accept only that which will, as one supposes, conduce to happiness in life. Or—eliminating any question about the correct word for the *summum bonum*—one may be finally bent upon that which will conduce, in the highest measure, to the quality or character of life by reason of which he would call it a good life as against a poor or bad, or dissatisfying, life to live. And perhaps some initial discernment of what he thus pervasively and enduringly wants will be conducive, in some measure, to his getting it. It is, indeed, only on such a supposition, that of a last and comprehensive criterion, that it could make any sense to say that the *uncriticized* life is not worth living, and it is only on some supposition of an overall critique that any critique or any code of conduct could well be justified. If we don't know what we want—and even what we want most and finally—we are unlikely to make headway in getting it. Having settled that, we shall then be confronted by the further question of *what items* embody this character of what we want, and which of them in largest measure, and what acts open to us will contribute most to our attainment of things which have this character.

The second pertinent point is that in the pursuit of any aim, there may be stages in the pursuit of that aim, which will involve subsidiary purposes and aims, and, accordingly, that the achievement of the ultimate end or aim may call for intentness, for the time being, on the achievement of these subsidiary purposes and aims. One who wants to drive a nail may have to find the hammer first, and the best way to find the hammer is to put one's mind on it and not think about the "nail driving" until later. Aristotle said that happiness is a blessing which adds itself to the achievement of other worthwhile ends. But he did not say that the ends may not be selected specifically on the ground that the attainment of them will make us happy. If he had, he would have been wrong. And it is the business of reflection upon the ultimate aims of life which is in point when the question is of the *summum bonum*, or of the critique of values, or the coordination and integration of our aims by a directing purpose. One can value beefsteak on the ground that it is food, and that the attainment of food is our controlling purpose. And one could value the concert to which one goes because hearing good music will contribute to a satisfying life. One who would emphasize the necessity of criticized living is in a poor position to overlook such points, or to raise this silly objection to the naturalistic conception of the *summum bonum* as a satisfied life.

But let us return to our directing interest here, from which we have digressed. It is difficult to say anything accurate about

perfectionism in general—as in the case of any other philosophic tendency—because of the diversity of views which fall
under this general head. But the point of its difference from
naturalism does *not* turn upon the question whether the attainment of the good life requires or does not require a critique of
purposes taken. The critique of desiring which is essential to
the validity of aims and purposes in order that they be directed
to the actually desirable as against what is desired in virtue of
a mistaken belief as to what will satisfy such a desire may be
called the cognitive critique. And that manner of critique of
valuing must be recognized as essential on any constructive
theory of ethics. It is implied in any view which would recognize intelligence as having any function in the direction of our
doing and in the selection of the ends of right action, and it can
be repudiated only at the price of moral skepticism. The distinguishing feature of perfectionism is the supposition that, in
addition to this cognitive critique, there is some *other* critique
which is essential before the *summum bonum* can be correctly
envisaged. Or perhaps it should be said that this cognitive critique is to be viewed as simply a part of, and as involved in,
another which is more fundamentally essential. The desirings
of men as they naturally find themselves must first be purged of
some original sinfulness, some allurement of what is bestial and
does not befit a man, or some lack of responsiveness to that
which has an intrinsic worthiness not to be confused with the
satisfaction of natural wants, or with the satisfaction of feelings with which we are endowed by nature, before that which
will satisfy can be taken as that which is validly to be aimed
at. Right-mindedness must first be attained before that which
will gratify or satisfy can be projected as the ultimately good,
Selbstzufriedenheit or *Seligkeit,* rather than *Glückseligkeit,* the
higher goods of self-realization, the blessedness of the saints, a
happiness which the natural man cannot naturally know—or
could not if his nature did not include some cultivable strain
which bespeaks his kinship with what transcends the merely
natural and earthy. We must define our nature not by what we
find ourselves to be but by reference to ideals which, though we
may not attain them, we nevertheless cannot repudiate, before
our human nature can be taken as the touchstone of the valid,

the correct, the genuinely worthy, or before we can project the ends which, in spite of all difficulties, it is imperative for us to pursue. The human capacity to envisage the "ought to do" and the "ought to be" contrasts with, rather than coincides with, what will please us as the other animals may be pleased. Self-criticism is self-transcendence; it reflects the leading light of a better self than we have as yet made real, and which it is our destiny to pursue. Until we set our compass to the direction of the ideal goal, we do not achieve that right-mindedness which is a prerequisite for the valid determination of anything as genuinely right and validly to be accepted as good.

It is possibly germane that, while the naturalist in ethics seldom finds it pertinent to his ethical doctrine to advert to any metaphysical thesis not implicit in common sense, and is usually an empiricist in epistemology, perfectionism is often coupled with some form of transcendentalism in metaphysics and epistemology, with the Platonic strain in Aristotle and with his teleologism of final causes, with Kantian or some idealistic transcendentalism, or with a claim that apprehension of the right is an intuitive insight not subject to the criteria of knowledge derived from sense experience.

It would be impossible to argue any issue which lies embedded in such a contrast between naturalism and perfectionism without proceeding to a particularization of particular theories which must run to inadmissible length here. And in any such attempt to "hit off" this contrast, we could make no warrantable claim to disclose any root of this matter correctly. We shall, however, venture to suggest one form which the issue might take, the question, namely, whether or not the naturalist's ideal of the *summum bonum* is, except for preferred vocabulary, identical with the perfectionist's ideal. The perfectionist characteristically clouds this issue, in the end, by claiming that the *summum bonum* as he would portray it represents a happiness or a satisfying life which to any who should adequately envision it would be found preferable to any other. He cannot resist the temptation to find an argument which will be convincing to those who argue from a premise he himself repudiates. Now, if this be true, that moral perfection is the "higher prudence," then any man who should fail to acknowledge the perfectionist's vision of the *summum bonum* as his ideal goal must be making a common-sense mistake. He fails to recognize the highest happiness, that which would satisfy him as would the achievement of no other goal open to him. And whether this insight is natural, transcendental, or supernatural, if it is open to him, he prejudices his own "natural" bent to achieve a life which will be, in the fullest measure, that which he would find it satisfying to live, if he fails to seek and to govern himself by reference to this ideal. Not to do so would be simply unintelligent, a failure of correct cognition of the validly desirable. If he must be critically observant of his own valuations in order to envisage correctly this valid highest good, that is the common sense of evaluation generally. Uncriticized value judgments are perennially subject to mistake. And uncriticized action is perennially likely to be prejudicial to the realization of what will be found most satisfying and genuinely desirable. The requirement to be converted to those aims which will be found satisfying in attainment, and to those ways of acting which will best achieve the ends for the sake of which they finally are taken, is no more than the requirement to avoid mistaken attitudes and acts which will prove self-frustrating of their final purpose, and not to be more stupid than we can help. If we do not see amiss in this matter, it is difficult to distinguish the perfectionist's ultimate goal and his criterion of the good and the right from that of the naturalist—*unless* the perfectionist claims that true insight into the highest values can come only by some manner of esoteric insight, not vouchsafed to men at large as they naturally find themselves, and not attainable as knowledge of other sorts is attained.

That question we shall not argue here, believing that the issue is justly obsolescent.

ESSAY 8

Right Doing and the Right to Do

Ethics concerns voluntary acts. And the character of them it would assess is the final rightness or wrongness of them. It attempts a decisive judgment of them as permissible or impermissible to do.

An act is a physical bringing about. Governable or directable thinking we may call an activity, but if it does not eventuate in any physical bringing about, we shall not refer to it as an act. Any voluntary act will be a corrigible commitment of doing with an expectation of consequences. These expected consequences, as envisaged in advance, constitute the intention of an act. Without such an anticipation, it would be a piece of behavior but not a deliberate act or even, in any strict sense, an act at all. As we have observed, the acting—the act as a doing—is to be identified with the commitment, the initiating of it, and as such the act is not identical with its consequences, either actual or expected, most obviously by being antecedent to them in time. But there is nothing by which an act can be specified, and one act distinguished from another, except by reference to what is done or to what the act was expected, and intended, to bring about. As an event merely, it may be determined by its space-time locus, but this unique predicate of it does not specify what act it is which happens then and there.

Let us pause here to observe—parenthetically and as a loose generalization—that gerunds, gerundives, and pronomials or adjectives otherwise derived from active verbs tend to occur in three verbally distinct forms. There are acting, action, and the enacted; intending, intention, and the intended; committing, commitment, and committed; doing, deed, and done; choosing, choice, and chosen. The variant idioms of customary usage doom the attempt to formulate any precise and general semantic statement concerning these forms, presenting exceptions to almost anything which could be said. But as something to be examined at least, and which may be illuminating in various contexts, we may remark that the '—ing' form refers to the doing, the committing as attributable to the agent's initiative, and the '—ed' form refers to consequences, as actual or expected. The middle member of the triad characteristically has two usages: first, it may replace, ambiguously, either of the other two, and, second, it may function as an abstract term denoting the "content" of the act or activity as something repeatable and of which there may be instances. For example, the "same action" may be taken on different occasions, or adopted by different persons. An action or act of which there may thus be instances represents a *way* of acting.

It is one important point in this connection that it is only as instances of *ways* of acting that acts are either governable or subject to any critical assessment. Any voluntary act must be one we *know how* to do at will. And what we thus control we must have *learned* to do from past like instances. It is as a repeatable way of acting only that we can voluntarily initiate what we do on a present occasion. And it is only as something whose desirability or undesirability is worth assessing, in the anticipation of *future like occasions,* that there is any point in the critical assessment of acts already done. But only by so learning the advisability and inadvisability of certain ways of acting, from past instances, can we deliberate, *i.e.,* criticize in advance of doing, what we presently consider or propose to do. It is an even more important consideration that, whether it be a unique act or a way of acting which is under consideration, it is only by reference to what is done, brought about, or to what it is intended to bring about, that any act is criticizable and could be called either right or wrong. It is the *acting,* the committ*ing,* to which this rightness or wrongness is strictly attributable, but the *ground on which* this attribution is determined must concern what this act is a doing *of,* or what it was intended so to do. What we intend is what we *decide to bring about*— the anticipated consequences. Again—and this is not the same point, though it is one which immediately follows—acts which are deliberate rest upon some present or past deliberation and the conclusion so reached, and this conclusion concerns the consequences of so doing. There is no deliberate doing which does not reflect a *judgment* having reference to the anticipated consequences of this committing to do, and to some specifiable and expectable character of them. Such a prediction is a cognitive judgment we have learned to make, and one which is criticizable as to its *cognitive* justification. It is a cognitively right or a cognitively wrong prediction. But the rightness or wrongness of the doing *also,* and particularly, concerns some predictable, and desirable or undesirable, character of the consequences as predicted.

Consideration of these points obliges us to recognize that any assessment of right or wrong doing is a complex matter, having parts or aspects which will call for separate consideration. It is by reason of this complexity that, up to this point, we have had to preserve a certain ambivalence with respect to the assessment of right or wrong doing. The critical judgment to be made of acts turns principally upon the intentions of them, the consequences as anticipated by the doer, and upon the character of these intended consequences. Such an assessment of acts by reference to the character of the consequences which the doer intended to bring about is, let us say, the primary mode of adjudging acts as right or wrong to do. But secondarily, the intending requires to be assumed a mode of cognitive judgment, which may be cognitively valid or an unjustified and incogent prediction. The *deliberation* reflected in a deliberate act may be at fault, and whether such a fault is or is not to be attributed to the doer, as a faultiness of his doing, is a nice point in the assessment of his deliberate act as right or wrong for him to do. Certainly for ourselves, in our own deliberation, it is not a point on which we absolve ourselves from responsibility in our decisions with respect to what we undertake to do. Cogent foreseeing of the foreseeable consequences and the foreseeable character of them is an essential part of the rightness of any deliberate doing. As we shall find, there are, consequent upon these complicating considerations, two different modes in which deliberate acts are assessed as right or wrong. We shall call these, respectively, the "subjective rightness" or "subjective wrongness," and the "objective rightness" or "objective wrongness," of deliberate action. Both of these modes of assessment we shall find it required to include and consider in any adequate doctrine of ethics. We must shortly return to examine more at length the consequences of these complicating considerations. But for the present let us observe only that any deliberate act is, for the doer of it, subject to critical assessment in two ways. First, there is an expectation of consequences which, like any prediction, is cognitive and assessable as to its cognitive justification. He will be responsible for this, in the same sense and measure that he is responsible for any conclusion he reaches or belief he holds, perhaps particularly so when he decides to act upon it.[1] Second, there is that manner of assessment of an intending and of a deliberate doing which is common to normative judgments at large and which turns upon the character of the consequences so to be brought about, as desirable or undesirable.

Otherwise put—and allow us to summarize this, from the conviction that it is an important and too frequently neglected matter—a deliberate act is a commitment to bring about, and as deliberate it involves a believing as to what consequences will follow. The primary and distinctively normative assessment to which such a commitment to do is subject is the critical appraisal of the consequences being such as it will be justified or unjustified to bring about deliberately. Secondarily, there may be a criticism of the expecting, the believing that consequences such and such, and not others, will follow upon this

---

1. This may suggest that the noncognitivists in ethics have been a little hasty, unless they are prepared to go the whole way with the skeptics in epistemology.

commitment to do. And this second mode of critical assessment is criticism of the *cognitive judgment* involved.

There is a third and subsidiary point of complexity.[2] Not only may a doer be criticized because of an incogent prediction of the consequences of his doing; he may also be criticized, on occasion, for inadvertence, for carelessness or thoughtlessness in his believing. It is so that he may be accountable not only for what he brings about intentionally, but sometimes for what he brings about without intending it. As we sometimes say to children, "You see, you did not think straight about what you were doing," or, again, "You did not stop to think." In either of these cases, the doer's act is criticizable for the faultiness of his expectation, which he could have helped by thinking. Or even if, this time, it is excusable by reason of immaturity or inexperience, still it is criticizable as a way of doing it is important not to repeat. And as a final such annotation, let us add that, in general, *not* doing, *not* expecting, *not* thinking, can be as wrong as wrong doing or thinking, by reason of the consequences of the *failure* of such an initiative, where such an initiative is possible and called for.

Before we plunge into any further complications—and there are others still to come—let us pause to take a few compass bearings. As the remarks just made must call to our attention, we cannot achieve the perspective necessary for any consideration of ethics as the topic of the final and decisive mode of assessing the right or wrong to do without first giving attention to the distinction between the cognitively right and wrong, since certain beliefs—expectations of consequences—are always involved in deliberate doing. These beliefs themselves may be right or wrong, and he who deliberately brings anything about may be criticizable for his believing, on the basis of which he makes his decision, his deliberate decision to do. Those who lack the capacity for deliberate foresight, as well as those who are incapable of being deterred by such foresight of consequences as is open to them, are not accounted responsible for their acts. Conversely, responsible doers are responsible for

---

2. The reader is asked to observe that we do not gratuitously introduce this further complication, but merely remark a further pertinent fact.

the determinations of cognitive conviction which are involved in their deliberate decisions to do. Rightness or wrongness of deliberate doing cannot be assessed without reference to rightness and wrongness of believing. And the critique of cognitive believing must be antecedent to, or else a part of, any adequate critique of right or wrong doing, in any sense in which doing is to be called right or wrong, whether, for example, the mode in which rightness is to be assessed is that of the morally right, prudentially right, technically right, legally right or any other such category of the right or wrong. Or if there be some sense in which doing is adjudged right or wrong *without* reference to the rightness of the believing involved, then this particular mode in which doing is assessed relatively to what *is* believed, whether justifiably or without justification, will call for some qualifying adjective, marking this peculiar limitation of it. (We shall proceed to that point shortly.) But even for the consideration of this peculiar manner of adjudging acts as right or wrong, it will remain a significant fact that there can be *no* deliberate doing without a cognitive judgment as to its consequences. A doer without foresight, correct or incorrect, could *ipso facto* bring nothing about deliberately.[3]

Let us also observe that right and wrong apply to whatever is decidable, whatever is governable or directable by our activity. And in the root sense, that and that only is right or is wrong the decision of which is right or is wrong. Right and wrong doing and right or wrong concluding and believing—commitments as to fact—represent the two major divisions of assessment of the right or wrong.

However, having remarked the two different grounds on which deliberate doing requires to be assessed, the justification of the cognitive expectation of consequences so to be brought about and the justification of bringing about those

---

3. In the light of this obvious fact, it may again suggest itself that noncognitivist conceptions with regard to the normative in general may have been a bit hasty, unless, as we have already suggested, those who propose them wish to go the whole length, join, say, with the Sophists and Cynics, and repudiate any validity of knowledge whatsoever, e.g., repudiate even that distinction of right or wrong which might apply to taking them seriously or believing what they tell us.

consequences, let us omit, for the time being, that mode of criticism which turns upon the cognitive validity of the predictive judgment in the light of which the decision to do is made. The justification of believing is a separate topic, to which we must later return. Confining attention to that rightness or wrongness of doing which turns upon the character of what is done, or intended to be done, let us observe that no doing or intended doing could be right or wrong without some character of the done or intended by reason of which what so comes about or is expected to result is something it is "right-to-do" or "right-to-intend-to-do." The rightness or wrongness is attributable to the do*ing* or the intend*ing*, but it is so attributable only on the ground of some "right-to-do-ness" or "wrong-to-do-ness" of what is done, or some "right-to-intend-to-do-ness" or "wrong-to-intend-to-do-ness" of what is intended. "It is right to bring A about" ascribes rightness to the act, the commitment to bring A about, but it also attributes "right-to-bring-about-ness" to A itself. And "Intending to do A is right" ascribes rightness to the intending, but it also attributes "right-to-intend-ness" to A. Otherwise put, if there were no discoverable character of anything, A, by reason of which bringing A about is right, or intending to bring A about is right, then a right-minded person, bent on confining his doings and intendings to such as are justified and right, could not choose anything in particular, as against anything else, on the ground of its being right to do or right to intend to do. The distinction between the "right-to-do" and the "wrong-to-do," and between the "right-to-intend" and the "wrong-to-intend," must be in what is *done,* or what is intend*ed.* And this character of what is brought about or expected to be brought about must be a character of the actual or expected consequences of action which is recognizable antecedently to and independently of any choosing to bring about such consequences. Otherwise there could be nothing discoverable in the nature of things by reason of which any choosing to do this rather than that would be ascertainably right or wrong. Without some discernible character of what the action is to bring about, as the ground of the rightness of bringing it about, any ascription of rightness or wrongness to the act of deliberately bringing it about must be groundless, arbitrary, subjective.

Absence of any objective ground of right choosing to do is, of course, precisely what the Cynic alleges. He claims that there is nothing in the way of objective actuality or cognizable fact by reason of which any deliberate act could be ascertainably right or wrong. Any who would escape such cynicism must find himself committed to the assertion of some determinable and objective factuality as the ground on which to bring about or intend certain things or happenings is right, and to bring about or intend certain others is wrong. Even those who would maintain that the distinction between the right and wrong, or, in particular, the morally right and wrong, is the ground of certain rules or principles, representing some insight which is nonempirical, cannot escape this requirement. Rules or principles of right doing must be applied to cases by some manner of empirical discrimination, for which these directives afford a criterion for application to the empirical factuality of *what is so to be done*, or *intended to do*. A rule which does not in some wise discriminate between the doing of this and the doing of that is one which no one could apply to action. We are not yet ready to discuss the fundamental issue between cognitivism and noncognitivism in ethics. But let us note in passing that without some manner of cognitive and empirical discrimination between the "right-to-do" and the "wrong-to-do," there can be no valid distinction whatever between right doing and wrong doing, in any category of the right or wrong to do.

It is a thought which will inevitably occur to us that this "right-to-bring-about-ness" or "right-to-intend-to-bring-about-ness," which must be attributable to the consequences of action, before any determination of the rightness of bringing them about, is some goodness of these consequences, and that the adjudication of the goodness of the consequences is the ground of the adjudication of the rightness of bringing them about. It suggests itself that there could be no rational ground for doing or attempting to do anything, except the expectation of thereby doing some good—some good of some kind and to somebody.

However, if such should be our initial thought, then we must promptly be aware that, however obvious it may be, it is too indefinite and too simple to be either accurate or adequate. For one thing, there are those different senses of the right—moral, prudential and the varieties of the technical—which we have already remarked, and there are others still to be noted. And there are at least as many senses in which 'good' is predicated. Very likely that will be already in our minds if we commit ourselves to this thought that the ground of ascribing any rightness to an act must be *some* goodness of its consequences.

Nevertheless this is too promising a thought, and too clearly suggests itself as pertinent, not to carry it forward, if only to see where we might come out. And being aware that we are as yet only at the beginning of an investigation which, so far, shows itself more complex the more we examine it, we can proceed somewhat experimentally, not expecting that the conclusions we can presently reach will be finally precise and decisive and need no further qualification, but hoping that our present and tentative findings may nevertheless prove useful.

If we may proceed, there is one matter which can now be clarified provisionally, using the vague term 'good' in the sense already suggested, that is, merely as a shorthand term for "that character of the objective of action by reason of which it may be recognized as right to bring about." Consideration of the relation between the right and the good in these terms can clarify the different senses of 'right' as attributed to acts. There are two such different meanings of 'right' whose distinction is necessary, particularly in ethics, and there is a third, the addition of which will help to clarify the other two.

Let us say that an act is *absolutely* right if and only if the consequences of it *are* good, or more good than bad, or better than the consequences of any alternative doing open to the doer's choice.[4]

---

4. Already we must remark that we are leaving open two distinguishable subvariants of the meaning here assigned to the expression 'absolutely good'. So be it: we cannot discuss everything at once.

Let us say that an act is *objectively* right if and only if the consequences of it are *cogently thought* to be good, more good than bad, or better than those of any other alternative.

And let us say that an act is *subjectively* right if and only if the doer *thinks*, whether cogently or not, that the consequences will be good, more good than bad, or better than those of any other alternative.

And now let us investigate these diverse possible senses of 'right' by way of an example—their applicability to the prudentially right to do. It is peculiarly patent that prudential rightness is to be adjudged by reference to a particular sense of 'good', the personally good, the good for some individual, in this case, good for the doer whose acting is in question. Clearly, what the doer, aiming to do what is prudent, *wishes* to do is what is prudentially right in the sense of absolutely right. He wishes to attain something good for himself, something findably good in his own future experience. This absolute prudential rightness is the *ideal* of prudence. It turns upon the *truth* about the consequences, what *will* happen if he does the act in question. In one sense of 'intend', we might say that this absolute good-for-himself is what the doer, choosing to be prudent, *intends* to do. But that would be a loose sense of 'intend', and we have heretofore used 'intend' and 'intention' to denote what the doer *expects* as the result of his action, not what he wishes or hopes for but may be aware that he cannot expect with any assurance, something whose attainment will be in some measure a matter of good luck. Let us stick to our narrower and commoner meaning of 'intended' as "*expected* to result from adopted action," not merely wished for or hoped for. Any judicious doer will be somewhat aware of the hazards of foresight and recognize that the absolute truth about the consequences of any contemplated act runs beyond any confident predicting, and may even on occasion betray his best assured expectancies. And we who observe his act, and to whom his predictions as to its results may be made known, will be unlikely to call this act of his prudent simply by reference to its actual consequences, good or bad, to himself. On occasion at least, both he and we will be more likely to say, when the consequences of it have occurred and have been observed, that the act was prudent enough, but proved to have been unfortunate, or, again, that it was not only prudent but lucky. The most frequent meaning of 'prudent' is not this sense in which it turns upon the actual consequences of it, the absolute truth about them. In the ordinary sense, being prudent is taken as a matter which turns upon what was foreseen by the doer, or, at least, on what was foreseeable—what could or should have been foreseen, at the time and in the circumstances in which it was decided. Prudence, moreover, would be less important to assess than in fact it is, if the character of the deliberate doing to which it referred were this absolute and usually less than certain character of the consequences as these later prove to be. This goodness of the forthcoming results to himself is what the prudent doer wishes to come as close to as he can in deciding his action. But insofar as it is something not open to determination when the doing has to be decided, it is not a character of the act for which any doer can take responsibility, and is not indicative of the quality of his self-determination in deliberate doing. Only such characteristics of action as are open to judgment at the time and in the circumstances of the decision to do are commonly ascribed to deliberate doings as pertinent to the prudential quality or character of them. Prudence, in the sense of an "absolute rightness," is not ascribable to an act as deliberate; this is because a prudential absolute rightness, although it certainly includes a reference to something which is indeed pertinent to the act done in the sense of being brought about, is something which could be fully determinable, if ever, only *ex post facto*; it is not determinable by any deliberation or any other manner of control which the doer could exercise in doing. The relationship between deliberate doing and good results is not a necessary one. It is contingent. Accordingly, good results cannot be ascribed to deliberate doing, except in so far as they might be consequent upon, or contingent upon, such doing. They are not themselves an essential element of, or a necessary character of, such doing, such governable acting.

This is a point in which the prudential rightness of an act and the prudential good of it stand in contrast. Whether it is prudentially *good* to do depends on what follows it, but whether it is prudentially *right* depends on nothing which happens after the commitment to do, and is not altered by the way it turns out. The good of it is something to be proved, something verifiable, or confirmable. The rightness of it depends solely on what was ascertainable before or at the time of the commitment to do, ascertainable on the *relevant evidence,* that open to the doer when he committed himself to do, that the doing would have good results.

In other words, an act is accounted prudentially right if it is objectively right, if the prediction that it would have prudentially good results was a prediction justified by the available evidence on which the decision of the doing had to rely. That is the usual and most precise sense of the statement that an act is or was prudent, and that the doer was acting prudently when he did it.

However, if we are speaking of the act in question *ex post facto,* and in the light of the observation that the consequences to the doer have been disastrous, there can be a nice question of what we may mean if we, say, should say that, as the consequences of it show, it was not the prudent thing to do. That kind of *ex post facto* observation may be illicit—may represent the human tendency to be wise after the fact: We would have thought of that adverse possibility at the time! But would we have? Shall we decide that the question whether it *really* was a prudentially right act depends on the evidence which was open to the doer at the time of his decision or not, and if we say that it was not really prudent, as the results of it show, what we mean is that the doer should have foreseen this adverse possibility and made his decision less carelessly, or else that, foreseeing it as a possibility, he assigned too low a probability to it, did not cogently weigh the evidence then open to his observation? That kind of judgment of the act will concern what we would here call the (prudentially) objective rightness of the act. It is an objectively right act (prudentially right) if and only if the relevant evidence open to the doer as to the (prudentially) good or bad consequences of it justified the prediction that the results of the doing would prove to be (prudentially) good. This relationship between the evidence, open to the doer, and the probable results as predictable on that evidence, is one which is a logical relationship—one subject to the rules of inductive logic—and it is one which is not altered in any way by anything which, in point of fact, subsequently happens. In other words, an act is (prudentially) objectively right if and only if, on the relevant evidence on which it had to be judged at the time of the decision and commitment pertinent to the act, the prediction that the consequences would be (prudentially) good was a *valid* prediction, whether this prediction later proves true or proves false—whether the actual consequences *are* (prudentially) good or not. That is the most obvious and most precise signification of 'prudent' as predicable of any deliberate doing or as ascribable to the agent in his so determining his act.

But now suppose that the act in question is something done by an immature person or by one with little experience of the kind of doing in question. The doer on this occasion has every intention of confining his acts to such as will not be detrimental to his own future welfare. But what he does turns out to be prudentially adverse. Or, to alter the illustration a little, this doer was well enough experienced in the kind of matter in hand, and he had every intention of being prudent, but he somehow didn't think, or didn't think cogently, about the relevant evidence open to him. Or, again, to change the example, the doer is a somewhat scatterbrained person, or a bit stupid, and given to failures of judicious awareness with respect to the predictable consequences of what he does. In any of these cases, there is a failure of cogency in the prediction of results, but no wish or will to commit an act having prudentially bad consequences. And there may be a question of the degree of competence of the doer in question to think cogently in prudential matters or, let us say, prudential matters requiring a prompt decision as to what to do. In all such cases, the point is, the present point, that there is no intention to bring about prudentially bad results, or any "imprudence" of *motivation*. The doer *thinks* what he commits himself to will have results which are prudentially satisfactory, but there is a failure of cogency in his so thinking and in what he intends. In any such case, the act is subjectively (prudentially) right, but not objectively (prudentially) right. The intention of it as a prediction is *not valid*; it is not supported by the evidence available to the doer in his decision to do.

Considerations of such subjective (prudential) rightness are not pertinent to the objective general question: "What acts, or ways of acting, are prudentially justified to adopt?" If our task were to elicit specific rules or maxims of prudence, we should set such considerations aside as not relevant. The question to which they are pertinent is that of the praise or blame to be assigned to doers in virtue of what they do. We might cover the case of a failure of cogency by reason of the immaturity or inexperience of the doer by saying that the relevant evidence was not, or not so fully, open to the doer, and that might argue that the point is already covered under the rubric of the objectively right. But where the failure is one of stupidity or some other congenital liability to incogent foresight, it will be a plain case of subjective rightness but objective wrongness, and the point is such that a failure in such a case may not be blameworthy.

There is thus a sufficient reason for preserving this category of the subjective rightness of doing as a distinct mode of assessing the rightness or wrongness of doing. It is pertinent, for example, to the justice of blaming or punishing children for imprudent actions, and for visiting our contempt of their prudential inadvertences upon others who suffer some limitation of cogent foresight.

The parallel considerations with respect to assessments of the technically right or the morally right may be sufficiently obvious. But there are minor differences to be observed.

Let us consider them briefly.

Any species of the technically right represents a subordinate mode of judgment of right doing. The end aimed at by prudence is an end in itself, the goodness of one's own living. Kant began to mislead himself in ethics by failing to distinguish the "good-in-itself" from the finally justified aim of action. If there be no character of that which is good for its own sake to be realized in the life of an individual, there could be none in anything. Society, as Herbert Spencer observed, has no central consciousness. Any goodness ascribable to a society is either an instrumental goodness, promotive of goodness in the lives of individual constituent members of it, or it is a creature of semantics and a myth. Any goodness of a society which is intrinsically desirable and good for its own sake is such only when and where it is possible to realize it as a quality or character of some existent—the goodness of such a society is then either a collective phenomenon, in the sense of being a phenomenon promotive of goodness in individual lives, or it is nothing. Kant recognizes this worth or dignity of the individual and speaks of it as an "absolute value." The validity of his Categorical Imperative is made to depend upon it: it is obligatory of, and indicates as required, a respect for the lives of others equally with our own, the root of the moral. But his denigration of prudence, as if acting from a concern for our good life were a falling off from the moral, instead of observing that such a falling off lies *only* in the failure of a like respect for the possible good life of others, is what leads him into the illogicality of treating the prudential imperative as hypothetical, like that of technically right doing. The technical end in view—the end which any technical rule is a rule for achieving—*is*, however, hypothetically good only. Excellence of technique serves some further end, *presumptively* good, though characteristically good only in the instrumental sense of "good-for," and on occasion "good for" something which itself is valueless or bad. As we might observe, there are technically right ways of making counterfeit money. The techniques manifested by a counterfeit bill may be excellent, though subverted to a bad end. And the judgment of technical excellence does not strictly imply any finally justified end of action at all. In this, technical rightness contrasts with, rather than belongs with, prudential rightness. The prudential end is always a valid end in itself, even when it is morally required to subordinate it to the demand of the moral. It is indeed contained in that end for which morals demands respect, and just why, or even whether, the prudential end should be subordinated to the moral is the peculiar problem of ethical theory.

The precise point is that the judgment of the technical rightness of any doing is independent of any judgment that the act which exhibits it is, in the particular instance, one it is justified to do. This is in spite of the fact that the cultivation of any technique argues *some* justified use for such a technical skill, that it evidences that on *some* occasions and for *some* purpose which is justified this manner of technical doing is called for. Technically excellent doings of the various types are useful for *some* purposes which are good—though almost any of them can be subverted to some purpose it is unjustified to pursue. And the technical rightness of doing strictly does not imply any justification of the act, or any goodness of the consequences in the particular instance. Technical excellence consists in the reliable *success* of the technical doing, for *whatever* purpose this manner of doing is invoked. And technical rightness is strictly to be ascribed without regard to the question whether the consequences of the doing are, in the particular instance, consequences which are good in any further sense.

What particularly needs to be observed here is that 'technically good' has no clear meaning *except* as a correlate of 'technically right'. It means no more than 'technically well done'. The expert in the Treasury Department who should say, "This is the best counterfeit twenty-dollar bill I have ever examined," would mean nothing but that this bill is such as could not have been produced except by a highly expert technique. It witnesses to expertness in wrong doing, an expertness which might have been turned to good use and produced a desirable result instead of this bad one, if the doer had so chosen. Such expertness is useful to command; it holds a potential for really good results. It does imply a capacity for some manner of doing which will be right in some cases and the potentiality for producing good results of some kind. But any technique can be subverted to wrongly taken aims. And technical rightness, by itself, argues nothing as to the desirability of the results, or the justification of doing what was done.

It might so appear that the ascription of technical rightness is not assessable at all in the other two modes above mentioned, "objectively right" and "subjectively right." But that would be an oversight. One thing we should so be overlooking is that expert doing, like any other, involves the cognitive expectation of results, and that such a cognitive expectation in the case of technical doing, as in that of any other, may be cognitively justified without being predictively *true*. Technical expertness most frequently involves special skills—manual skill, for example—but it *always* involves technical *know-how*, the guidance of deliberate doing by correct anticipation. In any technically directed doing, such an expecting of, and an intending of, results is involved in the determination of the responsibility or nonresponsibility for the actual consequences of the doing. A diamond cutter, for example—as the stories have it at least—may study a rough diamond of large size for weeks before giving it that decisive tap at an exactly determined point and angle. And then, instead of splitting in the desired plane, it may fly into comparatively valueless small pieces. There could in such a case be a fault of foresight, or it could be simply dire misfortune. The cutter's stroke may have been a wrong doing or not. If the assessment of it is that it was a wrong doing, then that assessment might depend on whether or not his intention was cognitively well taken on the basis of all the evidence open to his observation or it could turn, and perhaps simply so, on the question of belief—that this way of doing, whether cognitively justified or not, would have the desired result, all this aside from any considerations as to whether there was or was not any malice purposed or any culpable carelessness. An assessment as to whether the cutter's expectation of the desired result was cognitively justified or not, with respect to the evidence and with respect to correctly relating belief to that evidence, would be an assessment of the act with respect to objective rightness. This assessment would be independent of the actual and adverse result. But if the judgment made should concern merely what he *did* expect, whether correctly or not, and so decide and intend to bring about, then that assessment would be pertinent to the subjective rightness of his doing. A court which should be appealed to in a case such as this, where the act had unfortunate consequences, might have to assess the act in both of these modes, and decide whether simple damages, or triple damages, or no damages, were due to the owner of the stone destroyed. If the act was subjectively right, triple damages could not be legally assigned, the only wrongness of the doing being an error of cognition, and if it was an objectively right act, no damages, there being no fault of any kind on the part of the doer. But in either case the rightness or wrongness is not determinable simply by the results of the doing as good or bad.[5]

The point of major importance in this whole matter is that when any mode of technical doing is involved in deliberate action, the act must be so far forth technically right in the

----

5. [The basis of this passage, the handscript, is obscure in several ways. I have edited it in the interests of clarity. –Ed.]

objective sense in order to be prudentially or morally right in the objective sense, and must be subjectively right, blameless, in the technical sense in order to be prudentially right or morally right in the subjective sense. And, to cover every boggle which could arise: Whatever is in any sense objectively right is also in that same sense subjectively right. But the converse statement does not hold.

It is with the moral assessment of action that we are particularly concerned. And it is sufficiently evident without discussion that the assessment of an act as morally right or wrong is never to be determined in that mode which we have of "absolute" rightness or wrongness, simply by reference to the actual consequences of the act and their actual goodness or badness as eventually disclosed. Here as elsewhere, it is such absolute rightness or wrongness which we should like to be able to determine, and try to approximate as closely as we can. But it is judicious to recognize that it can be approximated more or less closely as the case permits, but never really and fully attained. But it is essential to ethics that *both* the objective rightness of acts and their subjective rightness be assessed. Judgment of the objective rightness of acts is peculiarly necessary when the question is "What ought I (or we, or anybody) to do?"—hence when the question is whether to do or not to do some contemplated act, and at the time of deliberation and decision, in particular when it is our own course of action which is considered. And the subjective mode of assessment is peculiarly called for when the question is of responsibility for what is done or has been done, and of what the doer so deserves at the hands of others, the question of praise or blame, reward or punishment, and, in our own case, of self-satisfaction or remorse.

There is a question just what the mode of right-to-do-ness, of goodness, is which is correlative with the moral rightness of doing. There are, of course, different views on this matter. But the antecedently most plausible suggestion is obvious: it is the goodness or badness of the consequences of the act to any and all those who suffer these consequences of it, and in measure as they are affected by it, for good or for ill. This is presumably what the utilitarians have intended by their shibboleth "the greatest good for the greatest number." (And it is regrettable that so many, with so little to offer except criticism of other people's suggestions, find so many exquisite and pointless objections to this good round phrase.) Plainly, weighing the consequences to others in measure as they are so affected is what is so dictated. And also, plainly, it is what is dictated by the Kantian dictum of the absolute, and in that sense "equal," worth of every individual and the criterion of doing as you would be done by, which is common to the Golden Rule and the Categorical Imperative. Since we are being a little experimental in our thinking in this essay, let us provisionally accept this suggestion that the goodness which is correlative with the moral rightness of doing—the right-to-be-done-ness of what is morally right to be done—is this goodness of the consequences of the act to all who are affected by it, in measure of its effects upon them for good or ill. It would be such consequences as actually do follow and are eventually disclosed which would determine an attempted moral assessment in the mode of "absolute rightness." It is the rightness of the intention of the act—such consequences as are justifiably predictable for the doer, on all the relevant evidence open to him at the time of doing, what he *correctly* anticipates or should anticipate as the consequences and the character of them—which would determine the moral assessment of the act in the mode of objective moral rightness. And it would be what the doer thinks the consequences in question will be, and with the character he thinks they will have, whether this thinking of his is right and a justified prediction or not, which will determine the subjective moral rightness or wrongness of the act.

As we have already indicated, *both* of these modes of the moral assessment of action are called for in ethics. But it is the reason why they are called for which is here the pertinent consideration. As also suggested, earlier, it is because *we* are called upon, on occasion, to judge the acts of others, and to praise or blame them, reward or punish them, in virtue of what they deliberately do, that the subjective mode of assessing the moral quality of action is called for. We conceive it to be neither just nor socially judicious to punish others for what they can't help. And some measure of cognitive error and stupidity is the common lot of all of us. The same could also be said of cognitive inadvertence, say, a failure to remark that there is more evidence which is relevant to our expectation of the consequences of action than we do in fact take cognizance of at the time when it would make a difference.

There may be a little difference here, relevant to these topics, between praising and blaming, and those more drastic critical responses called "reward" or "punishment."

Let us briefly consider such matters.

So much of praise or blame as may operate to correct future like cognitive errors and careless inadvertences may be justified by the future good that they may do in the way of preventing a repetition of them. But it is a nice point how useful and how just it is to visit our displeasure upon others for ways of acting incorrigible to the doer in the past case in question but corrigible to him on future occasions if we reinforce his notice of such matters and encourage the desirable manner of his later consideration in like cases. A slap on the wrist, perhaps, but no caning! And our like attitude to our own past lapses of justified cognitive expectancy in decisions to do: some serious reflection and firm resolution, perhaps, but no continuing remorse? It is the ethics of recrimination and self-recrimination which calls for the moral assessment of acts in the subjective mode. And otherwise it is out of place and even self-defeating. It can have no place where the question to be fronted is what we should choose to do—choose *now* when the decision requires to be made. In the subjective mode, our doing will be right just in case we now *think* it right. But we are *now thinking*, and thinking about what we *think* right is the recipe for self-frustration. What we must do, instead, is turn our deliberation to what we must think of, believe in, and expect—all this with respect to the thing to be done—we must turn our deliberation to the future eventualities, those to accrue as the result of the contemplated act, not dissolve into introspection, concerning ourselves with our own state of mind. Thinking about our present conviction will be a little *ex post facto* anyway, and out of place in any case. Either it is irrelevant to the matter in hand, or we know the answer to it already, and it is not the question we are now asking. The question is, "Would I be content to have others do to me what will probably happen to them if I should do this?" Or, say, "What will probably happen to others if I do

this, and would I be content if some other visited such consequences on me?" Kant supposes that kind of thinking to have
been done already. What *he* takes to be the question of ethics
still remains. Having *already answered* the previous question,
he would point out that the *criterion* of morally right doing still
remains to be identified; all this previous matter being understood, will it be morally right to do this act? And to *that* question he answers: the doer's doing will be moral just in case he
is minded to obey the Categorical Imperative in what he does.
The point is so simple as to be subtle: *What* is it that *ethics*
is supposed to teach? As a branch of study, what question or
questions does it address? His answer is, "The criterion of the
morally right." Our suggested answer is: "What the application
of this criterion dictates in various types of cases." He says:
"There is only one required principle of morals." What we
have been saying suggests: That isn't enough to make a branch
of study out of." Some third party may observe, "Why not
both: ethics seeks to elicit the basic principle of the moral and
paradigms of its application to specific and typical moral problems." We capitulate: that as a matter of fact is what is to be
taught to any who need to learn ethics—both the criterion and
paradigms of typical application. But neither of these requirements is satisfied, nor their associated questions addressed, by
answering the question, "Am I motivated in what I intend to
do by the will to do whatever is dictated by the moral law?"
Supposing I do not know what the moral law is—then I shall
not know what I am talking about; and supposing I do know
it—then it is not a question, unless for someone in need of psy-
chiatric help. Perhaps many need such help in identifying what
really moves them in their deliberate acts, but, in that case,
no study of ethics will meet the problem. The examination of
motives, in any sense which Kant intends, will answer *no* question, unless the question, "What sort of man am I, moral or
immoral?" The question of ethics is, "What should a moral
man *do?*" And, as we now admit, that has two parts, the identification of the moral criterion and its correct applications. But
neither of these is the question, "What moves me to do what I
do?" If I don't know the answer to that, in any given instance,
no study of ethics will help me. And if it is someone else who

asks this question about my motivation, the study of ethics will not help him either. Ethics applies to overt acts, such as affect what may happen to others. The application of ethics includes, as one type of problem, what it is morally justified to do to others in virtue of what *they* do, and to answer that particular kind of moral question, we shall have to guess at the motivations of their conduct. Ethics can answer it "in principle," supposing our guesses already determined. It is just such principles of a specific sort which ethics is supposed to provide, pertinent to a real question of justice, and an acute one as it happens. What this principle should be is obvious: we should govern what we do to others as a matter of retributive justice by reference to what they intend to do, rather than by reference merely to what they bring about. We shall, in this kind of case, deal justly if and only if we judge their acts as *subjectively* right or wrong for them to do, whether *they thought* them right to do, and intended or did not intend to do what is morally right. But it is in point that *if* they *thought* them to be morally right, *they thought* them to be *objectively right*. Even they were not thinking about their own motivations; they were thinking about what they proposed to bring about, and if they are in fact blameless, then presumably they thought wrongly because they are a bit stupid. It is *nobody's* moral problem what his own motivations are. The only problem concerns what he deliberately intends to bring about, the justifiability or nonjustifiability of doing that. Always and for everybody the question of morals is whether what he expects to bring about is or is not justified to bring about. When what he so expects to effect is reward or punishment of another for what that other has done, it is a material question what moved that other person to do what he did. But he can sensibly ask that kind of question about himself, expecting to get any answer, only by substituting for the question "What should I do now?" a different question, a different problem, that of examining his own active attitudes in depth. Commendably he may thus discover what makes him be that way, but that won't answer any present question, "What ought I now to do?"

It must appear that Kant has substituted for this question of ethics—"What ought I, and other men in my circumstances, to do?"—the different question, "What would the ideally just judge do to me for it, if I do what I now contemplate doing?" Kant appears to be preoccupied, in certain parts of his discussion at least, with the question of the moral merit and demerit of doers. That is a question of their intending to do what they *think* is right—the question of the subjective rightness of their doing, leaving aside the rightness or wrongness of their thinking. But no doer engaged with the question "What will it be right for me to do?" will find any answer to it by asking himself "If I do this, will I be doing it because I think it right?" unless he already knows whether he thinks it right or not, and *that* thinking is exactly the thinking he is trying now to do. He can't answer his question of his own motivation as a right motivation until he knows what he is thinking of doing as well as whether he thinks doing it is right in some sense in which the rightness of it is determinable on some other ground than the ground of this conclusion he is now trying to reach. He is now engaged in trying to think about *something* which is a fact independent of what he thinks about it; otherwise there would be no question for him to think about, with any expectation of finding out anything about it. He who thinks his contemplated act right to do thinks it right to bring about the consequences he foresees as the probable result of his doing—thinks that his act is objectively right. And if there be no determinable answer to the question of the objective rightness of doing—the rightness of *bringing about* what the doer intends and expects—there would be no genuine and answerable question of any kind under the label of ethics. Such an objective rightness is what any doer ascribes to his contemplated act when he *thinks* it right. His *ascription* of such rightness may be subjective, and not well judged, but that is what he *judges*. And that is what any ethics attempts to provide principles for the judgment *of*. *Amongst* such judgments there is the special class which concerns the rightness or wrongness of acts of retributive justice, a form of justice applied to others on the basis of what they do, a form of justice concerned with what it is objectively right to do to others in virtue of what these others do affecting the rest of us. And the objective rightness of retributive justice turns upon what those who are so rewarded or punished *intended* to do and whether they *thought* what they intended to be *objectively* right acts or not. That is, the moral rightness of retributive justice is the objective rightness of governing our retributive acts by reference to the *subjective* rightness of this doing of others for which they are to receive reward or punishment at our hands. Otherwise than in that way, the question of the subjective rightness of doing is not a question of moral rightness at all.

It may be correctly enough said that what is *judged* in judging that the act in question is objectively right to do is whether it is *absolutely* right to do. We judge whether it is or is not—on our supposition that the goodness to *be* judged is the good of all to be affected by it, in measure as they are so affected—that act open to us which will do the most good and the least harm to all. And that is what we here label "the absolute goodness of the act." But the point is that the best that the doer can do in so judging is to make the prediction on the basis of all the relevant evidence available to him at the time of the doing. And if he *cogently* so judges it, then, whether his prediction is *true or not*, the act *is* objectively right for him to do. In other words, if this judgment of *its* absolute rightness—of the goodness of the consequences—is *valid*, though perhaps not *true*, then the act is *objectively right* for him to do.

The word 'valid' here means what it means in logic. A conclusion is valid if it is correctly (cogently) drawn from the premises of it. And in such cases as we have to consider here, the premises are the relevant evidence available as the basis for this conclusion in question. A conclusion correctly drawn from the premises is *valid whether it is true or not.*

We here come as close as possible to delineating the meaning of "Act *A* is morally right to do"—unless or until we reexamine our provisional supposition as to what manner of goodness of the consequences of acts it is which is determinative of their moral rightness. Moral rightness is the objective rightness of the decision to do the act in question. That holds even when it is the subjective rightness of the act of another (or our own past act) which requires to be assessed. The subjective rightness of an act is to be assessed on the basis simply of what the doer of the act *thought* it right to do, whether his so thinking is a cogent conclusion or not. But such a judgment of the merely subjective rightness of the doing is not pertinent to the doer's own decision at the time when he decides. When any doer *thinks* his contemplated act right to do he *thinks* it is *objectively* right for him to do. His act *is* objectively right to do if and only if his *thinking* is cogent. He may *think* it cogent when it isn't. But one who deliberately decides an act is responsible for his deliberation—as well as for his commitment, taken in the light of it. He is responsible for being cogent in predicting the consequences of his act decided—if he *can* be cogent. (Nobody has a responsibility to do what he can't.) One may, by reason of his incompetence as a thinker, think his act objectively right when it isn't. But that is what he *thinks,* when he thinks it right to do; namely, he *thinks* it is objectively right. When a doer thinks his act to be objectively right, but it is not in fact objectively right, because his thinking is incogent, it is still subjectively right. We who observe another's deliberate doing (or reflectively examine our own past doing) may find this doing to be, or to have been, subjectively right doing. And in any act of *ours* which is retributive to the doer for what he did—our assigning of merit or demerit, praise or blame, reward or punishment—we should govern *our* such retributive doing by reference to the *subjective* rightness of the act on account of which this retributive action of *ours* is taken. *Our* judgment of *our own* doing must be made in the mode of *objective* rightness. Anybody's assessment of his own doing at the time of the decision to do requires to be a judgment of its *objective* rightness, in order to be a determination of its moral rightness. In the particular case of assigning merit or demerit to some other act than our own presently decided doing, we need to determine the subjective rightness of that other act, which is not the one we ourselves now decide to do or not to do. For any and every present moral deciding of our own action, the question is of the objective rightness of this contemplated act. It will be right to do if and only if it is objectively right to do—if and only if the consequences of it, as cogently predicted on the evidence now open to us, are good in that particular sense which is correlative with moral rightness—in the sense that it will, supposedly, be good for all whom it predictably will affect and as it will predictably affect them.

In conclusion, let us observe that one distinctive feature of the Kantian ethics is that Kant conceives that the distinction between right and wrong doing turns upon what we have here called the subjective rightness of the doing, on the motive—that which consciously moves us to do, the "reason why" we do what we do. The "reason why" of any particular act can be expressed as a maxim, and it is the justification of acting on this maxim which is to be assessed by the Categorical Imperative. He fails to remark the parallel fact that there is only one such basic principle of prudence likewise, "So act that you will thereby achieve the maximum possible betterment of your own life in the future." We could draw the same distinction between objectively right and subjectively right in the case of prudentially justifiable, prudentially right doing. There is only one prudential motive of doing, as there is only one moral motive of doing. But should we take it that it is this prudential motive only which marks the distinction between *prudent* doing and *imprudent* doing? In a sense, yes; it is this doing by reference to the expectation of prudential goodness, "good-for-me-ness," which reveals to us most clearly what counts with this doer, his character as a doer, and what we must with best assurance expect him to do on other occasions. But would any prudent father, wishing his son to follow in his footsteps, be satisfied that he had trained him to respond reliably to the expectation of good for himself, and that only? Presumably he would be also concerned with educating him to discern where his own best interests lay, and in so acting that the realization of them would be furthered by chosen ways of doing. A successfully prudent person must be discerning in predicting the consequences of what he does as actually contributory to his realization of his own good in the future. The prudential motive by itself is an insufficient guarantee of the realization of the prudent aim. "The best laid schemes o' mice an' men gang aft a-gley." Even the most prudent minded of men do not always achieve the aim of prudence. Absolutely prudent acts are those which absolutely do lead to the realization of the aim of prudence. Objectively prudent acts are those which it is justified to believe, on all the evidence available at the time of the doing, will lead to the realization of the prudential aim. Subjectively prudent acts are those the doer *thinks,* whether cogently or not, will achieve the aim of prudence.

It is an anomaly that Kant, who conceived the morally right to be rooted in reason and definable as the rationally justified to do, should have failed to mention explicitly the function of our rationality in determining what the consequences of our commitments of doing will in fact be. An intending to do is not rational if the expectation of what will be so done is not a rationally justified expectation.

It is a part of prudence to weigh what actually will follow on all the available evidence, as well as to weigh the first-person value of what is so expected. To be motivated by the anticipation of first-person value is the prudential motivation. It is imprudent *not* to weigh the matter of what the consequences will be, as well as weighing whether or not they will satisfy the aim of prudence. And we may say equally that it is immoral not to weigh the matter of what the consequences of the act will be, as well as weighing whether or not they will satisfy the aim of morals.

But what is the aim of morally right acts? According to Kant this aim is simply to be morally motivated: To do whatever you do because it is morally right. But what *is* it morally justified to bring about? Kant *does* give the criterion for determining that: Whatever you could will that any man in just your present case should choose to do. But what *could* you so will that any man in your case do, and why? To that, he gives no answer. That is the so-called emptiness of the Categorical Imperative. Bentham says, for example, "I could will that any man, in any case, should will whatever will contribute most to his own welfare and happiness: I don't believe in fact that any of us *can* will anything different from that." Kant would be obliged to reply to Bentham: "Then it is morally right for you to aim to do whatever will make you personally happiest." As a fact Kant does not conceive that Bentham's "psychological egoism" is an implication of the Categorical Imperative. We may guess that if he had read what Bentham later wrote, he would have thought Bentham self-deceived in his supposition that if all men *intelligently* followed their own best interest, it would lead to a high and desirable type of social order. He tended to agree with Hobbes, rather, about the consequences of universal egoism.

But in leaving it entirely open for each of us to decide what ways of doing, what maxims of conduct, we could will to be universally followed, how did he expect that *we* should decide that matter? He can only reply, perhaps, "According to your own expectation of what would be the social state of affairs if your maxim were thus universally adopted." And what will be our ground for a final decision, having *so* envisaged this resultant social state of affairs? His answer is, "If you could will that to be brought about." And what does he think we should, any of us who are in question, so decide what such social order we could be content to see come about? Is there any other possible ground for that last and decisive matter except that we should expect to find that social order good, one in which we should be happy to live, one in which we would be happy to take part? Our own utopia is Kant's last appeal in this matter; it is that in terms of which we must decide what it is morally right to do. He called it "The Kingdom of God on Earth," in his *Religion Within the Bounds of Reason Alone*. In it everyone would be morally minded, and that plainly would be essential in a society Kant would be pleased to live in. But plainly he did not think of it as a society of morally minded simpletons who could never bring off any project they set themselves to bring about. There is small ground, for any familiar with his writings, to suppose that he suffered fools gladly. He even turned away from his door the youthful Fichte with the project of his *Versuch einer Kritik aller Offenbarung*. (And if the publication of that work with the author's name omitted from the title page, giving rise to the common surmise that it was by Kant, gave Fichte his first great step up, it was romantic justice.) On what other ground than some prospective goodness could anybody rationally will anything to come about! Kant must finally appeal to some prospective goodness as the sanction of right doing. That is the only ground on which the "emptiness" of the Categorical Imperative can get any "filling," and dictate one way of acting rather than another, or any maxim of conduct.

ESSAY 9

We Approach the Normative Finalities

EDITOR'S NOTE: The text I have used for this portion of the "Essays" was written in the late summer and then the fall of 1963. It is the longest consecutively numbered text in the papers. On the other hand, despite the consecutive numbering, it contains, perhaps surprisingly, some disparate shifts in perspective and subject matter. These shifts, of course, have common relevancies to the project. I have referred to them, for better or worse, as "phases."

Phase I

The final surd of ethical theory is doubtless the question of any sanction for the subordination of what may finally appear to us as our own individual best good to the best good of all whom our action may affect. That aim, as we may be minded to think, is the peculiarly significant dictate of ethics, and one who does not reach to it but satisfies himself with egoism has abandoned instead of having achieved any final insight into ethics.

But even an egoist, like Bentham, must have his peculiar conviction of an ideal state of affairs—that which would come

176

down from Heaven, and be achieved on earth, if all of us should fully subscribe to, and conform to, the ethics he advocates. As Bentham strongly suggests, if he does not explicitly so put it, there would come about a social state of affairs with which every moral man could be completely satisfied, and in which he might find his Heaven on earth, if only his own, Bentham's, moral dictate should become that law of the land to which everyone unexceptionably conformed. What Bentham would point to as the pervasively besetting obstacle to the realization of this ideal is the failure of so many of us, so much of the time, and all of us some of the time, to understand what is to our own best good. And if he still envisages that each of us, doing what should truly be for his own best good, would still, on occasion be doing something which was *not* to the greatest possible good of all of us together, then at least he would be perfectly content to have it that way, neither expecting nor wishing that any other should make any final sacrifice to the good of J. Bentham. That—he surely conceives—would be the best of all possible societies to live in, even if not quite the best of all possible worlds. The morally ideal being attained, who would have it otherwise! Who would want anything in this Moral Heaven to be otherwise! And that being so, who is it who would find himself better satisfied if another should be deprived of even one stick of candy in order that this should fall into his possession instead! There being less candy in the world than amounts of all the candy anybody could want, he might be better satisfied to have one more piece, but would he be better satisfied to have it at the expense of another who should possess it morally, having come by it through clear-sighted pursuit of his own best interest, acting in that way in which everybody morally should? Anyone who could wish a redistribution of the social wealth in his own favor but in contravention of the moral ideal to which he is committed must be some queer sort of beastie, hardly to be called a moral man. Gratification with this departure from the moral dictate threatens to impugn the rationality of him who could so be made happy. And the mere mention of the possibility of this kind of anomaly, within a society which should achieve the Benthamite ideal, must—curiously—draw attention to that same kind of ambivalence in human nature which those moral theorists of the type most opposite to Bentham are wont to mention, the ambivalence between the "natural man," and his "natural desires" and "natural inclinations," and "moral man" or—in Benthamite terms—"completely rational man" and what he could be satisfied to have attained. It may be natural to be gratified with what you come by through a departure from what you morally approve, but can it be moral or rational to be so gratified? Even for an egoist, or egotist? It may be rationally gratifying to enjoy what you come by through some violation of what you acknowledge as the justified state of affairs, in which everyone conforms to your own accepted principles, but can it be ideally rational, to be glad that this principle has been breached in your favor? The possibility of being glad on one account but sorry on the other is just that ambivalence of human wanting "to-be-so" which the moral Salvationists would emphasize, whether they be rationalists or perfectionists. Which do you want more—or "more deeply"— the gratification of your sensuous drives and feelings or the satisfaction of your rational and moral ideal in your own case? The answer "Both" is ruled out wherever there can be any disparity of the two. And even the moral egoist, who accords to all others whatever privileges he conceives to be rightly his own, cannot quite escape from this ambivalence with respect to "his own best good." We want what we want when we want it, and we also and pervasively want to be in accord with whatever is our own insight of the right, and to move toward the realization, in all factuality and in our own case, of what will satisfy whatever principles we accept as right to follow. And whoever does not recognize any principles as right to follow could only be an angel or a fool. He absolves himself of any necessity for deliberate decision, of any and of every kind—including his decision to give heed to no principle of thought or action. It is just by the self-contradiction of a commitment to *that* manner of decision that we find ourselves in the predicament of the self-conscious animal. We can breach our recognition of the right but cannot repudiate it.

It is also characteristic of any egoist who should not repudiate his character as a social animal to include within his egoistic gratifications some which arise from empathic feeling—greatly in the case of some others, a little in the case of any fellow, or even any, recognized as such, conscious creature. To find some good in the satisfaction of another, and in our own contribution to it, is "natural" to any human and does not require the sanction of our "higher" or "rational" nature, or that of "conformity to our principles," in order to be felt. Bentham, as well as Hume, obviously takes pleasure in pointing out that such satisfactions naturally found in the good of others still fall within the scope of the egoistically justified. If one should put a penny in the beggar's hat, how else might one purchase so large a satisfaction by so small an expenditure! And if there be those who are naturally mean, how many of the possible pleasures of life they must miss by reason of it!

On the other side of things, the perfectionists simply capitalize on these two characteristics of our human nature, in particular, on the recognition that the pervasive and abiding satisfactions are those "higher" gratifications deriving from the self-satisfaction to be found when we are in accord with what we recognize, by our own insight, as the principles of right, in those decisions which are ours to make, and in those commitments of thinking and doing our responsibility for which is unavoidable. And even Kant, who can hardly be classed as a perfectionist, has left that passage in which he ponders whether *Selbstzufriedenheit* is not the *Seligkeit* which is the best of all possible goods in human life. The self-realizationist but emphasizes this. The satisfactions to be attained in virtue of the accord of one's practice with one's own insight of the right is a gratification outweighing any others, and there is no greater good to which any man could aspire, or which he could achieve.

Even the Stoic offers a variant on this kind of thought, though Stoicism must perhaps impress us as advancing its ideal of complete self-control *faute de mieux*. Life at best is a fairly nasty business, and your best hope for peace is to disengage yourself from petty hopes for childish pleasures. "Take away thy thought 'I have been harmed,' and the harm is done away." Our reaction to that is likely to be that that ideal is more lofty than we can measure up to: we doubt that if we were to die on the rack, we should be able to say, "How sweet."

And even in the case of the perfectionist, we may have our doubts that he is not already out of this world and describing a Heaven he aspires to rather than the earthly life either he or we can live. We do not ourselves expect to become so saintly— even in terms of rationality. There will be times when we would rather have ham and eggs than any satisfaction of our integrity, or a drink of water than any gratification in the complete justification, on the evidence we had, that this road was the right one for us to take. Offer us enough, and—we hate to say it but the truth must be told—we expect to be able to drown the thought that, if perfect justice had prevailed, it might have favored some other. The perfectionist has a little too good an opinion of us and what we can be happy about, and we have just a minim of doubt whether he does not think a little too well of himself. In any case, we have no illusion that the great body of humanity will ever rise to his level. When the fires of life grow dim, the old man may have nothing left to give any gratification stronger than *Selbstzufriedenheit,* but expecting the teenagers to buy that is overly optimistic: they are having too much fun. Rating the goods of integrity too low is indeed the commoner fault in these matters, but it is possible to rate the sensuous satisfactions too low, as well, and to take too little into consideration the evils of circumstance; it is possible to give such things too little of their due, and thereby to go beyond truth, to miss the truth, in these matters; such things, the realities of life, are important when we attempt to consider, or work out, the best life one could live in this vale of tears.

But, all things considered, putting aside Bentham and the perfectionists, we must commit ourselves to Kant's more characteristic conviction: adhering to one's own insight of the right *does* sometimes involve the sacrifice of our own best good in this world, as it is given us to judge of that. And the sanction of such moral sacrifices is precisely the obscurest point in ethical theory.

Or perhaps we should not too precipitately commit ourselves to that. It could be that there is some, and possibly an equal, obscurity with respect to each and every imperative of the normative. It may be that it is only in this case of the moral that our attention is likely to be drawn to this question of any ground of the imperative commonly acknowledged as valid, and the basis of validity in any sense. Perhaps we should examine the other outstanding imperatives—the prudential and the logical—with respect to any ground of them capable of discernment.

Let us begin with the logical—with deductive logic. The paradigms of logic stand as imperatives for our believing. It is true, of course, that these paradigms are not commonly formulated in the imperative mood, and also that it has become customary with many of those who presently discuss logic to regard reading these paradigms in the imperative as a kind of fault, a misinterpretation of what they say. But all will admit that they are to be classed as analytic statements, as tautologies. And it is a distinguishing character of an analytic statement that its denial (its contradictory) is *self*-contradictory, a statement which is self-inconsistent, knowably false regardless of any premise, or any other information. No statement which fails to have this character—that "to deny it is to reaffirm it"—because its denial, being self-contradictory, implies this statement itself—can be contentual to deductive logic. This character of being contradictable only by a statement contradictory to itself is the necessary and sufficient condition of being logically certifiable, certifiable without premises. And every paradigm of deductive logic has this character of the undeniable *per se* because to deny it is to imply it, implicitly to reassert it.

It can be said—and correctly, when what is so said is correctly understood—that deductive logic presupposes itself, because any deductive inferring presumes the distinction of valid inferring from asserting in the conclusion what does not logically follow from the asserted or assumed premises, and any *proof* that a paradigm considered has this character of being inferable from its own contradictory will require to draw this conclusion, itself, from this premise, its contradictory, *in accord with*, "by authority of," a principle or principles which themselves belong to logic. One cannot *prove* any principle of the logical without some use of, or reference to, or presumption of, *rules of proving*, which are themselves valid principles, formulatable as paradigms of logic.

It is thus true that you cannot prove basic logical rules without at least implicitly assuming them. But of the whole body of the valid rules of deductive logic, too, in the only sense in which such a whole body of such rules can be spoken of, there can be no such *proof,* too, without assuming some of them as *rules of valid deduction.* This kind of "circularity" in logic is unavoidable, but unavoidable precisely in the sense that there can be no deductive proof except by the tacit or explicit assumption of *rules of valid proving.* Even taken as a whole then, logic could have no significance if deprived of its "rule significance," and, too, we note, pushing the whole business of rules "upstairs" into "metalogic" does not alter the significance of the paradigms as *rules* of inference either. It is imperative *not* to contradict yourself, explicitly or implicitly; one must preserve consistency at least; hence, one must *not* commit oneself to what implicitly denies what it explicitly asserts. "Do not believe, or even take seriously as hypothesis, what contravenes itself by requiring that if it be true it must also be false."

What a statement implies is what it intensionally means. And one statement, *p,* so implies another, *q,* when and only when "*p*-true-but-*q*-false" is impossible, in the sense that the negation of *it* is "logically necessary," analytic.

Having now located this "root significance" of the paradigms of deductive logic—as consisting in the adjuration not to contradict yourself—let us ask what is the *ground* of this imperative.

We might say, parenthetically, to digress for a moment, that it also adjures us to *accept* the analytic, but that is stretching the facts a little. Logic provides no hortation to think of everything—or of anything in particular—the statement of which would be analytic. The central, or principal, imperative here is not to *deny* the analytic; that is crucial; to be sure, if one encounters the analytic, if the question arises, one must accept it; this is because its *denial* implies it; illustratively, as the disjunction of any statement with its negation is a logical truth, the disjunction exhausting all possibilities, the negation of such a disjunction, specifying an impossible state of affairs, must be a logical falsehood. One must thus accept the analytic, just as one must reject the contradictory. Being consistent is merely avoiding any and all self-contradictions, explicit or implicit. "Be consistent."—that, if it be understood what it requires, expresses precisely the logical imperative.

But why should we *be* consistent?

Why is that *imperative* if we be otherwise inclined—as, in some sense difficult to describe, we sometimes are? Or should we say that, squarely facing the alternative 'p or not-p', where 'not-p' implies 'p', we *cannot* repudiate any statement, 'p', such that 'not-p' implies it? If this kind of possible situation fails to have any bite, let us think of the Pythagoreans, committed to the thesis that numbers and ratio lie at the root of all that is, and the metaphysical understanding of all reality, when they discovered that if there be any fraction m/n which is the length of the hypotenuse of a right-angled triangle, this number, on *any* scale of measure, would have to be both odd and even. Their *rationality,* and the rationality of the universe, was at stake. But mathematicians, up to Dedekind, fobbed off this question with a phrase, "irrational number"—without any clear idea what they meant by it. Many of them today have no clear idea what they mean by 'implies', consistent with their usage, though implications are the things they deal with. Consistency is a tough business. And a trained intuition is not good enough.

But why, in our everyday attempts to think straight and to know, be regardful of consistency and alert to avoid any inconsistency? Is it because the human animal must live by his beliefs, and act in the light of what he thinks to be the case? And for such thinking, he requires a "reason," something in the way of premises? Excepting only analytic statements, assurable by the impossibility of what the denial of them would intend, he lives by his expectancies, the grounds of which he thinks to have assurance of already. He has good reason, if not an absolute assurance that p is the case. He now observes that "p but not q" is impossible, the very thought of it impugns it as out of the question. So q must be at least as assurable as his premise p. So he believes q likewise: it is as well assured as p at least. Expecting the impossible, or being afraid that it may happen, is silly. He has outgrown such infantile expectings. He *must* live his life and sometimes decide what he will do by this kind of critique: p is fairly sure; p but not q is impossible; therefore q is also fairly sure—at least as well assured as p. The step from p to q is that part of the matter which simply could not be otherwise.

That is the part which can be beyond all doubt, and is *logically* assurable. That step calls for the logical critique only. That part of it is what we can assure concerning any expectation of finding q true. But to leave that part of it unexamined, to ignore the logical critique, is unnecessarily hazardous. To do that would mean to proceed on groundless expectations; it would be no better than deciding what to do as fancy dictates, or by tossing a penny. And he who so lives—so, we feel sure—might as well say, "Here I am, Luck, now what are you going to do to me?" (If I fail to put this well, let the reader put it better.) The point is that being the kind of creatures that we are, obliged by our endowment to sometimes decide our acts, and bent upon the accrual of this rather than that in consequence of what we do, we have no practical alternative but to decide so as to avoid expecting the impossible, since to do otherwise would be no different, in effect, than abandoning ourselves to whatever may happen to us, with no anticipation whatever. (That this story calls for a more complex manner of telling, we shall all recognize. We attempt only to tell this little bit of it as truly as words can tell it.)

To ignore the imperative 'Be consistent in your thinking and belief' is to abandon all attempts at self-direction in life, in our believing and our concluding, and consequently in our doing. So to live would be simply idiotic—which is merely calling names but is literally and exactly the right name to call it. Being constituted as we are and human life being what it is, we simply "cannot" do that. The logical imperative is built in: we can contravene it, by mistake, if not deliberately, but we "cannot" repudiate it without repudiating the human vocation of partial self-control to which we are born. If something like this is not the validation of the logical imperative, then, we suggest, there is none. But he who pretends to repudiate the imperative to be consistent will show himself an idiot. We shall be charitable and believe that, like Epimenides, he really intends only to amuse. The appropriateness of attributing this imperative to our nature as self-governing and self-critical—rational—will be sufficiently evident. And let us note that to subordinate this imperative to any other, or to set it aside for any other, can have no excuse whatsoever, unless it be a confession of the loss of self-control in the face of an obsession of thinking and conviction. Not even the moral imperative can displace the imperative to avoid controverting the logical. Those who may appear to demand belief in the impossible in fact require only an admission of possibilities against which no *empirical evidence* may be sufficient to prove the impossibility. *Logical* impossibility is a very narrow thing. What is more frequently spoken of as "impossible" includes what would controvert empirical evidence we think we have—something we conclude from premises deriving from sense experience. And the transcendentalists characteristically rest their case upon the inadequacy of any empirical evidence to preclude the possibility of realities beyond the scope of any empirical investigation. That they still recognize the purely *logical* necessities as compelling is witnessed by their presentation of *arguments* which they believe must rationally constrain us to agree with them. Leave out the constraint to avoid self-contradiction and *no* argument could have any force whatever. Any who should refuse this constraint rules himself out from any forum whatever. He rules himself out even from the supposition that a transempirical revelation could have any *consequences*, either for believing or for conduct. Recognition of the logical imperative is the *sine qua non* for any significance of thinking and concluding altogether. The only alternative to the acknowledgment of the logical imperative is the admission of the complete and unexceptionable foolishness of any conviction at all—including *this* one, that of the universal idiocy of thinking. Any such universal skeptic of all validities would have dissolved the universe he consciously lives in into universal "blah"! And if he blat that out, the justified response might be, "So what? So nothing." The imperative to be consistent is not rationally or humanly repudiable, however often it may be contravened. We agree in advance with ourselves and with any to whom we would convey our thought—or with whom we can join in the consideration of anything—that if we be convicted of violating this imperative, we shall so far forth surrender our point, and recant our thinking. With any who should not tacitly, or otherwise, so agree, we can have no intellectual, and no human, fellowship, even though we may still commiserate with them in their miseries, as we may with other animals that suffer in virtue of their own unfortunate activity.

If considerations such as these—better and more fully spelled out perhaps—do not sanction and validate the logical imperative, what would it be that is called for, and could stand as the final ground in such matters, and the absence of which would allow skepticism with respect to such validity? And the trouble with any positive skepticism of the logical imperative is not merely that the assertion of such a skeptical conviction throws overboard what we cannot get on without; the decisive difficulty is that it says too much; if it were true, it would *declare itself* to be baseless nonsense—something nobody could possibly know to be true.

It is a temptation to pass by the matter of any imperative which grounds the rules of induction: that matter is not only complex but involves many points on which there could be doubt. We shall confine ourselves to two basically important points, and to statements which will not attempt precision, and, at best, must be left dogmatic, with the hope that they will be found suggestive, and that what they suggest will sufficiently indicate something which can hardly be gainsaid.

In the first place, we should be clear that nothing certifiable by the principles of deductive logic, or analytic, can be sufficient to assure any empirical and existential fact whatever, beyond the facts already pointed out, that whatever is actual is *ipso facto* possible, and that whatever is logically impossible cannot be actual. The contrary supposition that analytic truth assures *some* existential facts is common. But it is incorrect. Deductive logic can assure nothing beyond the necessary relations of our concepts, our principles of classification, explicable as the meanings we entertain and apply, formulatable as definitions.

One may, for example, say that 'All men are mortal' is true *a priori* by the fact that we should refuse to classify any being found not to be mortal as a man; and then, further, that this *a priori* and analytic diction implies that all existent men (the class of men) are (is) contained in the class of existent things which are mortal. Let us take 'All men are mortal' as true by our intent in using the terms 'man' and 'mortal'. The second locution, then, say, 'All existent men are contained in the class of existent things which are mortal', is also true. But neither of these locutions, nor both together, assures that there are any actual men or that there are any actual mortals. And neither do they assure that there are no men or are no mortals, or that there are no actual immortals that look and act like men and defy our powers to distinguish them from men. This analytic truth, or truths, here, assures only that if we discover any being to satisfy our concept "man," it will satisfy our concept "mortal," by reason of our classificatory intensions, those implicit in our application of the expressions 'man' and 'mortal'. And that if we discover any actuality to be immortal, that actuality, that actual thing, will *not* be a man, for the same reason, that of our classificatory intent. So long as our *concepts* "man" and "mortal" stand as they are, the actual universe may contain or not contain anything the most bizarre imagination can conjure up, but nothing so imagined could be a man but not mortal—if we stick to our usual concepts of "man" and "mortal." Furthermore, this *a priori* assurance of the relation between our two concepts—or any altered concepts we might choose to entertain—can in no wise determine that the concept "man" or the concept "mortal" applies to any particular actuality whatever. And it wholly precludes that we should first find out that our concept "man" applies to an actual and perceived thing, and be assured by this that the perceived thing is also mortal; *until* we have found out with certainty that this thing is mortal, we have not found out that it is a man, no matter how much we otherwise know about it.

In similar fashion and for wholly similar reasons, we never know with theoretic certainty that any of our concepts completely applies to any particular thing presented to us. Our application of any term to any thing is always subject to some theoretically possible doubt, *e.g.*, that what we presently see, on any occasion, is a man always implies *something* more which we do not presently and certainly assure by observation. Until *all* implications of being a man are verified, are actually satisfied by this object we observe, we are not certain that our concept "man" applies to it. Thus, knowing *a priori* that whatever

is a man is mortal does not certify for us in the case of any existent actuality in any particular instance that it is either a man
or mortal. Our knowing *a priori,* further, that every *actual* man
is an *actual* mortal is merely knowing that whatever thing we
observe is *not* a man *unless* it is mortal.

The point of this is not any absurd skepticism of common-
sense convictions: the point is that *we know no existential fact*
whatever without some *induction* which deductive logic alone
cannot assure. Only empirical premises, which are *not* analytic
statements, can assure, or even be a reason for believing, any
statement of existential fact whatever. Deductive logic, by itself,
can assure only that the logically impossible—the assertion of
which contradicts itself—does *not* exist, and is no actual fact.
Neither does inductive logic by itself assure any fact of existence or make it probable. Such assurances, or the attempt to
obtain such assurances, or to establish probabilities in such
cases, requires both premises of observation and concepts.
Conceptualization is presupposed; else observation would be
meaningless. In this sense, conception must be antecedent to
what we observe. There must be some classification, on some
level, even if at first it be primitive or elemental, of what we
observe. Is there a ground for this sort of classification? Certainly there is such a ground—it exists in the appearances of
sense experience, *e.g.,* if necessary, so simply as in observations
that this "looks blue," this "feels hard," this "looks the same
from every angle," as might a sphere, and so on.

The lower animals make inductions—without knowing
that that is what they do. If appearance *A* is regularly—or even
usually—accompanied by, or followed by, appearance *B,* the
occurrence of *A* "makes them think of *B,*" arouses the response
which *B* arouses, makes them feel as the appearance of *B* does.
Such associations of presentational elements and feelings is the
"conditioning" of animal behavior. Such conditioned response
is the basic law of all "thinking." That such conditioned
response is "adaptive," promotive of the animal's continued
existence is, of course, due to the way the world is. In reality,
some observable happenings are associated in existential fact.
Otherwise this fact of animal response by association would not
be "adaptive," would lead as often to "ill-fare" as to welfare,

to death as to the saving of life, to starvation as to nutrition, etc. This is no more, and no less, than the basic principle of probability: What has been associated in past experience will, more likely than not, be associated in future experience. That is the way the world is, and the way conscious creatures that succeed in living in the world are constituted. Otherwise creatures whose behavior is affected by their conscious experience would not continue to live in it. Or, at least, this effect of consciousness upon their behavior in it would have no effect with respect to promoting their continuing to live in it. This law, "What has been associated in past experience will with some probability be associated in future experience," expresses the indispensable condition for the persistence of conscious life in any world we can easily imagine. It could hardly be otherwise. At least we venture the dogmatic statement, that that is the way it is in this world in which we consciously live. And we cannot, further, imagine any world perceivable to conscious beings as we know them which could be otherwise.

Let us look at this same fact from another perspective, that of our own consciousness as we recognize it to be, *i.e.*, from the phenomenological perspective. In this world, as disclosed in our given experience, there are included trains of given appearances which repeat themselves, or repeat themselves with occasional variations. Otherwise we could find and recognize no *objects* disclosed in presentational experience. This law was stated by Berkeley as the condition of possible knowledge: One idea (presentation) is the sign of another which is to come. (He ascribed that to the goodness of God: we here ascribe it to the existence of a world of recognizable things. It is, in any case, the condition on which alone any manner of perceivable object could be recognized.) The true and adequate story is, of course, considerably more complex than this. But this is the root of the matter, and let us stick to this simplicity for the moment. Some presentational experience being given, there is some sequent and anticipatable further presentation which is likely to follow. Without that there could be no knowledge whatever. Without that there could be no actuality to be known, and nothing to be mistaken about. Without that, *Alles geht los*. The further complication, desirable to mention, though we must not here attempt to pursue it far, is that we can, by acts of will, intervene upon some trains of what is to come and alter what would otherwise be likely to ensue, *e.g.*, this thing looking like a cube will, if I walk around it, present a succession of different appearances; it will present a succession of different "looks," and in ways predictable by what I call the "laws of perspective." Such complex ways of anticipating, for example, expecting divergent appearances depending on the nature of our own activities, are essential to our possible doing—and also to our recognizing our own doing—essential to all that we can learn "by experiment," and to our distinction of "veridical perception" from "illusions of sense." But to revert to the simplicity which, by itself, is sufficient to our point, unless there be trains of observable circumstance in our experience in which what comes earlier is a more or less reliable sign of what is to come later, there could be no such thing as knowledge of anything and no such thing as acting with any reliable expectation. There being for us any object to know or any objective and apprehensible world of things, or any possibility of our behaving with the anticipation of a result, is completely dependent upon our being able to learn from experience that something, A, being presented, there is a predictability of something else, B, as likely to ensue. *Things* that exist, objects, are "coagulated clots in experience," trains of circumstance, observable to us, and predictable in their time-order. Recognizable happenings are merely such "coagulations," too, trains of circumstance in which detectable objects are involved. Indeed, within such a train of circumstance, a recognizable thing, as *experienced,* is a kind of recognizable order, the order of an unfolding experiential event, one having a recognizable pattern.[1]

One way of approaching this matter—the phenomenological—would be to attempt to trace the development of understanding—the emergence for us, in experience, from infancy on, of discovered predictabilities within the Jamesian "blooming, buzzing confusion" of the original chaos of

---

1. More accurately, it would be a multiplicity of such recognizable patterns correlated with one another in recognizedly "orderly" (reliably predictable) ways.

ongoing experience. We shall merely leave that for the reader to think about. That same kind of consideration may suggest the question of how far the emergence of predictable orderliness in experience is due to the "kind of minds" we have, and how far it is attributable to reality *an sich*. In this connection it may be well to remember that the residual and not further resoluble *disorder* of experience is our scrapbasket category of illusion, hallucination, and "mere chance." The "order" is the reality we cling to in experience, repudiating the nightmares and the hopelessly happenstantial, the unreal and the unintelligible which nevertheless continues to invade our apprehension, though largely meaningless. From that point of view the history of developing understanding is the history of the eliciting of predictable orderliness, which is the progressive human conquest of the unintelligible, or chaos, or the "intellectual construction," if you please, of an intelligible reality. But that leaves always some residuum of the not-yet understood, and therefore uncontrollable, areas of living experience, unfolding in its processes. The breakdown of this progressive conquest of the unintelligible or chaotic, the breakdown, if you wish, of this "intellectual construction procedure," in the face of given experience, is insanity.

As Charles Peirce has suggested to us, in various ways, the world has habits, and we have habits. Whether it is our habits in which this "order" is native, or the habits of the real world which provide the basis, the "original datum," in this matter, at least the one relates to the other, and there can be no cognitive emergences of a recognized cosmos, in contrast to a chaos, without the one communicating with, or deriving from, the other. As a final and farfetched puzzle, one can also ask, though perhaps not answer, this question: What is the chance that a world of chance should not, by chance, include enough strands of orderability to constitute an intelligible world, in its chaos of the apparent?

As we have seen, what is substantiable by induction cannot offer any theoretically demonstrable and complete certainty. Whatever the degree of its reliability, it remains always no better than theoretically probable. Let us state the root principle of inductive probability in a way which is naive but hardly could be incorrect: When any observable item, A, has been found to be associated with another such item, B, in a sufficient number of past observed instances, with a frequency represented by the fraction m/n, there arises a probability that further and not-yet-observed instances of A will be found to be associated with B with a frequency close to m/n.

Here then would be the associated basic rule: So act, when any hazard of action turns upon the association of what will be found, or is found, to be A being so associated with B, as would be desirable if this same measure of association, m/n, should hold of instances of A in general.[2]

Probable expectations are subject to another rule: Consider your expectation as determined by the basic rule to be the more reliable, the more trustworthy, the more extensive has been your collation of the past observed instances of A.[3]

We have formulated these matters of probable expectation as *rules,* imperatives. That we take to be their essential significance. They are the rules of rational thinking and behaving in matters in which decisions of thinking and of deliberate doing require to be made.

And now what is their sanction, their validation? Time out of mind, logicians have puzzled over this. And one observation, frequently made, is that we could regard the general reliability of induction as itself an inductive conclusion justified by our past experience at large. It proves to be a profitable way of making decisions. And John Stuart Mill did not draw back from the circularity of so concluding. But we suggest a more compelling consideration. The formulation of the procedure of inductive thinking is merely our self-conscious and self-critical

---

2. This rule is expressed in terms of the simple "straight line" projection of the future. We omit considering a further rule, namely, one expressible as follows: Whenever in your course of progressively observed instances of A, and your count of the instances of B associated with A, the *cumulative* count (m/n up to now) progressively alters in a certain manner, act upon the expectation that this mode of progressive alteration will continue. (That is, project your statistical curve of progressive determinations of m/n.)

3. There are other, further, rules of reliability. (See Chapter X, *An Analysis of Knowledge and Valuation.*)

formulation of those ways of learning from past experience by which alone we have ever learned anything recognizable as a fact of the world we live in. We are like Moliere's gentleman who discovered, to his surprise, that he had been speaking prose all his life. But that is what he had been doing, just the same. It is only by making inductions that we have come to recognize objective realities. And if it should ever occur to us that thinking inductively may provide no assurance of fact, the only test we could ever apply to the determination of that general suspicion would be the inductive test; the determination would either be corroborated by induction or would fail to be corroborated by induction. If we should wake up some morning beset by the obsessive conviction that we are not in fact lying in bed, with the sun shining in the window, and a floor beneath us to step out on, and so forth, what should we do in the light of this fear that induction has no validity, and all we have learned from experience to expect is simply without warrant? Humean skepticism is merely an idle dream which Hume enjoyed playing when not playing some more serious game, such as backgammon. The reason for accepting the validity of induction is that you have no alternative. There is no other kind of test you can even apply to any question of objective factuality. The inductive procedure is already implicit in those forms of animal behavior determined by association: they act as if they expected A and B to be associated in the future, as in their past experience. And Santayana calls our own thinking and behaving of that sort "animal faith," and suggests that humans cannot transcend it. The pragmatic question then is, "Why try, since you will only be playacting in making the attempt?" If this is all the "knowledge" of the world we live in which we can ever achieve, and this is the general way we come by it, the way we attempt to ascertain the facts of it, why not just recognize it, this "knowledge," as what alone we can ever claim as *knowledge,* and give up the game of playing God to ourselves, encouraging in ourselves some pretense of a divine humility, one which we can neither live up to nor act in the light of? Why not just say, "This is the only knowledge of their world humans can ever have, and these inductive principles are the only tests of its facts we can ever apply?"

There is something here which, with a good deal of liberty of interpretation, may remind us of Kant's "Deduction of the Categories"—except that Kant thought that it was synthetic judgments *a priori,* and not inductive concluding, which was required in order to elicit the justification of empirical knowledge. One major strain in his argument is that without this—in his case, the apparatus of categories, and such—we could have no "experience," and a careful consideration of his position suggests that by that word 'experience' he means the "experience-of-objects experience." And, as we have suggested, you could not find recognizable objects in experience, instead of merely the passing play of "phantasms" or a mere chaotic "stream of consciousness," without a "coming to expect on the basis of passing presentation," and your finding of such expectations to be generally indicative of (signs of) what is to come. In brief, without the habit of induction, you could not meet the passing show, and either think or act as humans do, and, indeed, cannot get out of doing. The only alternative is to throw in the sponge—and you can't even do that, unless in this same manner of "doing something with the expectation of something," as inductively indicated by your past experience. You have *no* alternative, certainly none with any shadow of what we call rationality. The philosopher who attempts anything serious in any other way should have it drawn to his attention that he is gracelessly attitudinizing, and his slip is showing. He is purposing to dismiss all purposes as not really significant.

Let us now turn to the prudential imperative.

The significance of the prudential imperative lies upon the face of it, and might well be regarded as the primordial imperative of life at large. When self-conscious, it is the root significance of rationality. So considered, what rationality signifies is—for one thing—a present concern for the future. Consciousness is as the firing line of life, and its battle is for its own perseveration, its self-projection into the future. Activity *ipso facto* is directed to the future. The future is that which alone can be affected; the past is but the reverberation of dead fact, important only as we can learn from it something about the possible future. Active concern for the past would be a kind of absurdity but concern for the future is the vital impulse, and the lack of it is a kind of absurdity. Any self-consciousness of living is, by its intrinsic nature, the felt imperativeness of activity directed toward a future to be realized and to be affected. Concern to affect the future is the essence of living; to lack such concern is to be dead. The animal consciousness *feels* this vital impulse of self-direction and acts it out, but without self-awareness. The awareness of it as being one's living self is the spark of rationality. We consciously live in the conscious intention to become, to realize in living what we desire and what we intend.

The other animals—we may suppose—though perhaps with some degree of error in the case of those nearest to us in endowment—have their wishful and their apprehensive *feelings,* but lack explicit foresight. Emotive drive or felt urge is the animal sense of the imperative, and they fatally do as they are so inclined. The objective of that drive or urge is just in front of their noses, within their range of immediate apprehension. To do as they feel impelled satisfies it, if it is satisfiable by anything that they can bring about.

It may be that we are prone to exaggerate our difference from other animals. Our own drives and impulses remain with us as similar felt urges, and we are natively inclined to respond to them automatically, and in similar fashion. But that deeper penetration of the future which gradually develops with human maturation brings about a felt hiatus between our felt impulses and inhibitions and the projected apprehensions of more complex trains of association. We apprehend matters "more objectively," with some detachment from *felt* concern. We pause to think upon what is to come. This anticipated future, relatively, lacks the felt urgency of emotive drive. The "thought anticipated," that which is anticipated in thought, lacks the vividness and driving impetus of immediacy and the emotive urge. To substitute a response to the "thought anticipated," to that which is anticipated in thought, for the impulsive drive, we must "move ourselves," must reinforce this apprehension of what lies beyond the horizon of immediate feeling and fails to evoke a response automatically. The human will and cognitive apprehension dawn together, and are two sides of the same thing. To govern ourselves is to subordinate emotive feeling to cognitive foresight, and to behave ourselves as intelligence directs. This capacity for self-government, possible to the human, is, at one and the same time, what we call our rationality, and the root distinction of human conduct from animal behavior, as commonly conceived. And it is correlative with the distinction between the recognized *imperativeness* of response to the cognitively discerned future and the not-self-governed doing of what we feel like doing, characteristic of that manner of response to stimuli which is common to ourselves and the lower animals. The root dictate of this rational imperative may be stated: So behave yourself as you would if the intelligently foreseen consequences of your doing were to be as vividly felt now as they will be when they become realized in your immediate experience. In other words, so govern yourself as to do now what you will later be satisfied to have done, instead of that which you now feel like doing but will later be sorry for having brought about or having allowed to happen.

Those who could commit themselves to emotivism or noncognitivism in ethics would appear to be better versed in animal behavior than human behavior, so much so that it might appear that they are insufficiently aware of the differences between animal and human behavior, and that they fail to recognize the difference, or superiority, of the human mentality; it seems, too, that they take too dim a view of their own intelligence, and too dim a view of the human will. They do not, we feel sure, present their own argument at the behest of an emotive drive merely, or merely say what they feel like saying, oblivious of the consequences. They have not—so we are convinced—sufficiently taken note of the grounds on which human self-approval is at least meant to be determined and taken to be justified. Or perhaps we overlook the source of their apparent shortsightedness: they are themselves already too cultivated in their feelings, and too intellectually well governed to be aware of those animal propensities and the solicitations of crude impulse which others of us have to set our wills against in order to win our own self-approval.

Concern for oneself tomorrow, and concern for another, have something in common; both are concern immediately felt for what is not immediate. We project, and believe in as actual, this self tomorrow, and we similarly believe in that other self today, and tomorrow, which likewise is not immediate, and in this case can never be so. Both concerns are, so to say, empathetic feeling for an absent self and, perhaps in the case of another, as for ourself in the future, a self which our present doing may affect.

Psychologically perhaps, the capacity for prudential concern is a prerequisite for any moral concern, sympathy for oneself a prerequisite for any sympathy for another. That might be suggested by the fact that certain hardy souls who sternly repress any self-commiseration are likely to refuse to be moved by sympathetic feeling for others. (Children in upcountry New England sometimes learn to appeal from Mother to Grandma, who has outgrown some of her responsibilities and allows herself to commiserate, retrospectively, with her own childhood.) But for us, in any case, the intent of any rational self-government has the character not of an emotive inclination—or not that merely—but of a recognized imperative.

To identify this imperative, as we have here spoken of it, with the prudential, would be overly simple. For one thing, we here come in sight of an ambivalence in human nature which has been for so long a cliché with moralists that to revive an observation of it smacks of the stale and the sententious. Our better selves want what we want when we want it, but we also want what we shall later be satisfied to have wanted and committed ourselves to. The animal—so we imagine—suffers no such schizophrenia by reason of which men may speak of "their better selves": he does what he wants to do when he wants to do it, and meets the sequel with no backward glance of self-recrimination. His foresight exists only in his immediate inhibitory feeling, induced by past experience but now moving him only as immediate feeling, immediately pressed upon him, and only so far as it overrides, in the now-felt force of it, any contrary impulse. Cognitive foreseeing, comparatively, lacks any such sufficiently impelling force. The cognitively anticipated has its own qualifying and perhaps deterrent force as feeling, but as premonitory feeling it does not measure up in strength to that of felt immediacy. And, in general, the further off this anticipated future eventuality, the less the force of it as anticipatorily felt now. Insofar as it is this fact which is in question, this is characteristic of the rational imperative as prudential. What marks the rational imperative as *imperative,* what calls attention to its imperativeness, as opposed to some experienced impulsive coerciveness, is just this failure of the cognitively foreseen to be as automatically moving as the presently felt; and the more remote the anticipated future eventuality is from the present, the greater this disparity between the rationally recognized to be done and the immediately felt to be done. The failure of prudence consists in the sacrifice of the future to the present, or the more remote to the nearer.

In common-sense terms, the sanction of prudence is obvious: you will be sorry if you do that, or if you don't do this now. And this avoidance, or disposition to avoidance, of the future regrettable or dismaying is "built in." This concern for the avoidance of the future regrettable or dismaying, either as animal automatic inhibition or self-admonitory prohibition by intelligent foresight, is of the essence of being an active creature. Without it, in one or the other form, even if only in a form so simple as that of the arrest or redirection of movement by premonitory animalistic inhibitory feeling, there would be no effect of consciousness on a creature's behavior; and for ourselves, a rational creature, a creature having some capacity for significant self-direction by reference to its conscious processes, it stands as the indispensable root "reason" for the alteration of what we do on account of what we think, and expect. Without concern for the future, no decision or determination to act would be meaningful. It is the future only which action may affect. If some incurable "question asker" ask, "But *why* should I be concerned for the future, if that runs counter to my inclination?," the only answer having any point must be: "But why should you do anything? Why not just go jump in the lake?" To resign one's concern for the future would be to resign the privilege of doing by deciding. And we "cannot" so *decide,* unless by the completest of all confusions of mind. There would be a kind of contradiction in any such repudiation of active concern, a kind which we shall call "pragmatic contradiction." And the nature of it will bear examination, since it is a little different from a purely logical contradiction.

There was once a philosophic sect—the Cyrenaics—who counseled repudiation of concern for the future: "Have no concern for the morrow, for tomorrow is another day." But why the *counsel*? Why the *exhortation*? They pronounced an imperative sentence, expressing a general directive of conduct, and even offered something which sounds suspiciously like a "reason" for it. Could it be that they so are taking a thought for tomorrow, and even, with kindly intent, a thought for the happiness of others than themselves? And this thought appears to be that all of us will be happier if we take no anxious thought for our happiness. But they appear to be just a trifle anxious in the matter. They are taking thought for their own and our tomorrows. If their counsel should be right, they appear to be doing wrong in concerning themselves in giving it, as well as in their own taking it to heart and acting on it.

Consider oddities such as these:

The decision to make no decisions; the rule of disregarding all rules; the imperative to give no heed to imperatives; the concern to have no concerns; the principle of repudiating all principles; the dictum to disregard all dicta; the resolution to give no heed to resolutions made.

All of these oddities, these strange decisions, rules, recommendations or such bear a certain analogy to the statement of Epimenides the Cretan, that all Cretans are liars, or, say, to the statement that everything I say is a lie, or to the statement that what I now state is false—to any declaration which logically implies that the declaration itself is false or should be disregarded.

There are many varieties of "self-negation."

The sort we will wish to consider presently is that which might be expressed in the imperative, and in an imperative addressed to oneself, one which is to be accepted or rejected by the one who pronounces it.

It would be more amusing than profitable, we should think, incidentally, to enter into all the detail, into all the involution, of this general class of self-vitiating pronouncements. They are not all of any single or simple kind, logically considered. And in order to make that clear, we might add to the preceding examples yet another type of self-vitiating pronouncement, one which C. H. Langford has offered: "Today is Monday, but I don't believe it."

A fundamental consideration here, connecting self-contradicting statements and self-negating imperatives, is that both represent, ostensibly, a commitment on the part of the one who pronounces them, a commitment to believe in the case of an indicative pronouncement, a commitment to heed or adopt a certain way of acting in the case of an imperative pronounced. In either case, the "pronouncer" ostensibly commits himself for the future—unless or until he gives—at least gives himself—notice of a change of mind. And on this point, it is the imperative significance of believing anything, instead of any cognitive sense of commitment to an imperative (a resolve), which serves to relate the two. A cognitive decision which should not operate to direct or modify one's own decisions of future action in any way would be a decision there would be no point in making. Any knowing which should be precluded from all directive significance for the knower's doing could have no more than an esthetic significance for him. It might please him to know—or merely to conjecture or to fancy—but so what! It is this consideration by reason of which Langford's kind of example belongs with the others.[4] And it is this consideration which is fundamental in the Epimenides example. One who advertises his own lack of commitment to what he says, gives notice that his pronouncement advises of nothing reliably indicative for the future. It expresses no credible *intention*, either logically—with respect to what its pronouncement implies—or practically—in the sense of affording any forecast of the speaker's future way of doing, unless it be that he is a person who lacks integrity, avoidably or unavoidably, and is not to be counted on in any cooperative enterprise. He cannot be believed; he cannot be trusted to do what he says. Integrity is continuance in commitments taken—whether of belief or of formulatable ways of doing.

It is as an *act*—a commitment taken—that the assertion of Epimenides, or the pronouncement "What I now assert is false," or "Today is Monday but I don't believe it," is self-vitiating.

---

4. [Lewis had deleted the reference to Langford in this sentence. I have restored it, thinking that in the best interest of the text.–Ed.]

P. H. Nowell-Smith has called such "implications" of *acts* of asserting—"contextual implications." A simpler way of putting it would be to say that an act of stating so "implies" what an observation of the act affords evidence of—including the speaker's presumptive intention in saying what he says.

When one says "Tomorrow will be Monday," he gives presumptive evidence that he believes it—although what he says does *not* logically imply that he believes it.

It is in this sense of belying an active commitment that an imperative pronouncement may be self-vitiating, comparably to the assertion which logically implies its own negation, and that logical self-contradiction is subsumable under the broader classification of self-vitiating intentions, self-negating commitments, which belie themselves by requiring a departure from themselves, and are impossible to adhere to. And it is this broader category, *inclusive* of logical self-contradiction, but not confined to it, that we would designate 'pragmatic self-contradiction'.

It can be further illuminating to observe the connection between this narrower category of the self-contradictory and consistency in general. And such consistency in general, as applicable to ways of acting, formulatable as rules, imperatives, is an important topic for ethics. It is not merely self-consistency in *each* of our statements, or assumptions, but consistency with one another amongst *all* our statements, or assumptions, and amongst all of our beliefs and our intensions, which it is important to submit to the critique of logic if we would think rightly and confine our convictions to that only which has some possibility of being true. And if we would be moral, or even prudent, it is similarly important to submit the whole body of our *intentions to do* to the critique of "consistency"—to aim at the compatibility of each intention with all the others, to attempt bring them, as a total set, to consistency, insofar as that is possible, insofar as it can be attained.

'Consistency' in this sense, in which it applies to acts and to purposes, will turn out to be a different thing from the logical consistency of any set of beliefs.

But first let us give attention to the homology which obtains between the two. And under that head, the first topic may but be the connection between self-consistency and consistency in the more inclusive sense.

Let us first think of logic. Logic applies to indicative sentences, which could express beliefs. Let us represent these as 'S_1, S_2, S_3, ...'. And let us represent 'S_1 is self-consistent' by '<> S_1'. And let us represent the *conjoint* statement of any set of statements (*e.g.*, a set of assumptions for a mathematical system) simply by writing them one after the other, e.g., 'S_1 and S_2 and S_3' as '$(S_1 . S_2 . S_3)$', and so on.

We may then observe that '<> $(S_1 . S_2 . S_3)$'—the statement 'S_1 and S_2 and S_3 is a self-consistent statement'—says exactly the same thing as 'S_1 and S_2 and S_3 are all of them consistent with each other; they form a consistent set' and, accordingly, it would be consistent to assume or believe all of them together. That a set is self consistent, e.g., '<> $(S_1 . S_2 . S_3)$', is, of course, a much more demanding requirement than that each member be self-consistent. A statement which is not self-consistent, of course, is not consistent with any other statement, or with the consistency of any set of statements of which it is a member. If, *e.g.*, it is false that <> S_2, then it is false that <> $(S_1 . S_2 . S_3$ ...). But even if it be true that <> S_1, <> S_2, <> S_3, and so on— '<> $(S_1 . S_2 . S_3 ...)$' might still be false. What '<> $(S_1 . S_2 . S_3$ ...)' requires to be true is that each member of the set be consistent with the *conjoint statement* of all the others, for example, that '<> $[S_1 . (S_2 . S_3 ...)]$' be true, '<> $[S_2 . (S_1 . S_3 ...)]$' be true, '<> $[S_3 . (S_1 . S_2 ...)]$', be true, etc.

To state this matter fully without any use of symbols: For any set of indicative statements to be self-consistent, it is a necessary and a sufficient condition that every member of it be self-consistent and that for every selection of members the conjoint statement of the selected members be consistent with the conjoint statement of the remainder of the set.[5] More briefly put, if everything you can say at one time is to be a wholly consistent set of remarks, then there must be no statement, and no

---

5. This matter sounds complicated, as stated without symbols, but will be obvious to those who are familiar with the manner of testing the consistency of a set of postulates for an abstract mathematical system by the use of "interpretations," which can be imposed upon this set.

combination of your statements, which is not consistent with all the rest of what you say. And if *anything* you say fails to be self-consistent, or any *combination* of statements you make fails to be consistent, then that vitiates the consistency of your whole discourse. This is a "very large order," but plainly nothing short of it will satisfy the requirement of being completely consistent.

Perhaps it will strike us as fairly obvious there is such a thing as being consistent, and such a thing as being inconsistent, in what we decide to do or try to do. And it may seem equally obvious—or perhaps only a little less so—that this whole story of consistency in what we believe, or commit ourselves to asserting, applies to any course of conduct, any set of purposes taken, any plan of doing some set of things, of performing some set of acts, in pursuit of some whole result, one intended to be consequent upon such acts, taken together.

This is indeed the case, except for one point, the point, namely, that the consistency of two acts, or of any set of acts, means something different from the consistency of two assertions or two beliefs. But let us postpone that basic consideration and observe that, allowing for it, this whole story of what holds for statements—and hence for our *beliefs*—holds *pari passu*, for decisions to do. To do is to bring about something, and to act is to *try* to bring about something. Doing, and trying or *intending* to do, are not identically the same thing, but they are alike on the point of purposing or intending. And one may ask another—or we may ask ourselves—"What are you doing?" or "What are you trying to do?" And the answer will be to name, specify, formulate a *state of affairs* expected or intended to result. And any state of affairs which is intended could be stated. If or when brought about, it becomes something *assertable—as* accomplished. When one is acting to bring it about, it is future, hoped for, and expected. But it is the *same* state of affairs, whether intended, hoped for, expected, or (later) brought about. Making an apple pie intends an apple pie made. The apple pie made is the same state of affairs when now aimed at, when worked for, and expected, and when or if later realized. Insofar as any act is successful the achieved result *is* the same as the aimed at, intended, and expected result. A

sufficiently efficient and confident doer whose confidence is
wholly justified intends and expects to bring about just what he
does bring about. The competent cook says, "You shall have an
apple pie for dinner," and the later-realized state of affairs she
names "You having apple pie for dinner" is identically what
she intended, what she brings about by doing, and what later is
a realized fact. "You having apple pie for dinner" is, let us say,
the *name* of the state of affairs in question. It is identically what
you wished or hoped for, what the cook intended, what she
brought about, and what both of you realized in the result, and
what both of you were talking about, both before and now,
when the apple pie is on the table. That state of affairs is the
state of affairs in question, in this whole matter of wishing and
wanting and doing and later realizing. Otherwise you and the
cook would have been talking at cross-purposes, and the doing
would have lacked pertinence to the intending and effecting
and realizing. There is a difference in tense in the conversation
at different times, but "You having apple pie for dinner" is the
state of affairs in question throughout this whole matter. Your
deliberately intended doing *is* what you expect to bring about;
and so far as your act brings about what you intend, what you
intend *is* the consequence; and the consequence *is* what you
intend. If then, you *know* what you are doing or intend to do,
state it. And what you state will be something which happens
in the result, if you succeed in your achieving the object of your
intention. Anything you *intend* to do is a result you *expect* as a
consequence of your doing; and anything you expect as a result
of your doing is included in what you intentionally do. You do
not always or wholly bring about what you intend; and you
do not always or wholly intend what you bring about. But so
far as what you intend happens as a consequence of your act,
what you intend and what you bring about are identical. And
whatever you so deliberately bring about is exactly what you
deliberately do. There are any number of *other* and conflicting
considerations pertinent to deliberate doing, but none of these
can falsify what we have just said.

All this leads up to the point in question: the relation
between states of affairs, any one of which could be *asserted*

(truly or falsely) as being the case, and any deliberate doing bringing about any of the states of affairs in question. And the initial consequence of these considerations, which we may now observe, is this: If the assertions (statements) of two states of affairs as being the case are consistent, the one with the other, then the intentions to bring them about are consistent intentions, and intending both to do this and to do that would, so far forth, constitute a consistent plan of action. To put this matter more briefly, we can observe a general connection between consistency in thinking, concluding, believing or expecting, and consistency in doing intentionally, by remembering that deliberate doing is deliberate bringing about. And what it would be inconsistent to believe or expect cannot be consistent to *intend* to bring about, *expect* to bring about, think that you *can* bring about. It so becomes quite clear that there is a good and useful sense in which deliberate acts may be consistent or inconsistent. And consideration of the consistency or inconsistency of different intentions to do is a highly important part of the critique of deliberate doing. Intending to bring about A and intending to bring about B are inconsistent intentions if the assertion *of A* as being the case is inconsistent with the assertion of B as being the case. You cannot do both A and B if A and B are incompossible, *i.e.,* not consistent as factual accomplishments.

Perhaps that would have been obvious if we had said it at the start. But that there is a direct connection between the consistency or inconsistency of thinking and what may be apparent, the consistency or inconsistency of doing, is a point on which we should have faced almost endless controversy if we had not spelled this matter out a little. (And—let the reader be warned—it is only a little that we have so far spelled it out. And we do not expect to spell it out fully in these essays, for fear of burying the main points in logical considerations which can be spun out *ad nauseam* by those who pursue logic for recreation instead of for use.[6])

---

6. I am a little fond of such logical recreations myself, but am able to restrain my enthusiasm on occasion.

However, if it is now clear that there is an apposite and important sense in which purposes, intentions, and deliberate doing may be consistent or inconsistent, let us now turn to the point mentioned at the outset, that the meaning of these terms, the *useful* meaning, is different as applied to our governed doings from the usual and useful meaning of them as applicable to what we think and believe. This will become clear if we observe that the consistent is the compossible, the inconsistent the incompossible. The *logically* possible is a very wide category as compared with the practically possible, what can be brought about, and conversely the practically *impossible* is a far wider category than merely the logically impossible. This is not a matter of metaphysics; it is basically a matter of the use of words, in the "logical" and the "practical" context. But there is a basic reason for this difference of common usage: it is the difference between what we can certify *a priori*, the "logically necessary," and the range of "what we know" and take for granted in practical doing.

Logic rules out *nothing* except what is provably contradictory in conception, the self-contradictory. And as we have seen, the logically consistent (the noncontradictory) *set* of statements is any such that the conjoint statement of them involves no self-contradiction. But when we speak of a consistent *belief,* the set we are thinking of is the totality of "what we know." It would be "inconsistent" for us to believe anything which is incompatible with *anything* we know or believe. And we presume knowledge of many things which are *not* logically certifiable, not such that their negation is a self-contradictory statement. Indeed, the whole body of our common-sense knowledge and the laws of the natural sciences, all empirical knowledge, is of this description. The denial of the law of gravitation is not self-inconsistent, nor is the denial that the sun is shining when I see that in fact it is.

There are, however, empirical statements which are self-inconsistent, because they imply the contravention of some statement which is analytic, for example, 'Today is Monday but tomorrow will be Wednesday'. This is certifiably *false a priori* because, barring the crossing of the international date line, today's being Monday implies tomorrow's not being Wednesday.

By the meaning of 'today', 'tomorrow', 'Monday' and 'Wednesday', it is logically certifiable that today's being Monday but tomorrow's being Wednesday is *logically* impossible. Similarly, 'The opposite sides of this rectangle are not parallel,' is a self-inconsistent statement because 'Whatever is a rectangle has opposite sides which are parallel' is an analytic statement. Every empirical statement has *logical consequences*—various implications, and an empirical statement having any two logical consequences which are contrary to each other is certifiably false.[7] What is *logically* impossible can be guaranteed *not* to be the actual and empirical fact. That things of a certain description do *not* exist can, in consequence, sometimes be logically certified. But that anything of a certain description *does* exist can never be certified without some premise which deductive logic, by itself, cannot assume.

Similarly, there could be intentions of doing whose *failure* can be logically guaranteed, *e.g.*, nobody can fit a round peg to a square hole, and this logical critique is important because we can stupidly waste time trying to achieve such a self-inconsistent aim. And it is further important that two different purposes, both continuously entertained, may be logically inconsistent with one another, one of them calling for the achievement of *A*, but the other calling for the avoidance of this consequence, *A*.

But the further, and perhaps more important, consideration is that when we speak of two acts, or two intentions, or two purposes of action as being consistent or inconsistent with one another, we commonly use 'inconsistent' in a wider sense than the logical, and 'consistent' in a narrower sense than that of the merely logically consistent. The "consequences" we are so thinking of, in determining our acts, intentions, and purposes of action are not the purely logical consequences of the formulation of what we intend to bring about, but the *empirical* consequences of bringing them about, what will happen as a result, by reason of the laws of nature or of some other empirical generality we take to be common-sense fact.

---

7. Two statements are contrary if and only if both could be false but both cannot be true. Any statement contrary to another implies the contradictory of that other.

To make what could be a long story shorter: what we characteristically intend by saying that two intentions or purposes, *A* and *B*, are inconsistent is that the empirical consequences of so acting as to bring about one of them will prevent or militate against the achievement of the other. And our knowledge of this relation of the two is, characteristically, empirical cause-effect knowledge, not merely knowledge of logical relationships.

Let us try to pin down, as precisely as we can, just what it is that is characteristically intended when we speak of two intentions or purposes deliberately to do as being inconsistent, first, in logical terms, and then in terms of common sense.[8]

As we have already observed, in terms of logic, one intention is distinguished from another by what it is that we intend (expect) to bring about. Including in our intention *all* that we expect the intended act to bring about, there is *no* way in which we could distinguish one act from another except (1) by what it is expected to bring about, or (2) by the date of it. And two acts distinguished by date but having identical expectations would be what we mean by 'two attempts to bring about the same thing' and by 'doing the same on two different occasions'.[9]

---

8. "Intention" and "purpose" are not in general identical. We *intend* to do whatever we *expect* to bring about by our own contemplated act, and we may expect (intend) *certain* consequences of it which we do not care to bring about, or may even wish we could avoid while still attaining our purpose. The *purpose* of an act is that *part* of our intention in doing *for the sake of which* we do the act. Two different acts may have the same intention but different purposes, and two acts may have different intentions but the same purpose.

9. An act and doing the same again are, literally, deliberately acting twice in the *same way*. But comparing "acting twice in exactly the *same way*" with "two *events* of doing the same," we may observe that any deliberate act is an abstraction. The two occurrences are to be distinguished by their difference of temporal context. But the *to be deliberately done* content is identical in the two cases. We *know* "what we do or attempt to do," in our deliberate act, in the doing of any act, only as an abstraction (a particular *way* of acting) which may recur in two contexts, just as we may know two roses to be different roses because they were picked in different places at different times, but could not tell them apart if put side by side. The plausibility of the Leibnizian principle of the identity of indiscernibles turns upon the predicament of knowing as confined to abstractions—to "universals," "properties" instanced by individuals.

Logically considered, the difference between the logical consistency of two propositions and the consistency of two deliberate intentions or purposes is that the question of the consistency of the two propositions is confined to the question of the self-consistency of their joint assertion. But the consistency of two aims to bring about is not decidable merely by finding or failing to find the supposition of a supposed realization of both as an attempt to bring about the truth of a statement which is logically self-consistent. It is further required that the statement of both as realized should be compatible with *everything else we know.* That one cannot eat one's cake and have it too, or be in two places at once, is determinable merely by the contemplation of what it would *mean* to 'eat but have left' or 'in two places at the same time'. There are, we may say, *logically* inconsistent supposals and hence supposals *logically* inconsistent as aims or purposes. But that eating this for dinner and enjoying good health tomorrow are incompatible, if that should be the foreknowable fact, turns upon *something else* we know, like "Every time I eat spice cake I have indigestion the next day." Knowing that, it is inconsistent for me to intend both to eat the cake and to avoid indigestion. If there is *anything* else I know, K, such that "I eat the cake and K is the case" implies "I shall not escape indigestion," then, in common parlance, my deliberately eating of the cake but intending to avoid indigestion is for me an inconsistent way of acting. Let E be 'I eat the cake' and I be 'I avoid indigestion', and K be everything else I know, which will include whatever is pertinent. Then I deliberately act in an inconsistent way just in case '$\Diamond (E . I . K)$' is false, and '$\Diamond (E . I)$' should be true; there is no *logical* inconsistency in the conjunction of the two statements E and I, omitting K.

This—we suggest—is the *general* difference between the mere *logical* consistency of two statements expressing two intentions to bring about, and the "practical consistency" of two intentions. We are practically consistent in entertaining or acting on two different intentions, I_1 and I_2, if and only if, adding K (all the rest of what we know), we are *logically* justified in believing '$\Diamond (I_1 . I_2 . K)$'.

There is one point which is a bit subtle and is truly involved in what we characteristically mean in imputing consistency or inconsistency to purposes and intentions of deliberate doing. It *could* be that, in point of fact, I cannot eat some viand without having indigestion, though I do not know that—this fact is not included in K. And in that case, we should *not* say that my deliberately eating but at the same time intending to avoid indigestion was "acting inconsistently." Consistency of intentions and of deliberate doing requires reference to whatever else the doer knows (which is pertinent), but it does *not* require that the consequences of the two deliberate doings should be in point of fact both realizable. One who "has no reason to believe that"—does not know it—may be acting consistently in intending two different bringings about which in point of fact are not coincidentally possible. So we have been exactly right in including, as K, whatever else the doer knows, but *not* whatever else that is pertinent may in fact be *true*. What a doer may consistently intend does require reference beyond the statement merely of what he expects or wishes to bring about, but the further reference required is limited to his further knowledge or cogent belief, and does not require reference to anything which may be pertinent fact, but beyond his knowledge.

It is to be observed, with respect to practical consistency, as with respect to logical consistency, that our account above of the consistency of any *two* intentions coincidentally entertained can be extended to the consistency of any number of intentions. Any intention is an intention to bring about some state of affairs. Any two intentions will be consistent just in case the propositions formulating, or the *assertions* of, these two states of affairs are consistent. And that will be true just in case the *joint* formulation of the two propositions, or assertions, will be self-consistent. Similarly, any three such propositions, or assertions, or any four such propositions, or assertions, and so on, will *all* be consistent just in case they form a *self*-consistent *set*. And any set will be a self-consistent set just in case the joint statement of *all* the propositions, or assertions, together will constitute a *self*-consistent statement. (Two propositions are consistent if and only if the joint assertion of the two is self-consistent, and vice versa.)

And all of these statement just made will hold whether the consistencies in question are logical consistencies or practical consistencies—because a *logical* inconsistency names a state of affairs which involves a logical contradiction, and what is logically impossible is something which could not be bought about in any world anybody could imagine and so cannot be brought about in this world we live in; and a practical contradiction is one which, in virtue of certain things we know about this world of ours, we can know cannot be accomplished, though whether we know that or not depends on how much we know and on the nature of what we know about this actual world of ours. We know, for example, that any straight line we can draw can be prolonged in either direction, so *a priori,* there is no *logical* contradiction in *supposing* a straight line of infinite length. But we also know from experience that we can*not* draw a line of infinite length, and it is a *practical* absurdity to attempt it. What is logically impossible is practically impossible, but many things which are not logically impossible are practically impossible, impossible in practice, and he who does *not know* their practical impossibility may find that out by trying—by experience, or by knowledge of our world established by scientists and imparted to us as information about the way our world is. Logical knowledge is analytic, knowable *a priori.* Practical knowledge *includes also* empirical knowledge found out by the past experience of men, but not knowable *a priori,* not self-contradictory to suppose to be otherwise than in fact it is. Thus practical impossibility is a far wider category than logical impossibility; it *includes* the logically impossible but also includes much the impossibility of which could only be found out by drawing upon "the laws of nature" or other knowledge established by experiment and observation.

As we have already pointed out, the connection of the two—of logical possibility with practical possibility—can be summarized by adding to our propositions or suppositions (or our intended aims) "what we know" (fact that is pertinent). Let this body of our non-a *priori* and empirical knowledge be represented by K. Then any supposition of a state of affairs, P, is *logically* consistent just in case the assumption of its truth is *self*-consistent, involves no contradiction, which we may symbolize as '<> P'. But it is a *practically* consistent supposition if and only if '<> $(P . K)$' holds. But if '<> P' is *false,* then

'<> (P . K)' will be *false, no matter what* knowledge 'K' stands for. Thus we can define practical consistency in terms of the *logical* consistency of a *set*, namely, of the *set* "(P . K)." That is, P expresses an aim it is practically consistent to attempt to realize just in case, knowing what we otherwise know, this aimed-at state of affairs, P, is logically consistent to suppose—to take as possible—*and also* is logically consistent with all the rest of what we know (which is pertinent).

As we have already suggested, however, we should not confuse practical possibility or impossibility with *metaphysical* possibility or impossibility. Practical possibility or impossibility is relative to *what we know* about the world by observation and experience. There will be those who object to this; they will say, "No, a thing is practically impossible to achieve if it impossible to achieve it, no matter whether we know anything which allows you to infer the impossibility of bringing it about or not. But that is simply a different way of using the words 'possible' and 'impossible', one which is just what we would here express by 'metaphysically possible' and 'metaphysically impossible'—something "fixed in the total character of reality, whether you know it or not." But we do *not* here mean that by 'practical possibility' and 'practical impossibility'. We intend to use 'practical' in a practical way—as concerning the justifiability or unjustifiability of *intending to bring about* a state of affairs in question, allowing or disallowing ourselves to entertain the *intention* to bring about so and so. And *that* kind of practicality or impracticality depends on what you know. It may be *metaphysically* impossible to bring about P. But if we know nothing which allows us to infer that, it is not practically inconsistent to *try* to bring it about. But if we know something, K, in the light of which the impossibility of realizing P is *inferable,* then it is practically inconsistent to attempt to bring it about.

One reason for carefully distinguishing practical possibility and practical impossibility from metaphysical possibility and metaphysical impossibility is the plausibility of the thesis (often advanced in philosophy) that if *you knew everything* which is pertinent to expecting to bring about anything, P, you would either know that it is fated to come about or know that it is fated *not* to come about. That is the timeworn thesis of metaphysical determinism. Our point here is that, so long as you don't know whether *P* is fated to come about or not, and can't logically infer that from what you know, it is perfectly consistent to attempt to bring it about, and perhaps find out by trying whether it can be brought about or not. That is what scientists are continually trying to find out—by making their experiments. If nothing is metaphysically possible except what is metaphysically actual, still that holds no dictate whatever concerning what it is reasonable to attempt. But your complete body of achieved information about the world *does* have a bearing upon what it is practically reasonable to attempt to bring about. And this last is exactly what can have importance for the rational criticism of our aims to do—our deliberate decisions of action. That being the case, this kind of consideration is basic for any prudential critique and any moral critique. The basic criticism of action must at least include the rational imperative: Do not attempt anything you know to be impossible, either because it is logically impossible and the supposition of it not even self-consistent, or because it is inconsistent with something you already know to be the case, and therefore is a practically inconsistent aim to entertain.

There is a corollary of these facts, to which it is desirable to draw attention, because of the presently more or less prevailing tendencies in logical study. Consistency and inconsistency are considerations basic for the distinction of what is rational from what is irrational. Much of current logical study is based upon an unfortunate and even ludicrous dogmatism which would preclude what will be obvious to any common-sense mind not already prejudiced by this current dogmatism. The question, "What is deducible from what?" and "What is inconsistent with what?" are always questions which can be settled *a priori,* by reference to statements which are analytically true, and can therefore be assured by anybody who knows what he means by what he says and has the capacity to "be logical." "Being logical" means nothing in the world but avoiding any and every belief which would (logically) lead to a contradiction. And in cases which are not too complex, we can all of us do that without more than elementary instructions which, once given, and utilized, we can see what is true, and necessarily true, for ourselves. (We would not say, of course, that this is true for complex cases, which might be found, for example, in extensive mathematical systems.)

In these current "logics" to which we refer, it is not possible, in their vocabulary, even to *define* the relation "*q* is deducible from *p*" or "*p* is consistent with *q*" except in ways so abstruse and complicated that attempts to determine them, in complex cases, as in certain extensive mathematical systems, run into paradoxes, such as that if this system were to be "complete"—contain all the consequences of its assumptions which could be written out—it could not be self-consistent throughout. This dogmatic attempt to confine logic to truth relations (certifiable from a consideration of the truth or falsity of propositions alone) and ignore simple relations like "p is self-consistent," "*p* is not self-consistent," "*q* is deducible from *p* alone," and so on—this attempt to reduce logic to so-called "truth functions," or "extensional functions," is a hopelessly perverse and injudicious logic, false to our simplest and most obvious logical insights. The whole of what logic can certify to be true and what it can certify to be false turns upon consistency and inconsistency. In fact there is nothing which logic itself can certify which does not turn upon that. Even this perversely defined "truth logic" turns upon that, upon the fact that whatever is admissible to *any* system of logic must be *analytically* true, and the negation of it a self-contradictory statement. It is only in what is now called "modal logic" that one finds explicit reference to the analytic or logically necessary as distinct from the merely true, and explicit reference to the consistency or inconsistency of a pair of propositions, or a set of propositions, and reference to the deducibility or nondeducibility of one proposition *q* from another *p*. In these terms *q* is deducible from *p* just in case the joint assertion '*p* is true but *q* false' is a self-inconsistent statement, having some self-contradictory statement as a logical consequence of it.

At this point, let us remind ourselves of certain logical relationships.

We should observe that it is one thing to ask, "is *q* consistent with *p*?" and a different one to ask, "Does *p* imply *q*?," but we should also observe that these two are related. That q is deducible from p means precisely that p is *not* consistent with the *denial* of q, which is also equivalent to "the denial of q implies the denial of p."

Let us symbolize "q is deducible from p" by '$p < q$' (p strictly implies q). And then let us consider the following formulas:[10]

$$\sim <> (p . \sim q) = (p < q) = (\sim q < \sim p)$$
$$<> (p . \sim q) = \sim (p < q) = \sim (\sim q < \sim p)$$

"p implies q" is thus definable in terms of negation and consistency. To reiterate the point, two propositions, r and s, have the relation "s is deducible from r" ('$r < s$'), just in case r and the negation of s are not consistent, that is, '$\sim <> (r . \sim s)$' is true, or, alternatively, dispensing with symbols, it is false that r and the negation of s (the contradictory of s) are conjointly consistent.

Let us consider now the relevance of these logistic considerations to matters of commitment and belief.

---

10. [A brief remark on the following formulas is in order, as logicians often differ with respect to notational conventions. The curl or tilde, '$\sim$', will indicate negation, '$<>$' is retained as the modal operator for consistency. '$<$' will stand for "strictly implies," or "logically implies," as indicated above, which is to be distinguished from "materially implies." (In "material implication" any conditional statement with either a false antecedent or a true consequent counts as a true statement.) In Lewis and Langford's system of "strict implication," '$=$' stands for the relationship of logical equivalence, rather than that of material equivalence. (Two propositions are materially equivalent if and only if they have the same truth value, either both true or both false.) In Lewis' rough text he seems to use dots for bracketing, as he and Langford often did in *Symbolic Logic*, but he also, here, as is quite common, uses them for conjunction. Whereas, strictly, the formulas are, in context, unambiguous, it seemed to me preferable to eliminate the dots as brackets, as they might be initially confusing, and not to supply additional parentheses, as they might, strictly, be supplied in more than one way. This is innocent, given the associational equivalences involved. Accordingly, here, following the precedent of various logicians in similar contexts, we will accept a formula such as '$A = B = C$' as well formed. Each of the formulas in each of the rows is to be understood as logically equivalent to each of the other formulas in its own row. –Ed.]

What will it mean to say, "I am consistent in believing P, for any proposition P?" In the first place, being consistent in believing *P requires* that *P* itself be *self*-consistent, that '<> *P*' holds. (If *p* is consistent, it must be self-consistent. Since 'p = (p . p)' is true, it follows that '<> p' logically implies '<> (p . p)', i.e., that the conjunction of *p* with *p* is consistent, and thus, if *p* is consistent, then it is consistent with itself, or self-consistent.) But it is *not sufficient* to assure what we ordinarily mean by saying, "I am consistent in believing P" to simply assure that P, all by itself, is a self-consistent supposition. Ordinarily whether I am consistent in believing *P* would require, first, that I am *not* also believing its negation, '~ *P*', but also that I am not believing anything from which this negation of *P*, '~ *P*', is *deducible*. And that, of course, depends on *what else* I believe. It requires that *everything else* which I also believe at this same time be consistent with *P*, which I now believe. It depends on what else I *know*, accept as true. Let us represent this whole body of our beliefs (what we know) by *K*. Then we can say that I am consistent in believing a certain proposition just in case the total statement '*P* and *K*' would be a self-consistent statement, that is, just in case '<> (*P* . *K*)' holds. We do not have to repeat here the requirement of the *self*-consistency of *P*, that '<> *P*' is the case, because a statement which is not self-consistent is not consistent with any other. '~ <> *P*' logically entails '~ <> (*P* . *K*)', and the requirement "<> (*P* . *K*)" *includes* the requirement "<> *P*."

To assure that what one is believing, *P*, is consistent with everything else I now know or believe is, of course, a tall order, but is there anything short of this which would satisfy what we mean in asserting, "I am consistent in believing *P*"? The only other thing we might be intending by that statement would be the very much narrower thing mentioned above, namely, that this supposition, *P*, all by itself, and without reference to anything further, is a *self*-consistent supposition. Ordinarily we should mean the broader requirement of the consistency of *P* with all the rest of what we believe.

And in these terms, we can immediately characterize the consistency or inconsistency of an *intention to bring about* any state of affairs *P*. In the *narrowest* sense of *practical* consistency, the intention (expectation) to bring about P is a self-consistent intention just in case it's supposition, '<> P', is true. However, "I intend to go to the moon tomorrow" would hardly be spoken of as a *self-consistent* intention.[11] But why not? The answer is, because I know something by reason of which "I go to the moon tomorrow" expresses an expectation which will prove *false*. The expectation all by itself is not a *self*-inconsistent expectation. (Some men may hold it a thousand years from now and carry it out.) It is an inconsistent expectation because it is inconsistent with something else I know to be true, namely, K. Accordingly, '~ <> ("I go to the moon tomorrow." . K)' is the case. There is no briefer or narrower way of the saying of any intention to bring about a state of affairs, P, than this formula. An intention to bring about a state of affairs, P, is an inconsistent intention just in case '~ <> (P . K)' is the case, where K is the body of my knowledge or other beliefs.

An intention to bring about is consistent or not just in case the expectation of bringing it about is consistent. And an expectation of bringing about is consistent just in case the belief that it will be brought about by our contemplated act is a consistent belief, and we would *act* on that intention—with the *consistent expectation* of bringing it about.

Thus *the consistency or inconsistency of acting on intentions is wholly describable in terms of the logical consistency of our intentions.*

However, there is a narrower thing which might be—and often is—meant by the consistency or inconsistency of two intentions simultaneously entertained. As we have already seen, what it means to say that a *single* intention—to bring about P—is consistent already involves more than merely the logical self-consistency of the expectation "My contemplated act will bring about P." It requires that nothing else I know has the consequence "If I so act, P will still *not* come about." It requires that '<> (P . K)' be true. But it is a different question whether *two* intentions—to bring about P and to bring about Q—are

---

11. [The text was drafted prior to July 20, 1969. To keep the spirit of the example, Lewis, if writing today, would presumably have substituted something else, say, Mars, for the moon. –Ed.]

consistent intentions. But, as perhaps the reader will already see, what the consistency of two different intentions, to bring about P and to bring about Q also, requires is that '$<> (P . Q . K)$' holds. And it could easily be that although '$<> (P . K)$' and '$<> (Q . K)$' both hold, '$<> (P . Q . K)$' does *not* hold, *i.e.,* that you can bring about P (and know you can) and can bring about Q (and know you can), but you *cannot* bring about *both* P and Q (and know that you cannot). It is the following *three* convictions which would ordinarily summarize what is meant by saying that two intentions, to bring about P and to bring about Q, are not consistent—"$<> (P . K)$" and "$<> (Q . K)$," but "$\sim <> (P . Q . K)$." Just occasionally, saying that two intentions, to bring about P and to bring about Q, are not consistent would be to say "$\sim <> (P . Q . K)$" alone. But let us observe that if either '$\sim <> (P . K)$' or '$\sim <> (Q . K)$' should hold, then it follows from that fact alone that '$\sim <> (P . Q . K)$' will also hold. Any self-inconsistent intention is inconsistent with *any* other intention, whether that intention is inconsistent or not. The main point, however, is that any two intentions, each of which is by itself a consistent intention, may be incompatible, inconsistent, with each other. And that is what is symbolized by the three expressions above, respecting what is most commonly meant by calling two expectations inconsistent with each other.

We should also observe that what is said about the consistency or inconsistency of *two* intentions can readily be extended to any set of intentions, whatever their number. For any set, "$(P . Q . R . . . .)$," this set will be a consistent set just in case '$<> P$', '$<> Q$', '$<> R$', '$<> . . .$' all hold, but will be an inconsistent set if any member of the set, say, R, is self-inconsistent, and *also* will be self-inconsistent if any member of the set, say, Q, is inconsistent with the conjunction of all the others. And the set will be thus inconsistent if there is any *pair* of these intentions, say, P and Q, which are inconsistent with one another, *i.e.,* if '$\sim <> (P . Q)$' holds, or if any included triad, or n-ad of them, fails to constitute a consistent set. Being completely consistent in *all* our intentions, at any one time, is a very large order indeed, and being consistent in all our *continuing* intentions, or in all those purposes to which we would hold, is so large an order that it is implausible that anyone ever has or ever will achieve it. But that is the ideal requirement we would fain achieve, that of being completely rational in all our intentions, in all our purposes, coincidentally entertained. But that is precisely our continuing rational intent, an imperative we respect and would conform to so far as in us lies. Any departure from it hazards somewhere attempting the impossible without our notice. But being finite, that is, of course, exactly what all of us, some of the time, are pretty sure to attempt deliberately. We do not expect to be *completely* consistent in all we attempt to do, but we hope to correct our doing every time we notice that any intention of ours fails to be consistent with others to which we would commit ourselves. Rationality itself, whether in believing or in deliberate doing, remains our nonrepudiable ideal, and unqualified imperative, even if such complete rationality is more than we can expect of ourselves. And rationality, in commitments to believe, and in commitments to do, is coterminous with consistency in believing and consistency in our self-governable doing. The *critique* of voluntary doing is, throughout, completely parallel with the critique of believing and concluding, and is essentially the critique of our convictions and of our intentions (our expectations of bringing about) and is subject to the same logical principles, differently applied. (Please note that we say 'subject to', not 'reducible to', here.) Whether there are *additional* imperatives of rational doing which are other than, or more than, logical, we do not as yet say.

If we are correct in this, if right doing must be rational doing, and our intentions to do must be logically self-consistent and consistent with each other in order to be justified as rational, then that conclusion, all by itself, must constitute a refutation of any emotivist theory, and any noncognitivist conception, of ethics. What we know, what we believe, and what we expect, intending to bring it about, must preserve the integrity of self-consistency, and must depend on what we know and hence also, in some measure, on what we do *not* know. We do *not* take anything to be a rational aim of doing, and in *any* sense right to do, regardless of the critique of consistency. And what we think a right aim, valid to aim at, justified to bring about, can*not* be determined independently of the rational critique and without reference to consistency in our purposes or without reference to what we know or believe. The critique of logical consistency and the critique of rightness in believing are presupposed and necessary to apply in any determination of what is to be called right (justified) to do. And any who would relegate the moral and prudential considerations to the category of the emotive and nonrational must in consistency (!) likewise relegate the logical critique, and the critique of scientific convictions as well, to the category of the emotive and nonrational. It is just as true or just as false to say that 'A is right to do' means only 'I approve of doing A; do you so as well' as it is to say, 'A is right to infer' or 'A is right to believe' means simply 'I approve of inferring A; do you so as well' or 'I approve of believing A; do you so as well'. The *act of* inferring A, or the *act of* asserting A, is, indeed, good inductive evidence that the speaker approves of inferring A, or of believing and asserting A, but the point is that he also must evidence some rationality of his so inferring, or believing and asserting, in order to have any claim upon the credence or argument of his hearer, and that what he *means to "imply"* is *not* that he is so emotively bent, but that he is so convinced for some reason which no other rational being could well repudiate.

The prudentially or morally right to do may be a matter of sentiment, but if it is merely an emotive and noncognitive sentiment, so is your grandmother. To change the figure, the emotivist and noncognitivist in ethics have gotten confused as to which is the dog and which is the tail, and what wags what. It is the conviction of rationality which rules our prudential and moral convictions, or at least it would better be, if we have any intent to convince (not "persuade" irrationally) any other whom we venture to address. It remains as true as when Aristotle said it, that it is the function of reason to control our emotive inclinations. Adherence to the rationally justified is humanly imperative. Any for whom it should not be so belongs in some home for the feebleminded. If there be no other and more decisive ground for the settlement of moral issues than the emotive and noncognitive, then those who disagree about them have no final arbitrament left open but force, even to the bomb.

In this too brief discussion of the relation between the right to do and the logically and cognitively justified, we have, up to this point, left unremarked one complication of the basic factualities, to which we must now give notice, though we can hardly follow things through in detail here. We have passed it by, above, for fear of introducing so many considerations at once as to prejudice even provisional clarity. We have so far spoken as if "what we know" which may be pertinent to decisions of doing would or could be known with certainty. But, as will have been clear, the knowledge pertinent to decisions of action which is over and above what is certifiable by logic alone, and is represented in our formulas by "K," is *empirical* knowledge. And empirical knowledge, as we have noticed, is never better than theoretically probable. That fact must qualify what has so far been said, and it must, on occasion, also qualify what it is rationally and cognitively justified to choose to do.

In common-sense terms, what we have said might be more briefly put somewhat as follows: Decisions of action are decisions to bring about. And the intentions of such decisions to do comprise that and only that which, in taking the initiative of the action in question, we foresee as the consequences of this commitment to do. Any simple such intention will be self-consistent if and only if it will not, foreseeably, lead to the self-frustration of, instead of the achievement of, its aim. And any two purposes or intentions—simultaneously regarded as desirable ends of action—will be consistent with one another just in case the achievement of the one aimed-at state of affairs (one purpose) and that of the other state of affairs (the other purpose) are compatible, and the expectation of achieving both is self-consistent. In the simplest common-sense terms, our various aims of action, conjointly desired and purposed, must not conflict. Judgment as to whether two such aims will, in the active pursuit of them conflict, or not—and the expectation of achieving both be self-consistent, or not—turns upon the predictable consequences of the two acts, upon whether or not the expectation of achieving both is consistent. And knowledge pertaining to such matters, turning as it does upon the consequences of action, is always empirical—never more than probable. It can never be certified by deductive logic alone.

Such compatibility—the nonconflict as ends, consistency in the sense of the word which we apply to acts and

their intentions—can never be assured with theoretical certainty, because the truth of the involved predictions can never
be assured with certainty, and it can be theoretically assured
that two purposes *will* conflict only in the exceptional case in
which the mere joint formulation of them would involve a *logical* inconsistency, *e.g.*, "I wish to sleep until nine but to start
work at seven." (And even this is not a strict contradiction
in terms.)[12] Incidentally, it might be remarked in passing that
simultaneously entertained ends may be two consequences of
one act, or of two different acts, both intended to do. But this
does not affect the question of consistency in action, except by
the difference between the self-consistency in one act and the
consistency of two acts, both intended to do.

Knowledge of the consequences of action will, in some
cases, amount to what we call "practical certainty," but never
to theoretical certainty. And practical certainty, of course, will
involve "theoretical doubts." These, as would be expected, are
logical and empirical. Both logical and empirical aspects are
involved in questions as simple as the following: "Will consequence C_1 accrue as a result of action A_1?"

Consider the following example:

I wish to run a belt from pulley A to pulley B so that when
pulley A revolves clockwise, pulley B will be driven counter-
clockwise. These are two purposes of one (or parts of one)
comprehensive doing (having parts). Are the two intended purposes consistent? Yes, it is quite often done, but it takes a bit of
know-how to do it. Knowing how, the conjoint purpose being
practically consistent, the result—"doing it right"—is a practical certainty—given dexterity and a bit of luck. But with flat
pulleys it may take three tries, even by a knowledgeable and
skillful belt-man. Is the determination of the conjoint attain-
ability or conflict logical or empirical, or both? A part of the

---

12. [This is an example, it seems, of the unfinished nature of the text,
    for Lewis appears here to undercut his own example. It seems he would
    need an example of a logical contradiction here, but his own example,
    as he admits in passing, does not furnish, strictly, a logical contradiction.
    –Ed.]

answer should be evident—purely logical knowledge is to be presumed in *any* empirical knowing; without the knowledge of *logical* impossibilities, like "both C and *not-C*," there could be no practical certainty that *anything* is practically impossible, no knowledge of the practical inconsistency of two aims. The practical consistency of two aims, say, A and B, requires (1) their logical consistency and (2) that there be no known fact which, together with logical "*a priorities*," implies that if A is the case, then not-B is the case.

This kind of consideration, that having to do with the limitations on human knowing, requires no qualification of what has been said above, except one which will accord with the fact that that which we say we know we recognize we know to a degree no better than that of a "*practical certainty*"—but this degree of practical certainty, near enough to theoretic or absolute certainty, is more than sufficient to justify action, is such that hesitation to act upon it would be unreasonable. If we can—as indeed any who must decide his action by the guidance of his empirical "knowledge" is under the necessity to do—take it that the K (what we know) in all our formulations above is known only to the point of practical, and not theoretic, certainty, then we will surely proceed—as indeed we must—on the basis of that accommodation. And, of course, as one previously dealt with notions such as "consistency," "inconsistency," and such, one would now, in a completely similar fashion, deal with, and understand, notions such as "practical consistency," "practical inconsistency," and "practical entailment," the inductive inferability of one state of affairs from another.

Phase II

We must observe that, over and above the divergent meanings of the verb 'to be' which are well recognized, there is another which it is necessary to acknowledge.

First, however, let us note that there are those who insist that any statement of the form "A is —" be construed as equivalent to "A exists such that A —," and implies "A is real,"

"A is actual." This is a serious oversight, condemning them to being incapable of saying for any A whatever, "A does not exist," "A is not actual," "A is not real," "A is purely imaginary," and so on.

In such cases, the "nonexistence cases," they have forbidden themselves to *truly* ascribe *any* predicate to that of which they are thinking. They are thinking of something which does not exist, and cannot tell what it *is* of which they so think. According to them, to say that an entity *is* anything (answers to any description) implies that it *exists,* that it is real.

Given the automatic uncritical nature of their existential commitments, they would reduce any assertion of their own to the effect that "A exists," were they to make such an assertion, to a meaningless pronouncement; it would deny nothing; it would repeat; it would be no more than a linguistic pleonasm.

And if centaurs, Zeus, round squares or such be mentioned, and they think poorly of what is said, they can say nothing to the point of this adverse conviction of theirs because they can attribute no predicate to any such subject as "Zeus," or "centaurs," etc. and so cannot say that of anything that it is mythical or imaginary because any such assertion, if true, would commit them to a claim that such an entity exists, and, indeed, that they ought to believe in it as real.

They are infinitely ingenious in being wrong. We simply say to them, "You do not speak English (or any other natural language) as it is spoken. And you have no excuse to deny to others a use of language prevalent wherever men of common sense address one another."

This claim that any form of the verb 'to be' must imply the actuality of the subject is, of course, a pure dogma, and a piece of semantic silliness. Anything thought of can be mentioned and some character of it specified by reference to which it is to be what is spoken of, what is connoted by any sense of the subject term, what is implied by such mentioning or else what is said is said of nothing and is senseless.

There is a meaning of 'is', or of any inflected form of the verb 'to be', in which the intent is merely explicative, to say what it is of which one thinks and speaks, to characterize it as the speaker thinks of it, and as it must be understood by any hearer who is to understand what is spoken of and to be thought about. A centaur is a mythical creature, half horse, half man. In so saying, that it is mythical, it is implied that centaurs do *not* exist. But we have indicated what it is that does not exist.

It is quite true that we oftentimes imply the existence of A in saying "A is —." It is likewise true that oftentimes we intend no such implication. And we ordinarily understand what is intended, in either case, by reason of the linguistic context, or by reason of some other context.

It is also commonly, though not necessarily, the case that the use of 'to be' in the purely explicative sense is uninflected for tense. We use the uninflected present: "There are no centaurs." (There never have been and never will be). "There are cows." (There have been for centuries, and presumably will continue to be.) The tenseless present is one usage extending not only to the indicative but also to the interrogative, *e.g.,* "Are there any such things as centaurs?"

All terms and all linguistic expressions have meaning in the sense of indicating what the speaker is *thinking of* and *intends* to convey by using this language, stating what he thinks or believes. And nothing can be conveyed by language at all unless what is thought of and what is thought about it is conveyed. Meaning in this sense of conveying what is intended (implied in the strictly good and precise meaning of 'implies') is intensional meaning. (We retain the old-English spelling—'intension'—to mark it as a technical term.)

Thinking and doing are both governable activities.

The relation of intentions in doing and intensions in thinking is not merely a metaphorical extension of linguistic usage; the connection of the two is of the essence. And it is faithfulness to intention which is in both cases one requirement of integrity—of rightness. Adherence to intentions is a prime requirement of rightness.

You must say what you mean and mean what you say, and doing what you do not intend, linguistically or otherwise, is always a blunder, even if it should be a fortunate one. Correlatively, keeping to the same meaning of terms in the same sentence or paragraph is a requirement of clarity, a requirement for understanding—even for understanding oneself. Doing otherwise is either a joke or a blunder, or perverse.

There is a logic of *extension,* as we have suggested, a logic of terms, and relations of terms, of propositions and their relations, confined to their meaning as denoting, as applying, to what exists only. But that is *not* the logic pertinent here; it is not the logic of strict implication; and within such a logic, an actually extensional logic, considered by itself, it is impossible to say even what is deducible from what, as that relationship, the deducibility relationship, is essentially one of meaning, one which is essentially intensional. In such a logic it is not possible to express, to say nothing of *defining,* that relation *of p* to *q* which holds when and only when *q* is inferable from *p* without any added premise; that logic cannot give any correct meaning to this most important of all logical relations.[13]

In a sense, however, it is the logic of intension *only* which is logic; there is nothing certifiable by logic alone which cannot be certified by reference to *intension*—the reason being that, as already indicated, what is strictly inferable from what is statable *only* by reference to the intensional meaning of the expressions so related.

The logical consistency of propositions or statements is, like strict implication, a purely intensional relation. It is only in a logic including the intensional relationships that self-consistency or the relation of the consistency of two or more propositions or statements can even be expressed and symbolized.

Accordingly, what is to be said, following, as it pertains to matters of logic, is to be understood in terms of the logic of intension, not the logic of extension; and when we speak of implication we are to be understood as referring to, and

---

13. In the history of the development of symbolic logic, which dates from Boole's algebra of 0 and 1, a most extraordinary logical blunder was committed. It was perpetuated by oversight and today the greater number of those who specially devote themselves to the subject have so much time and so much of their written work invested in this logic of extension that they attempt, by extravagant conceptions, and a little frantically, to argue away the logic of intension, in which this abysmal blunder is easily corrected.

presupposing, not "material implication," but strict implication, in terms of which we shall also understand deduction.[14]

Those whose logical sense has not already been perverted by overexposure to exclusively extensional logic will find what is said here intuitively evident, with a little care taken in grasping what precisely is intended.

The two outstanding notions of logical intension are, as already indicated, those signified by 'implies' (the converse of 'is inferable from') and 'is consistent with'. These two are related to each other, very simply, if we introduce the additional idea signified by 'contradictory of'—e.g., '~ p' would be the contradictory of 'p', meaning '*p* is false', 'it is not the case that *p*', or, say, simply, 'not-p', for brevity. If we then, as noted earlier, symbolize '*p* strictly implies *q*', '*q* is deducible from *p*', by 'p < q', and symbolize '*p* is consistent with *q*' by '<> (p . q)', then:

$$(p < q) = \sim <> (p . \sim q).$$

That is, *p* implies *q* if and only if it is *false* that *p* is consistent with *not-q*—if and only if '<> (p . ~ q)' is *not* the case. To review a familiar example, one notes that 'Today is Monday' implies that 'Tomorrow is Tuesday' just in case it is *false* that 'Today is Monday' is consistent with the denial (the contradiction) of 'Tomorrow is Tuesday'. Admitting that it *is* false that 'Today is Monday' is consistent with 'Tomorrow is not Tuesday', 'Today is Monday' strictly implies 'Tomorrow is Tuesday'.[15]

---

14. It might be noted, in passing, that this involves no loss of the logic of extension, for the whole of the logic of extension can be included in and *deduced from* the logic of intension; the reverse, however, is not the case. The logic of intension is, thus, not only the only logic which is strictly deductive but also the only logic which is *comprehensive*, the only logic in which *all* logically certifiable relationships can be symbolized and the principles governing them accurately stated.

15. *Please note* that if you happen to think of crossing the International Date Line at midnight—*everything* asserted above regarding consistency and implication relations will still be absolutely correct and absolutely true. You would be merely observing the possibility that this particular example, in such a case, would *not be an example* of a strict implication 'p < q', and, accordingly, would not be an example of the inconsistency

Let us amplify and remind ourselves of a few points.

Whatever can be mentioned, referred to, by the use of language, must be thought of, and what is said must be thought by the speaker and by any who understands what he means, in the same way. The language used must convey this intended meaning. Either then, there must be expressions referring to nonexistent things and conveying this specific intended reference, or there is nothing which can be truly said about centaurs, Zeus, unicorns, etc. One must be able to characterize, describe, what, say, 'centaur' or 'Zeus' is intended to refer to. There must, then, be true sentences like, 'A centaur is a mythical creature, half man, half horse', and 'Zeus is the ruling god in the Greek pantheon.' There are indeed such true sentences; one might even find them in the dictionary.

In spite of this plainest of all plain facts, there are "logicians" who commit themselves to the doctrine that any sentence of the form 'A is —' must be so interpreted as to be false if what is meant by 'A' does not exist. Or they so interpret statements of this form in case 'A' is a proper name like 'Zeus'; and in case it is a common noun like 'centaur', they so interpret it that 'A centaur is —' will be true no matter how you fill the blank, *e.g.,* 'A centaur is the cousin of an aunt,' 'A centaur is a six-sided pentagon', etc.

The sense in which 'A centaur is half horse, half man' and 'Zeus is the father of the gods' are true, and 'A centaur is a woolly lamb' and 'Zeus is an early Greek philosopher' are false, is the sense of intensional meaning, once again spelling the word with an 's' in the old-English fashion, and therewith again marking it as a technical term, and appropriately suggesting that it has reference to the meaning of language in the sense of what any user of it intends to convey, what the user connotes or implies by this use of words. Intension is thus conceptual meaning; it is not reference to what the terms used would point

---

of *p* ("Today is Monday") with *not-q* ("Tomorrow is not Tuesday"). One might, of course, insert "here" after "Monday" and after "Tuesday," making both statements precise. Given that, the example becomes impeccable. But, most importantly, the *equivalence* noted above, that of 'p < q' with '~ <> (p . ~ q)', stands, *with* or *without* this correction.

to, denote in actuality, something confined to *existential* reference, which in the case of 'Zeus' and 'centaur' would be nothing. Meaning in this latter sense, that of *actualities* indicated, existent entities denoted, is *extensional* meaning. It is quite different from the crucial modality of meaning with which we are here primarily concerned, namely, intensional meaning. It is important that these two modalities of meaning not be confused. It is important that extensional meaning be distinguished from, and contrasted with, intensional, or conceptual, meaning.

The logicians above referred to attempt to confine logic to the logic of extension, a procedure which is peculiarly anomalous, since no statement "belongs to logic" or can be certified by logic alone unless it can be certified by reference to its intensional—its conceptual—meaning, which is the same as to say "unless it is analytic, it is not true *a priori.*" The attempt to argue away the distinction between intension and extension, and confine logic as written to the logic of extension may, thus, remind us of Lewis Carroll's "For I've been thinking on a plan to dye my whiskers green; and then to use so large a fan that they cannot be seen."[16]

The reason for our necessary interest here is that, on the one side, so much of the exact logic in symbolic form now current being confined to the logic of extension, a failure to remark our divergence from it could cause confusion; and, on the other side, we are obliged, in the interest of ethical conceptions to

---

16. They accomplish this feat by confining their assumptions for logic to postulates which are *analytically* true, and definitions—a definition being—by the "definition" of definition—an analytic statement, certifiable by the intensional meaning of words, and by confining their procedures of "derivation" (sanctioned by their *metalogical* rules) to such as, the premises being analytic, the consequences derivable from them will also be analytic, that is, to such procedures (or rules) as will allow no statement to be derived from an analytic assumption unless that consequence is likewise analytic. This last is easy to do since it accords with our intuitions of the logical.

Incidentally, the logic of intension includes the whole logic of extension—the *logical* facts about such relations being truths of intension; intensional logic is, thus, logic at large, extensional logic a part of it only. [Cf. note 14. –Ed.]

be considered here, to speak of consistency and deductive implication (of "*p* implies *q*" as meaning "the conclusion *q* is validly inferable from the premise *p*") and neither of these relations can be defined in the vocabulary of the logic of extension exclusively.

This point can be haggled over endlessly. And there is a temptation to haggle further here. Instead, let us go very far out on a limb and express our objection to the supposed adequacy of any purely extensional logic in a form which we think cannot be met. Write down any indicative sentence in plain English with "centaur" or "centaurs," or "a centaur," or "some centaurs," or "all centaurs," as its subject. Try then to construe this indicative sentence in the symbols of extensional logic exclusively (by the substitution of values for the variables in the formula) in such wise that, in this symbolic form, this sentence would be true but would become false if, whenever the word 'centaur' occurs, you strike it out and substitute the word 'unicorn'. That, we venture to assert, cannot be done. In the vocabulary of a purely extensional logic, there is nothing sayable which is true of centaurs but false of unicorns. The difference between a unicorn and a centaur is not expressible: what it would require for a thing to be a centaur instead of a unicorn cannot be said at all in the language of extensional logic. In English, it is expressed, in part, for example, by saying, "To be unicorn, a thing must have a horn in the middle of the forehead, but to be a centaur, it must not have any horn." You cannot say 'must' in extensional logic; it ignores the difference between 'must be', 'necessarily would be', 'is logically required to be' and contingent, existential fact; the difference between the actually, existentially true or false merely and the necessarily true or necessarily false of statements certifiably true by logic or certifiably false by logic; the difference between the contingently true and the necessarily true—certifiable by reference to intensional meaning, the *a priori* true; between the analytically certifiable and the contingently true; between the logically contradictory and the contingently false. More exactly, the *asserted* relation in any statement must be a relation which is certifiable as holding by reference to intensional meaning, if that statement is one which belongs to logic. In other words, no statement which is contingently true but not necessarily true, which is not analytic, is a statement properly subsumable under the caption "Logic." Logic comprises only *a priori* truths.

Phase III

The arch imperative of all governed and governable doing is: Do nothing deliberately unless from conviction that it will bring about some good.

And this covers not only that physical bringing about to which we would confine doing in the narrow sense of acting. It applies as well to commitments of governable thinking.

Should we make concessions to our own frailties?—to our own lack of control over our emotions? That amounts to a kind of schizophrenia at best—a surrender of selfhood. But the self which *makes this decision* must at least do so from a conviction that such a surrender will do some good! He must say to himself: "Being what I have to admit that I am, it is better for me not to face the devastating truth."

The "Will to Believe," as James used this term in his essay under this title, would have better satisfied many of us if it had been apologetic for dismissing inhibitory doubts, doubts which may prevent our best efforts in resolutely acting on the only supposition acting upon which has any chance of doing some good—if the counsel had been, in situations where the only ways of acting open are doubtful as to their outcome, so still continue to act in that way which offers the best hope of doing some good. If dwelling upon the doubt that even this way of acting will do no good inhibits your best efforts, put such doubts from your mind, since they are bootless, and act with single-minded resolution to bring off this sole effect of action which offers any possibility of doing good. Hold firmly in mind this best possible thing to do, and dismiss from your mind alternatives which hold no hope at all for doing any good at all. That remains as the dictate of rationality, and the adherence to integrity. *Make believe* if you must to summon your best effort, but do what is rationally dictated, as offering the highest probability open of doing some good.

But we shall all wish to add that we do not take this issue lightly, or wish to dissemble our human frailties touching this point. One eventual bearing of it, which James had in mind, touches our attitude toward life at large, in view of our common human predicament.

Phase IV

Let us try to discern what we commonly mean by consistency in our voluntary doing. One thing involved is adherence to our own deciding—unless or until we have reason to believe a past decision ill-judged—and this involves the conformity of what we willingly do to what we believe. And saying what we do, and doing what we say—to ourselves, even if to nobody else—would seem to be involved.

The man who is unreliable in what he says to others is socially anathema; his way of speaking undermines the foundations of any social order. Even that pretender to extremist cynicism, Hobbes, elevated the dictate that covenants made must be kept to a position above his dictate of egoism in conduct. Otherwise his whole "social contract" theory would have fallen into ruin. It is a primary social imperative without respect for which no social order could endure.

The "social contract" is in fact the product of our intuitive recognition that nobody can diddle everybody all the time, and we shall all be best off if each is willing to give a little in the expectation of gaining a little. It is reserved to our own enlightened age to have to find that out by mathematical game theory and have it implemented by a conference of experts.

The practical point of thinking is in believing, and the practical point of believing is in determining what to do. It is our value assessments which are proximate to our decisions to do—without them no doing of this rather than that, or doing nothing, would have a reason—any justification.

"Act only on the justified expectation that what you decide upon will probably do some good."

We do not—not yet at least—say, "so that it has the highest probability of doing the most good." That matter is altogether too complex to be concluded at this point.

The good is that which is worth attaining, that which will satisfy if achieved. That is as concrete as water for the thirsty man and as abstract as the millennium. It is definitive of what we intend by 'good' and preclusive of any less adequate verbal rendering. 'Pleasure' is the word for the sensuously good, 'happiness' for the emotive good, 'integrity' for the good of self-direction, 'a good life' for the mundane aim, and 'the kingdom of heaven' for the mystic's insight. For all, there is no better word than 'good', whatever segment of that may have the strongest appeal and be the best exemplar of it for any given individual. And the good is, for each and any individual, the rational and self-justifying aim of action. If the good be not imperative to heed, then there is no saying what is imperative to heed; words are futile and insight worthless. If it need be established, then there are no premises which are adequate and no conceivable manner of its proving.

Phase V

Grasp of the fact that a dimension of experience, *e.g.*, "blue," has a multiplicity of "contraries"—incompatibles—each of which, in being attributed, implies the "contradictory" of blue—that requires an appeal to the sensory aspects of experience, and is incapable of any logical proof. It can be established only by an appeal to imagination. What cannot be imagined cannot be seen, heard, felt, sense-apprehended. I am certain, antecedent to any experience, that nothing can be both red and green—in the same place, at the same time, and in the same respect—because I cannot imagine what 'both red and green', under those restrictions, directs me to image. Red has alternatives, a plurality of contraries (not red), each implying its contradictory (not-red), but also each implying the contradictory of each other, and each implying the contradictory of "colorless." And let it be observed that this kind of fact, pertaining to this kind of category (*e.g.*, color), is not to be explained by correlation with the separate senses, because there is no correlation with the senses which could be established prior to the recognition of it.

Some seem to have an addiction to confusing the contrary of red, "incompatible with red," with the contradictory of red, "the negative of red." Any contrary of red implies the contradictory of red, but the contradictory of red does not imply a specific contrary of red. *e.g.,* "blue" implies "not-red," but "not-red" does not imply "blue." On the other hand, all of the contraries of red are comprehended by the negative, or negation, of red, *i.e.,* blue, green, etc. are all subsumed under the "not-red." And red is contrary to green and red is contrary to blue, but also green and blue are contrary to each other. And of red, green and blue, each is contrary to the other. And each one has one contradictory only, comprehensive, as above, of all its contraries.

"Consistent with" means "compatible with," compossible with, and "inconsistent with" means "incompatible with," not compossible with.

To give a "sense filling" to the contradictory, we must find some contrary. To negate "red" by any evidence of sense, we must find some positive "sensible" incompatible with red; this is not difficult; any one of several will do, since all have it in common that they imply the negation of red. (And we must not forget the contrary, "uncolored.") But there is no positive finding, negative of "red," except some particular of the incompatible.

*In*consistency is the positively findable fact; consistency is a privative fact only, the absence of incompatibility. It is *permissible* to think or suppose something, there being no positive evidence to the contrary, which implies the contradictory. This relationship is to be defined in negative terms. *A* and *B* are consistent predicates (for any entity) just in case the attribution of *A* does not imply the contradictory of *B*. Symbolizing the consistency of *A* and *B* by '$<> (A \cdot B)$'—it is logically permissible to think *A* and *B* both—and the contradictory of *X* by '$\sim X$', and "implies" by '$<$', then:

$$<> (A \cdot B) = \sim (A < \sim B).$$

Propositions are semantic entities—linguistic expressions having meaning. Specifically the proposition is an expression which signifies a thought-of (or to-be-thought-of) state of affairs, something which could be the case or not the case, in actuality, and could be asserted or inquired about, or believed or doubted, and so on, in any sententional mood, the expression of which would then be a full sentence.

We apply 'consistent' and 'inconsistent' to conduct in various ways, inconsistency, for example, when one speaks for something but acts to prevent it or indicates an attitude of *laissez faire;* when one takes one action to prevent something but another to bring it about or let it happen, or when one attempts to face both ways in any matter of decision. The connection with logic may seem obvious; a thing is or is not, cannot both be and not be; one cannot have it so and not so. And to evince an attitude both pro and con is "illogical," "irrational." The obvious connection is between valuing and doing, or between believing and acting in accord with the belief. Or it is between one act and another. To be inconsistent in action is to act as if attempting to realize contradictory aims—or as if attempting to bring about the impossibility of something being so and also not being so.

The connection between deliberate acts and the believings which must be submitted to the critique and the imperatives of logic lies of course in the consideration that both concern "states of affairs." Logic directly concerns, we may say, their being the case; deliberate action concerns bringing them about, or preventing them from coming about, and it involves the intentions of acts, the expectations of bringing about. Deliberate acting evinces, evidences, both the wish and will, and—reasonably—some expectation of bringing about. And we may say that the basic adjuration of logic for deliberate doing is: Do not expect or intend what, since it involves a logical contradiction, is impossible. That, obviously, is an imperative of rationality. The connection between the logical relations of propositions and deliberate doing is through the relations of the propositions expressive of the states of affairs the deliberate doing is aimed at bringing about, the proposition intended or expected to make true by doing.

On closer examination, however, it will become clear that, although this is the gist of the matter, we use 'consistency' and 'inconsistency' in connection with the aims and intentions of action in a somewhat wider way than this might indicate. And this is the case, because the expecting, the foreseeing, of the consequences of action itself involves something more than the critique of logic as deductive inference; all such predictions of action include at least inferences incapable of being guaranteed valid by deductive logic, and requires inferences called 'inductive', applying generalities learned from past experience to what has not yet been observed and, in the case of the consequences of action, have not yet happened. The final critique—applying simply to the anticipated or "willed to follow"—may be purely deductive, and the consistency or inconsistency of the expected this or that, or of both some this and that—that critique of consistency may be purely a matter of deductive logic. But the rationality, the reasonableness, of the *expecting,* the foreseeing, must include what is criticizable only if the critique of *inductive* validity be appealed to as well.

Another way of putting this same matter would be to observe that when we speak of the "possible" and the "impossible," we have in mind not only the deductively impossible of the contradictory, or the possible in the sense of that which entails no such logical contradiction, but also the "physically impossible," or the "psychologically impossible," that which contravenes the "laws of science," or even what contravenes well-established generalities of common sense.

We can, however, express this whole matter succinctly, and in terms which bring it under the purely deductive critique, if we allow ourselves a manner of representing it which includes a reference to whatever empirical (inductively established) knowledge is pertinent and presumed. Let us represent this, as before, by the letter 'K'. Also, we may remember that any item of knowledge is "pertinent" to any conclusion if and only if the *addition* of that item to our premises makes a difference to the justifiability of a conclusion, an inference, in question. So, if we should add to and include under what "K" represents the *non-pertinent* as well as the pertinent, that will make no difference for any consistency or inconsistency in question. So we might just as well represent by '*K*' "all the knowledge one has" or "all the evidence available," pertinent or not pertinent. Inclusion of the nonpertinent will not count one way or the other.

Phase VI[17]

Let us consider consistency.

Utilizing certain notational devices may help to clarify the matter in question, in spite of any "looseness" or "imprecision" of such devices. Accordingly, "P is possible," consistent to assert or believe, first, in the narrow sense of the purely deductive critique, and, second, in the wider sense of the inductive critique, inclusive of reference to scientific or other generalities (*K*) which we coincidentally *assume as true* and *not to be denied*, might be represented as follows:

"P is possible"—consistent to suppose, assert, believe or expect:

$$\text{Deductive: } <> P \qquad\qquad \sim (P < \sim P)[18]$$
$$\text{Inductive: } <> (P . K) \qquad \sim [(P . K) < \sim P]$$

---

17. [In this section of the text, I have introduced some notational revisions in the formulas, largely in the interests of uniformity, and, I suspect, greater ease of interpretation by readers, particularly those who might be unfamiliar with the use of dots as grouping devices. (As before, '<>' will stand for consistency; '~' for negation; '.' for conjunction (subject to the exception noted below); and '<' for strict implication. Similarly, as before, inessential grouping signs may be omitted, *e.g.*, we will count 'P . Q . R' as well formed. Note here, however, Lewis' use of commas for separating elements in a set. This allows him to utilize dots, in such a context, for indicating not conjunction *per se* but "more of the same," rather as if saying, "Etc." For example, the set containing P, *Q*, R., and *further possible members* could be indicated as 'P, Q, R, ...'.) –Ed.]

18. [Here we see a dramatic difference between Lewis' system of strict implication, and the notion of material implication. In material implication, neither the formula 'P ⊃ ~ P' nor '~P ⊃ P' is inconsistent. The first would be logically equivalent to '~ P' and the second would be logically equivalent to 'P'. Accordingly, in material implication, '~ (P ⊃ ~ P)' and '~ (~ P ⊃ P)' would be logically equivalent, respectively, to 'P' and '~ P'. –Ed.]

And one might note, as well:

"P is impossible"—inconsistent to suppose, assert, believe or expect:

Deductive: ~ <> P   P < ~ P
Inductive: ~ <> (P . K)   (P . K) < ~ P

Note that if 'K < ~ P' is the case, then '(P . K) < ~ P'; and also if 'P < ~ P' is the case, then '(P . K) < ~ P' is the case. This last covers the point that what is deductively inconsistent is also inductively inconsistent.

"P and Q are compossible"—consistent:

Deductive: <> (P . Q)
Inductive: <> (P . Q . K)

Nothing here implies that any of the formulas are false, *e.g.*, it is not the case that, say, 'P' implies '~ Q'.

Similarly, the set "P, Q, R, ..." is a consistent set:

Deductive: <> (P . Q . R, . . .)
Inductive: <> (P . Q . R, . . . , K)

As above, nothing here implies that any of the formulas are false. For example, for any chosen member of the set, say, 'Q', it is not the case that any members of the set, including 'Q', either singly or conjointly imply '~ Q'.

Similarly, consider:

[<> (P . Q . K)] < <> (P . Q)

and

[<> (P . Q)] < [(<> P) . (<> Q)]

Whatever is inductively consistent must be deductively consistent. And whatever is consistent with something else must be self-consistent. But the converse of those implications does not hold. That *P* and *Q* are each self-consistent does not imply that they are consistent with each other. And that *P* and *Q* are deductively consistent with each other does not imply that they are inductively consistent with the rest of what we know. For example, I may plan on spending the evening, and expect to spend the evening, in my wife's company and also plan on hearing, and expect to hear, the concert this evening. But the realization of both these expectations may be incompatible with the fact, which I do not know, that she has an unbreakable engagement for the evening at home.

Phase VII

But here we encounter another consideration. We have spoken of the self-consistency of a proposition by itself as its logical possibility, and of the logical consistency of two propositions as their compossibility.

Is possibility or compossibility a metaphysical fact, or is it an epistemic fact, dependent on what the person in question knows?

Whether there is any such thing as a metaphysical possibility which is not also a metaphysical actuality has been a metaphysical problem throughout the ages. The question is whether there is such a thing as "absolute chance." We wish to avoid metaphysical questions of that kind, and we merely remark in passing that natural science, after a century or two in which the possibility of knowing the world in a natural-scientific way had been supposed to depend upon the truth of physical determinism—no absolute chance—not even a smidgen—has discovered that it can, and apparently must, get on with statistical generalizations, and the particle physicist now cheerfully admits that, so far as any possibility of determining it goes, the locus of a particle is a "probability smear."

We shall not attempt a discussion of whether there is a metaphysical distinction of possible from actual, and between the merely actual and what "necessarily exists." Instead, we would here point out that we can avoid these metaphysical issues; their solution is not required for ethics. We can so avoid them by considering what, exactly, is meant by saying that an aim, or intention, or an expectation, is one which is consistent or is inconsistent for one of us to entertain and to act in the light of. I may be perfectly consistent in expecting to spend the evening with my wife *and* at the concert, so long as I do not know that she will spend it at home, but when I find that out, these two aims or expectations become inconsistent for me to entertain coincidentally. I am obviously inconsistent if I plan both to attend the concert and to stay at home—because, as everybody knows, you can't be at two places at once. (Whether that is *a priori* or not—an analytic statement or not—might be a nice question; that depends on how much meaning you import into "at the concert" and "at home." Everybody is supposed to be able to know what he means, though on occasion any one of us may be stupid enough not to realize what his own conceptions imply.) But perhaps none of us ever knows all the empirical facts which bear upon an expectation which he entertains and affect the "possibility" of his realizing it. For one thing, nobody knows what he is going to do while he is still engaged in deciding it, and not even a determinist denies that our actions cause what we call the effects of them. He maintains instead that the fact of what we are going to do is metaphysically determined before we decide it; our deciding is already fixed by causes of it unknown to us before our act of deciding. If it were *known* to us, the deciding would be silly.

Whether there is a *metaphysical* distinction between the possible and the actual, and between the contingently actual and what is necessarily the case, there is the distinction between what our concepts imply, and what we know implies, and all the implications of what we do not conceive and do not know. There is a distinction between what is inferable from our own knowledge and what necessarily follows from what we conceive as we conceive it, and what is not so inferable.

And *whether* we think of the distinction of possible from actual, and actual from necessarily so, as a *metaphysical* distinction or not, we can be sure of their epistemic (epistemological) distinction.[19]

---

19. The logicians who try to reduce logic to purely extensional (existential) relations are—whether consciously or unconsciously—attempting

But *if* we use 'possible' and 'impossible' in a seemingly metaphysical sense, as something fixed in reality whether we know it or not—and we sometimes do, being wary about pertinent facts which we do not know—at least we use 'consistent' and 'inconsistent' in this epistemic, or epistemological, sense, use them in ways which are limited by what we know, or what we *could* know, some evidence of it being available to us at the time of our decision. As long as I do not know my wife's engagement for the evening, or "have no reason" to anticipate her being engaged at home, my aim to go to the concert *and* spend the evening in her company is a perfectly consistent intention. It is inductively consistent, as well as deductively consistent.

When, therefore, we are speaking of consistency or inconsistency, as attributable to *us,* and not to the universe or separate factualities of the universe, consistency in conceiving (purely logical consistency) and inductive consistency are matters which are decidable within the scope of what we conceive and what we know, 'deductive consistency' being confined to what is decidable by reference to our conceptions alone—what we intend in the sense of what we mean by what we say, or by what we think and believe—and inductive consistency decidable on this ground of meaning together with the pertinent empirical information which we have. Nobody could well be said to *be* consistent or to *be* inconsistent on any other terms than these, either in his believing or in his intentions to bring about.

And such consistency in our believing is a first requirement of any deliberate decision, whether of believing or of intending to bring about—since our believing that we *can* bring this about is a first requirement for the rational expectation of bringing it about.

Consistency is essential to the rational, moral life. As self-governing creatures we must strive to be deductively consistent, inductively consistent, and consistent in our intentions and purposes.

What is required?

---

to reduce it to terms of metaphysical determinism, and whether they are right or not, they are scientifically rather old fashioned.

Our being consistent in what we think of—what we can seriously *suppose* as possible, as consistently thinkable.

Our being consistent in what we believe as contingent fact, as non-a *priori*, nonanalytic fact.

Our being consistent in what we intend to bring about, in what we intend to do.

With regard to our concluding, our inferring, we must be consistent with *our premises,* whether they are true or false. That purely logical consistency is the first and minimal imperative of rationality. But in our believing, we must not only be consistent at each and every step of any concluding, but we must also, in each such conclusion, in each such belief, be consistent with all our other beliefs, with all the other beliefs to which we are coincidentally committed. This is a second and further imperative of rationality. And this includes any expectations, any predictive beliefs, we entertain. And in this last sense, as will now be obvious, we must be consistent in our decisions to do, consistent with what we believe it possible to bring about. We must believe this, that we are being consistent, in the light of all that we know. Otherwise our intention to do will be inconsistently taken.

There is even a further requirement: we must in what we intend to bring about be consistent with every *other* aim we would preserve and hope to achieve. The total body of our continuing aims must constitute an inductively consistent set. Otherwise we should know ourselves condemned by our intentions to fail somewhere, and in some way and measure, to the disappointment of our aims; we would find ourselves self-condemned to some frustration. This is a third requirement of rationality in intentions to do, and such rationality in each and every deliberate decision is a requirement for rightness of doing in any sense of the right to do. It is a general imperative of voluntary doing. And that none of us will completely attain it is nothing to the contrary; it remains imperative for us to try to do this, on each occasion of doing, so far as in us lies. The integration of our continuing purposes into some self-consistent set of aims to bring about is a requirement of rational living for any self-governing and deliberate doer. It is one of the outstanding problems; indeed, it is a problem comprehensive of all problems, since what is beyond all possible control by us, and not possible for us to affect, by any decision or action, is not a real problem, though it could be mistakenly conceived as such.[20]

Be consistent in all you think, and all you believe, and in all you undertake to do, and consistent with your thinking and believing in your doing: that is the comprehensive imperative for every rational being. And this is no grandiose sketch of sentiment: it is the simple common sense of life, writ large.

---

20. "Intention," like most "-tion" words, is ambiguous as between the intend*ing*, which is the act or activity of intending, and the intend*ed*, that which is intended. We use "intention" here in the latter sense, as signifying the content, the referent, of any intent, what is intended.

Appendix

Datings, Pertinent to Lewis Materials:

The Lewis Materials, housed in the archives of Stanford University, are abundant and complex. The materials drawn on for the book are dated as follows, the dates usually, but not always, occurring on the first page of the material in question.

Preface—and Confession (12/15/63)
Chapter 1. Introduction: About Philosophy in General and Ethics in Particular (1/6/64)
Chapter 2. The Good and Bad in Experience: Prolegomena (1/30/63)
Chapter 3. The Good and Bad in Experience (7/7/63)
Chapter 4. Semantics of the Imperative (11/20/61)
Chapter 5. Ethics and the Logical (6/6/62)
Chapter 6. Deliberate Acts (1/21/62)
Chapter 7. Right Acts and Good Acts (6/16/60)
   (Much is not dated here. The first fully numbered page is that above.)
Chapter 8. Right Doing and the Right to Do (4/17/62)
Chapter 9. We Approach the Normative Finalities (9/18/63)